Plato's Statesman

Books by Stanley Rosen from St. Augustine's Press

The Ancients and the Moderns: Rethinking Modernity.
G. W. F. Hegel: An Introduction to the Science of Wisdom.
The Limits of Analysis.
Nihilism: A Philosophical Essay.
Metaphysics in Ordinary Language.
Plato's Sophist.
Plato's Symposium.
The Question of Being: A Reversal of Heidegger.

Other Books of Interest from St. Augustine's Press

Seth Benardete, *Achilles and Hector: The Homeric Hero.*
Seth Benardete, *Sacred Transgressions: A Reading of Sophocles'* Antigone.
Aristotle, *Aristotle – On Poetics.* Translated by Seth Benardete and Michael Davis.
Plato, *Symposium of Plato.* Translated by Percy Bysshe Shelley
Thomas Aquinas, *Disputed Questions on Virtue.* Translated by Ralph McInerny.
John of St. Thomas, *Introduction to the Summa Theologiae of Thomas Aquinas.* Translated by Ralph McInerny.
Francisco Suarez, *Metaphysical Demonstration of the Existence of God: Metaphysical Disputations 28–29.* Translated by John P. Doyle
Francisco Suarez, *On Creation, Conservation, and Concurrence: Metaphysical Disputationss 20–22.* Translated by A. J. Freddoso
Leo Strauss, *Xenophon's Socrates.*
Leo Strauss, *Xenophon's Socratic Discourse.*
Mario Enrique Sacchi, *The Apocalypse of Being: The Esoteric Gnosis of Martin Heidegger.*
Rémi Brague, *Eccentric Culture: A Theory of Western Civilization.*
René Girard, *A Theater of Envy: William Shakespeare.*
Friedrich Nietzsche, *On the Future of Our Educational Institutions.* Translated by Michael W. Grenke.
Friedrich Nietzsche, *Prefaces to Unwritten Works.* Translated by Michael W. Grenke.
Zbigniew Janowski, *Augustinian-Cartesian Index: Texts and Commentary.*
Leszek Kolakowski, *My Correct Views on Everything.*
Leszek Kolakowski, *The Two Eyes of Spinoza and Other Essays on Philosophers.*
Jean-Luc Marion, *Descartes's Grey Ontology: Cartesian Science and Aristotelian Thought in the* Regulae.

Plato's Statesman
The Web of Politics

Stanley Rosen

ST. AUGUSTINE'S PRESS
South Bend, Indiana
2009

1 2 3 4   15 14 13 12 11 10 09

Library of Congress Cataloging in Publication Data
Rosen, Stanley, 1929–
    Plato's Statesman: the web of politics / Stanley Rosen.
     p.   cm.
    Originally published: New Haven: Yale University Press,
    c1995.
    Includes bibliographical references and index.
    ISBN 1-58731-627-7 (alk. paper)
    1. Plato, Statesman. 2. Plato – Contributions in political
    science. I. Title.
JC71.P314 R67 2002
320'.01 – dc21   2002069968

∞ *The paper used in this publication meets the minimum requirements of the*
International Organisation for Standardization (ISO) – Paper for documents
– Requirements for permanence – ISO 9706: 1994.

St. Augustine's Press
www.staugustine.net

Contents

Preface

It is my hope that the present volume will be of interest not only to Plato specialists but to a wider philosophical public. Although it is an independent work, this book can be read as a sequel to my study of the *Sophist* and is also intended to supplement the discussion of Platonism in *The Question of Being*. The central theme of the *Statesman* is the relation between *phronēsis*, or sound judgment, and *technē*. The attempt to determine whether political experience is amenable to and clarified by quasi-formal methods of analysis opens an ambiguous path to the future on which we are currently stumbling and seem to have lost our way. The scientific Enlightenment of the early modern epoch is a critical point on this path, as is illustrated, for example, by Condorcet's extension of the Cartesian *mathēsis universalis* to the conceptual mastery of human affairs. On this path we are faced with the enduring question of the degree to which human experience is a technical construction or, as one might say today, whether our common historical experience is a myth—namely, the myth of the given—and so is merely a mistaken theory.

One should not expect these questions to be discussed by Plato in modern terminology or with the peculiar directness of modern revolutionary rhetoric. At the same time, if we are willing to submit ourselves to the careful mastery of Platonic rhetoric, and so to detach ourselves from the imaginary Platonism of contemporary ideological debate, useful surprises await us. The *Statesman* can and should be understood as a detailed if by contemporary standards eccentric reflection on what is today called the problem of philosophical methodology. I have accordingly devoted considerable space to the discussion of the related topics of diaeresis, paradigms, and the two kinds of measurement—arithmetical and nonarithmetical, which kinds may be said to correspond to what Pascal calls the *esprit géométrique* and the *esprit de finesse*. These topics are the hinges of the Stranger's technical argument.

As the title of the dialogue indicates, the question of methodology arises with respect to the art of politics. The issue is not simply what constitutes the appropriate method for the analysis of political knowledge, but also the extent to which the application of *technē* to human experience is an act of production rather than discovery. We may approach the further question of the relation between Socrates and the Eleatic Stranger by observing the constructive elements in the Stranger's teaching. The Stranger applies *technē* to the task of defining politics as the art by which human beings produce artifacts, in particular the artifact of the city, in order to protect themselves against a hostile nature. A careful study of the *Statesman* thus provides us with a deeper and richer portrait of Plato's complex teaching than is usually exhibited.

Plato has frequently been criticized as a utopian thinker on the one hand and a voice of conservatism on the other. I doubt that these two charges are mutually compatible. Philosophy is by its nature a revolutionary activity, whereas conservatism is at best only a tactic. Another central theme of the *Statesman* is the possibility of philosophical rule or, in the terminology of the Stranger, of the rule of *phronēsis* unencumbered by *nomos*. The Stranger concludes that such rule is impossible, a conclusion that is not without relevance for our understanding of the *Republic*. His account of political construction, with which the dialogue concludes, is accordingly both pious and conventional. But this resolution is rendered unsatisfactory by the partial emancipation of humankind from the rule of nature.

Politics is understood by the Stranger almost exclusively in defensive terms, and the enemy is nature, or more precisely, the disjunction within human being of a friendly and a hostile nature. The absence of a sharp distinction between practice and production casts its shadow over theory or (as it is called in the *Statesman*) gnosis as well. The art of commanding, of which politics is an instance, is defined by the Stranger as for the sake of generating a previously nonexistent body. Despite its classification under gnosis, politics is accordingly from the outset an applied or practico-productive theory. In addition, diaeresis, the principal tool of the theoretician, is silently detached by the Stranger from the Socratic doctrine of Ideas and applied to the analysis of human affairs in such a way as to blur the distinction between the discovery and the construction of formal elements. Diaeresis evolves into concept-construction.

Despite the many points of agreement between the Stranger and Socrates, as well as the conventionally "Platonic" ending of the dialogue, the *Statesman* presents us with a striking anticipation of the modern problematic of theory and practice. No doubt Plato's resolution of the problematic is quite different from ours. But he is much closer in thought and in spirit to the moderns, and in particular to the contemporary situation, than is Aristotle. The aforementioned disjunction between the friendly and the hostile dimensions of nature underlies the dramatic character of human life, and our effort to bridge that disjunction may be viewed either as a tragedy or a comedy, but certainly not as an expression of the *Heiterkeit* that marks the pages of Aristotle's writings on human affairs. The fundamental difference between Aristotle and the Eleatic Stranger may be expressed as follows. For Aristotle, *phronēsis* is the expression of the difference between practice and production. Human affairs are subject to the rule of *phronēsis* in a way that requires the mediation neither of the productive technician nor the philosopher. Aristotelian sobriety is the political face of philosophical *Heiterkeit*. The Eleatic Stranger, on the contrary, exhibits the Platonic madness by arguing that *phronēsis* could rule only if it were omnipotent; since this is impossible, *phronēsis* must submit to legislation and thus to the productive art of the statesman, who combines the theoretician and the productive technician. This is the Stranger's revision of the Socratic invocation of the philosopher-king.

This is the philosophical motivation for the patience that is required to master the Stranger's peculiar rhetoric. In order to facilitate immersion in textual detail, and thereby to bring the reader directly into the philosophical horizon of the *Statesman*, I have dispensed with the traditional footnotes indicating my agreements and differences with the secondary literature. The interested reader will find a brief discussion of the relevant scholarship in the Bibliographical Appendix.

One consolation of advanced age is freedom from the need to demonstrate a superfluous erudition. This freedom carries with it the obligation of paying one's debts. I have been studying the *Statesman* for forty-odd years, beginning with an extraordinary introduction to the dialogue in a graduate seminar conducted by Leo Strauss. However different the substance of my interpretation may be from his, I want to acknowledge here, especially at a time when his work has been silently appropriated by so many of his critics without a hint of obligation, and even with an explicit denial of debts incurred, that it was Strauss who taught me how to read a Platonic dialogue. There is no way in which I, or any of his former students, can identify with accuracy the countless details that he was the first to call to our attention. I owe him more than I can ever say. And I mean it as a statement of my reverence for a great teacher when I say that part of what I owe him is disagreement.

It is not clear to me whether Strauss has suffered more at the hands of his enemies or his disciples. However this question must be answered, it was he who largely initiated the serious study of the *Statesman* in the United States. I have conceived of this book as an *Auseinandersetzung* with Strauss, and for that reason among others, I have been unwilling to burden the text with references to works which, whatever their merits, played no role in my understanding of Plato. In any event, debates between scholars are of interest only to other scholars, and I prefer to address this book to philosophers.

I therefore conclude my preface with a special plea to the philosophical reader. The maxim "God dwells in the details" applies to Plato in general and especially so to the *Statesman*. Those who prefer unadorned argumentation to intricate textual decipherment will be tempted to criticize parts of my study as excessively ingenious in the best case and tedious in the worst. Why, it will be asked, must we spend so much energy in mastering Plato's baroque presentation of the art of weaving, with the attendant lists of productions, possessions, servants, and the like?

The answer that is contained in the following pages is that the excessive ingeniousness of Plato is at once part of his general teaching and a kind of playful testing of our right to penetrate into the most radical levels of his thought. If there is at least some truth to the observation that the history of Western philosophy is a series of footnotes to Plato, there is still more truth to the correlative assertion that a Platonic dialogue, and in particular a late dialogue like the *Statesman,* is a series of footnotes to its main text, footnotes that correct, qualify, and sometimes even contradict that text.

We live in a time that both characterizes itself as anti-Platonist and prides itself on its hermeneutical subtlety. Neither of these claims can be justified by a reading that generalizes fragments of the Platonic text, however dramatic the expression or famous the content of these fragments. I invite those who, regardless of whether they believe themselves to be Platonists or anti-Platonists, wish to know what they are talking about, rather than to repeat fashionable platitudes, to join me in the very difficult task of thinking through the *Statesman* in its entirety.

CHAPTER ONE

Setting the Scene

THERE can be no doubt that the late dialogues of Plato are more difficult in content and style than their predecessors. The displacement of Socrates from his role as principal interlocutor by a series of strangers from Elea, Locri, and Athens, respectively, is accompanied by an increased ponderousness of language, a greater proliferation of technical detail, and the consequent diminution of the erotic playfulness and Attic urbanity that mark the earlier dialogues. The initial predominance of sunlight and lucidity, even in conversations that take place at night such as the *Symposium* and the *Republic,* and notwithstanding the continuous irony of the main speaker, is replaced by chiaroscuro and baroque ornamentation on the one hand and the substitution of professorial discourse for dramatic dialogue on the other.

It is true that Socrates returns to prominence in the *Philebus,* traditionally acknowledged to be a late dialogue, but this is the exception that proves the rule. Having been subjected to the punishment of silent audition by Timaeus and the Eleatic Stranger and to the retrospective dialectical gymnastics of the old Parmenides, the Socrates of the *Philebus* is like a disembodied phantom of his previous incarnation. The dialogue between Socrates and historically anonymous youths takes place in an unknown dramatic setting; it has neither a beginning nor an end but exists as a headless and limbless torso of fluctuating dimensions, mysterious transitions, and linguistic obscurity. After his Odyssean wanderings and encounters with wise strangers who seem to rob him of speech, Socrates returns from a metaphorical Hades into the sunlight, but as a talking ghost who is about to be transformed for one last appearance as the Athenian Stranger (as Aristotle seems to identify him; see *Politics* II, 1265a10).

The *Statesman,* although not the last of Plato's productions, is prominent among the late dialogues for its obscurity. Much of the conversation is devoted to a minute and seemingly tedious analysis of the art of weaving, selected by the Stranger as a paradigm of the royal art of politics. The Stranger employs diaeresis—the art of division and collection in accordance with kinds—in order to arrive at a definition of the statesman's art, but with a cumbersomeness and tendency to error that testifies either to a heavy-handed playfulness or a technical incompetence for which we were unprepared by his previous exhibition in the *Sophist*.

Having taken us through a long and puzzling diaeresis, the Stranger identifies it as a mistake, which he will rectify by telling a myth: conceptual analysis is to be rescued from disgrace (268d2–3) by a bizarre fairy tale of the reversal of the cosmic revolution and the age of autochthonous mortals. The myth turns out, on the Stranger's own testimony, to have erred on the essential point and must itself be replaced by a series of difficult, sometimes even eccentric, topics, ranging from the nature of paradigms and the art of measurement to the discussion of weaving and correlative analyses of tools, possessions, and craftsmen associated with the art of clothesmaking. By an act of rhetorical legerdemain, the Stranger somehow gathers together the threads of his tangled web into a conventional, one could even say pious, conclusion that might have been established at the outset, without our having been subjected to the starts and stops of the error-laden middle.

Our initial survey of the peculiarities of the *Statesman* allows us to doubt the adequacy of those interpretations that see the dialogue as a technical exercise in definition. It would be more accurate to take the dialogue as a demonstration of the inappropriateness of diaeresis to the study of human affairs. From this standpoint, the shift from Socrates to the Eleatic Stranger takes on a richer and deeper significance than is imputed to it by those who see it as Plato's way of announcing a new stage in his thought. To anticipate, the Stranger evidently agrees with Socrates on a number of fundamental points. For example, the concluding thesis that the city must be woven together from the two opposing natures of courageous and temperate human beings, who if allowed to flourish separately decay into madness on the one hand and the lethargy of the cripple on the other (310d6–e3), is anticipated by Socrates in the *Republic* (VI. 503b7–504a1), where he indicates the need to mix together the quick and the steady in the souls of the guardians of the just city.

There are, however, two critical points of difference between Socrates and the Stranger. The Stranger exhibits no interest whatsoever in Eros, whereas Socrates claims to understand nothing else. The word *eros* appears just once in the *Statesman*, at 307e6, where the Stranger refers to the inappropriate desire of the temperate natures for peace. The erotic dimension of existence, which is pivotal for Socrates in the construction of the beautiful city of the *Republic*, is represented in the diaereses of the *Statesman* only indirectly, in the form of the breeding and nurture of herd animals, among whom human beings are included.

The second point of difference is related to the first; it is perhaps most immediately visible as a difference in pedagogical style. Socrates is fastidious in the choice of his youthful interlocutors. His manner of interrogation is not only playful and coquettish but is rooted in a serious concern with the *ēthos* and the intelligence of the youth, as well as in an ambiguous interest in his physical appearance and the distinction of his family. The Stranger, however, asks only that his interlocutors cause him no pain and be docile or "obedient to the rein." Otherwise he prefers monologue (*Sophist* 217d1–3).

The Stranger is more dogmatic than Socrates; he fills the void left by a disregard of Eros with a proliferation of technical doctrine. We cannot, of course, take Socrates literally when he tells us that he knows nothing but Eros, or only that he knows nothing. The *Republic*, to cite the outstanding example, is a continuous exposition of Socrates' detailed mastery of the Greek literary tradition, as well as of his high competence in mathematics and science. Furthermore, the dialogue is not aporetic but contains a circumstantial account of the manner of constructing the just city and educating philosopher-kings. Nevertheless, there is a discernible difference between Socrates and the Stranger that goes beyond questions of erotic interest and discursive playfulness. When Socrates introduces the most difficult section of the conversation in the *Republic*, devoted to the Idea of the Good, the divided line, and the nature of philosophical dialectic, he makes it clear that he is taking a "shorter way" that accommodates to the youth and intellectual capacities of Adeimantus and Glaucon (VI. 504b1–8 and 506c2–507a6). The Stranger exhibits no such reticence in his analysis of nonbeing and false assertions in the *Sophist*. The situation is more complicated in the *Statesman*, but again, whereas the Stranger seems to be error-prone and sometimes even to lose his way, he never suggests that he is withholding the truth or accommodating it to the undeveloped understanding of Young Socrates.

In addition, the Stranger not only shares Socrates' admiration for the method of diaeresis but goes beyond him in applying this method to human affairs, whereas Socrates employs it, or recommends its employment, for the articulation of formal structure (*Republic* VI. 510b4–9; *Phaedrus* 265d3–266b5; *Philebus* 16c5–17a5). Socrates furthermore recommends the method of diaeresis and praises its merits, but he never actually presents us with an extended example of its employment. The only two such examples in the Platonic corpus are assigned to the Stranger in the *Sophist* and the *States-*

man. These examples, or rather sets of examples, are extremely ambiguous and only marginally effective in achieving their stated goal; and they apply, to repeat, to human types rather than to pure forms. Nevertheless, whether successfully or otherwise, they distinguish the Stranger's practice in the dialogues from that of Socrates.

The Stranger is a man of *technē* in an extended sense as Socrates is not. He reminds us of a professor who is full of his own learning and the originality of his doctrines and who expounds these doctrines to young and old alike, regardless of their personal attributes. This is of course an exaggeration, but it points us in the right direction. What is not at all an exaggeration is the fact that the Stranger's approach to the *technē* of politics makes fully visible an ambiguity that is implicit in the Socratic teaching: the problem of the relation between knowing and making.

Again it is necessary to anticipate a point that will be developed more thoroughly below. Nowhere in Plato do we find the Aristotelian tripartition of the sciences into the theoretical, practical, and productive. In Plato, the distinction is always between the theoretical or gnostic arts on the one hand, represented most characteristically by arithmetic and logistics, and the practico-productive arts on the other, of which architecture serves as the paradigm in the *Statesman*. In Aristotle, the productive arts result in the genesis of an artifact that is distinct from the act of production and is the end or purpose of that act. The practical arts are activities in which the act is its own end or purpose; the examples are ethics and politics.

Since Plato does not distinguish between practice and production, it looks very much as though politics is a productive art, or, in other words, as though the city and hence its citizens are artifacts. And, in fact, although his interlocutors speak of the nature of the city, as well as of the diverse natures of individual human types, nowhere in the Platonic corpus is it stated that man is by nature the political animal. In the *Statesman*, the artifactual status of the city is underlined by the central paradigm of weaving. The art of the weaver produces clothing to defend the body against the rigors of nature. If it is permissible to speak of life in accordance with nature, we must also recognize that nature seems to be divided against herself and that human existence is the locus of this division.

Socrates uses the expression "art of politics" (*technē politikē*) on two occasions. The first is in the *Gorgias* (521d6–8), where he says that he is virtually the only living Athenian who practices "the genuine political *technē*." As the context shows, he means by this *technē* his usual practice of interrogating his fellow citizens on the question of their manner of life, and not at all the art of governing the city. The same passage makes explicit that

Socrates regards his art of politics as equivalent to the medicine of the soul (521e3ff), or to private rather than public practice. The second use occurs in the *Protagoras* (318e5–319a5), where Socrates applies the term to the art of the famous sophist, an art described by Protagoras himself as that of giving good counsel in the home and in the city, and which Socrates plainly identifies, here and elsewhere, as rhetoric in the pejorative sense of the term.

In a slightly paradoxical formulation, we can say that Socrates does not attribute technical production to the *technē* of politics. The term *technē* means here a kind of wisdom rather than the productive activity of the craftsman or demiurge. Nonetheless, the language he uses to describe the production of the just city in the *Republic* is filled with metaphors derived from the productive arts. To restrict ourselves to one example, Socrates says that the philosopher will be a good demiurge "of temperance, justice, and all the demotic virtues" (VI. 500d4–9); in the same context, he refers to the need to paint the city in accordance with the divine paradigm, of which the discursive version in the dialogue is a mere image (VI. 500d10–e4; cf. 501a2–b7). In the same vein, in an earlier passage he establishes that "we were making [*epoioumen*] the paradigm in speech of a good city" (V. 472d9–e2).

These passages and others like them suggest that the philosopher studies nature not simply to imitate it, but to produce the demotic or political virtues, as demiurges produce artifacts, but not wisdom or philosophical virtue, which are not artifacts. Otherwise put, the diverse human natures are the raw materials out of which the city is constructed. It is not the human being but the citizen who is a work of art. Even the philosopher, to the extent that he or she is a guardian of the good city, must be produced by the education of music, gymnastics, and, eventually, mathematics, an education that is carefully codified by the original lawgiver. In the *Statesman,* this suggestion is carried much farther and becomes virtually explicit in the detailed comparison of politics to weaving.

The Stranger's conception of the political *technē* is thus practico-productive in a sense quite different from the Aristotelian notion of *phronēsis* or sound judgment; so too the city is not in accord with nature for the Stranger in the same sense as it is for Aristotle. And the technical predilection exhibited by the Stranger takes him beyond the hints and metaphors of the Socratic formulation of the disjunction within human existence between theory and practice. A very similar point obtains with respect to the method of diaeresis. Whereas the Stranger repeats Socrates' general description of the art as classification in accordance with kinds, his own use is manifestly a prototype of what is today called conceptual analysis; more precisely, diaeresis is employed not to sort out the formal elements of abstract structure, but to construct new classes or concepts.

In this vein, it is instructive to compare the stated intentions of the main speakers in the *Republic* and the *Statesman*. According to Socrates, the main intention of the conversation in the *Republic* is to defend justice (V. 472b3–5) and more particularly to assist the potential philosopher in undergoing a "revolution of the soul" (VII. 521c6: *tēs psuchēs periagōgē*) as the necessary preliminary to a return into the cave, as political existence is represented there. In the *Statesman,* the Stranger says that the purpose of the conversation has been to administer a training in dialectic to all concerned, not simply with respect to the art of politics but in all cases (285d4–7). The intention of the Stranger is to provide technical training in dialectic, not to effect a revolution in the souls of his auditors. From this standpoint one could say that the *Statesman* is a more theoretical book than the *Republic,* although it makes more explicit the practico-productive nature of politics than does its predecessor.

With the preceding remarks on Eros and *technē* in mind, let us reconsider the question of the dramatic relationship between Socrates and the Eleatic Stranger. At the beginning of the *Sophist,* Socrates asks Theodorus whether the Stranger is not a kind of elenctic god who has come to Athens in human disguise "to observe and refute us because of our weakness in discussions" (*en tois logois:* 216b3–6). He prefaces this question with a reference to Homer, who speaks in particular of gods of strangers who observe the hybris and lawlessness of mankind (216a5–b3). At 229a3ff, the Stranger develops at some length the thesis that the art of punishment is suited to the correction of hybris or evil, whereas ignorance is addressed by teaching. There are different types of teaching that correspond to the types of ignorance; the greatest and most authoritative form of teaching is the art of elenctic (230d6–8).

These passages provide us with a textual basis for the suggestion that Plato invents the Eleatic Stranger for the sake of indicating his own refutation or punishment of his former teacher. Some who make this suggestion connect the discursive punishment of Socrates in the *Sophist* and *Statesman* with his trial and punishment by the city of Athens, which are described in the dramatically related dialogues *Euthyphron, Apology, Crito,* and *Phaedo.* We could strengthen this suggestion by observing that when Socrates was himself a young man, he was subjected to a punitive exercise in dialectical gymnastics by the old Parmenides, the Stranger's teacher (*Parmenides* 135d3ff). It would be in keeping with Platonic irony to subject the old Socrates to a renewal of his original punishment by Parmenides' student, a punishment that is delivered obliquely but significantly through the mediation of a boy named Young Socrates.

The imaginative reader might go a step farther and suggest that the Stranger suppresses Eros by *technē*, thereby fulfilling in speech what the Athenians are about to fulfill in deed, namely, the punishment of Socrates for corrupting the young, exactly as predicted in the *Gorgias* by Callicles, who links the charge of pederasty to the philosopher's inability to defend himself against political accusations (484c5–486d1). In sum, are we to assume that Plato in the last period of his philosophical development came to reject the erotic rhetoric of his teacher, and with it the doctrine of the Ideas as the objects of philosophical Eros, in favor of new and more powerful technical elaborations of discoveries introduced but not perfected by Socrates?

This preliminary survey of the peculiarities of the *Statesman* is intended to introduce the reader to an aspect of Plato that is rarely noticed and that contradicts the traditional oversimplifications of Platonism by friend and foe alike. The Eleatic Stranger represents neither the pure mathematicism admired by the great scientist-thinkers of the Renaissance nor the denigration of production and the celebration of an unchanging and friendly nature that is anathema to the twentieth-century descendants of Nietzsche. And he certainly cannot be explained as a prototypical version of the post-Fregean philosopher of language. The Stranger is neither an ancient nor a modern, if we use those terms to designate a rigid and total opposition of fundamental orientations. He is an expression of the inseparability of apparently contradictory philosophical doctrines.

To make this assertion more precise, we can say that the Stranger not only champions diaeresis as a prototypical *mathēsis universalis* but shows its shortcomings by a kind of *reductio ad absurdum* that implicates him in the obscurities of mythical discourse rather than in the clarity and distinctness of eidetic intuition. The constructive powers of *technē* are employed in the attempt to defend human beings from the disjunction within nature that they themselves exemplify but which for that very reason they can never master. The Stranger anticipates Nietzsche's famous characterization of the human being as the not yet fully constructed animal, without forgetting that to be partially constructed is already to possess a nature.

It is true that the Stranger concludes his dialectical exercise with what today would be called the message of a reactionary conservatism. The very attempt to preserve human nature by spinning the web of politics leads not to freedom but to the bondage of common beliefs, honors, and opinions (310e5–11); in other words, the Stranger's political doctrine is scarcely different from the views of Socrates in the *Republic* or the Athenian Stranger in the *Laws*. The human animal cannot finally escape its herdlike nature but must be guided by philosophical shepherds or their surrogates. But this is not because the cosmos is bound by transcendent Ideas, the noetic apprehension of which provides us with an eternal paradigm. It is rather because there are no such transcendent bonds that protect human beings from the dissolution of cyclical change that we must spin our own bonds. Underneath the pious rhetoric of the Stranger, which surfaces most fully in the conclusion of the dialogue, is a clear perception of the tragedy of human existence, which does not cease to be tragic simply because, if we view it from a sufficiently high perspective, it becomes a comedy.

The Eleatic Stranger comes to Athens with a modification of the Socratic teaching: erotic playfulness is an irrelevant diversion to the serious business of technical expertise. But just as the deep seriousness of the founders of modernity in their effort to emancipate the human race from the discontinuities of nature has culminated in the *absurdisme* of postmodernist discontinuity, so it would seem that, at least within the Platonic cosmos, Socrates has the last laugh if not the last word. In carrying out his effort to punish Socrates, the Stranger comes closer and closer to Socratic doctrine, until finally, despite all differences in character and rhetoric, one can scarcely distinguish between the contents of their speeches.

It may seem frivolous to suggest that the *Statesman* is an elaborate Platonic joke, but the suggestion is in no way intended to suppress the serious philosophical arguments of the dialogue. The joke is on those, whether philologists or ontologists, who lack the wit to appreciate Plato's elegance or the playful seriousness that is required to penetrate the initially tedious details of the *Statesman* in order to enter the presence of its enigmatic author.

Opening *Scene:* 257a1–258b3

The main conversation of the *Theaetetus* opens with Socrates asking Theodorus, the professor of geometry, if he has encountered any unusually gifted students. Theodorus begins the *Sophist* with a speech in which he refers to his agreement yesterday to a subsequent meeting with Socrates, but announces a surprise; he is accompanied by the Stranger from Elea. The *Statesman* opens with Socrates expressing his gratitude to Theodorus for these introductions. It is a bit odd that Socrates requires the mediation of a stranger (Theodorus is from Cyrene) in order to be brought into contact with the gifted young Athenian; the oddness disappears when we understand that Theaetetus, although he has heard about Socrates' conversations with other talented youths, has never himself been moved to seek out the philosopher's company. This raises a question about the Eros of Theaetetus. Apparently his physical ugliness, in which he resembles Socrates, has contributed to isolating him from erotic encounters. But what of his soul? Whereas Socrates is extremely pleased to have met Theaetetus, the young man gives no sign that he derives the same pleasure from his encounter with Socrates. I do not mean by this that the topics of conversation are uninteresting to him, or even that he does not respond with excitement at various points of the discussion. The reverse is the case, as we can tell from his frequent oaths and statements of perplexity. But excitement and perplexity at problems of philosophy are not necessarily sources of pleasure to young mathematicians.

In the case of the Eleatic Stranger, the situation is more marked. Again Socrates says that he is very grateful to meet the Stranger, whom he compares to a god in the *Sophist*. This could mean either that Socrates accepts his punishment or that he is grateful to have learned that the Stranger's refutation was unsuccessful. The Stranger never says that he is very grateful to Theodorus for the introduction to Socrates. He responds politely about his duties to his hosts but seems to take Socrates' compliment as his due. Otherwise stated, the Stranger is willing to exhibit his wisdom to Socrates by means of a rather mechanical-appearing discussion with two other persons, in the *Sophist* with Theaetetus, who looks like Socrates, and in the *Statesman* with Young Socrates, who bears the philosopher's name. He does not seem to have any interest in conversing with Socrates. And curiously enough, Socrates, who is presented in the *Theaetetus* (169b5) as sick with the desire to dispute with everyone he encounters, makes no effort to engage the Stranger in conversation. Instead, he suggests that the Stranger expound the Eleatic teaching with the assistance of Theaetetus (*Sophist* 217d5ff).

Why does Plato decline to present us with a conversation between Socrates and the Stranger? This is a particular version of the general question why we have no account in the dialogues of a conversation between two mature philosophers; instead, we are allowed to witness the exercise to which Parmenides subjects the youthful Socrates. Some have explained the absence of a conversation between two mature thinkers of the highest order as a sign of Plato's esotericism. Without rejecting that suggestion, I nevertheless wonder whether it does not prevent us from considering a deeper question. In what sense does one thinker of the highest rank ever seriously listen to another? Do Aristotle's writings, for example, reflect a fair-minded, open, or, as it would be put today, "objective" conversation with his teacher? Despite his expressed respect for his own teacher, father Parmenides, does not the Stranger rebuke him by accusing him of having spoken "carelessly" (*eukolōs*) about beings? (*ta onta: Sophist* 242c4–6). I suspect that Plato's attitude toward other philosophers is very much like that of the Stranger toward all of his predecessors. Fair-mindedness and objectivity are (sometimes) the traits of scholars, not of thinkers of the highest rank.

Philosophers educate nonphilosophers; they punish other philosophers for their mistakes. The connection between education and punishment is brought out in the opening exchange between Socrates and Theodorus as follows. Socrates says that he owes Theodorus a debt of gratitude for his acquaintance with Theaetetus and the Stranger. Theodorus replies that Socrates will soon owe him three times as much, when his companions have finished their work "for you" (*apergasontai soi*) on the statesman and the philosopher. Theodorus does not count as part of the debt the conversation in the *Theaetetus*, which was conducted by Socrates and led to no *ergon* other than aporetic speech. Since Theodorus has already heard what the Stranger has to say, the two conversations in the *Sophist* and *Statesman* are for the benefit of Socrates.

Socrates replies that he cannot believe what he has heard from the man who is best at calculation (*logismous*) and geometry. Theodorus has miscalculated by attributing equal worth or dignity (*tēs isēs aksias*) to three human types "who differ more in honor [*tēi timēi*] than is in accord with the analogy of your art" (257a1–b3). *Analogia* is a ratio or proportion: *a:b::c:d*. Theodorus has implied that it is equally gratifying to hear about the sophist, the statesman, and the philosopher. Since there are only three terms, the analogy may be this: the sophist is to the statesman as the statesman is to the philosopher (with *b = c*). There is no need for the proportion to be one of equality unless the statesman is equal to the philosopher. It is therefore unclear why Socrates refers to *analogia* in his ironical punishment of Theodorus. Furthermore, Theodorus followed the Stranger's instructions in abstracting from the honor due to the three types, since these conversations are presumably exercises in diaeresis, which disregards honor and is concerned exclusively with community of family (*Sophist* 227a1off).

The serious content in Socrates' statement is his tacit rejection of the diaeretic method as an adequate means for presenting the nature of the three human types. He himself does not employ diaeresis in this way, but only in the analysis of formal structure. One of the peculiarities of the *Sophist* and *Statesman* is that the Stranger employs diaeresis on human beings and that despite his apparent sobriety, these diaereses are extremely comical. This will be made explicit at 266b1off, where the method classifies human beings with pigs and the statesman with the swineherd, a result identified by the Stranger himself as a joke. It is hard to say whether the Stranger is intentionally satirizing the diaeretic method of Socrates or whether his application of it to human beings is a sign of his theoretical madness. Perhaps he is attempting to advance beyond his teacher Parmenides by assimilating the way of *doksa* (in other words, the study of genesis and, in particular, of political existence within genesis) into the way of truth by an appropriation of the Socratic instruments of diaeresis and myth-telling.

In any event, Theodorus acknowledges his error, the first of many to be encountered in this dialogue. In so doing, however, he makes another, unnoticed error. Theodorus does not see that Socrates is wrong to deny the applicability of proportion to persons or types of unequal honor. The error is instead to treat all three as of equal worth. Theodorus indicates his displeasure by swearing—he refers to the Cyrenian god Ammon, the Libyan Zeus—thereby descending from geometry to politics. Theodorus says that Socrates has spoken justly and in accord with memory (*mnēmonikōs*) in punishing him for his error in calculation (*peri tous logismous*). The allusion to memory presumably means that Socrates has correctly remembered the difference between mathematics and the estimation of human beings (257b5–7). *Logismos* is used by Aristotle in connection with *boulēsis* or deliberation, and so with *phronēsis* or practical intelligence, which, as we shall see, is the main theme of this dialogue. Just as proportions can be used to express inequality of honor, so too calculation extends from numbers to human beings. This suggests that it may be possible to employ diaeresis in the study of human nature, provided we do not abstract from inequality of honor, as does the Stranger.

Theodorus again playfully indicates his irritation by warning Socrates that he will take his revenge, in other words, equalize the honor due to each, on another occasion. He then turns to the Stranger and urges him not to stop gratifying them because of fatigue, but to carry out the exposition of the statesman and philosopher in whatever order he chooses (257b8–c5). Theodorus did not seem to be enjoying himself in the *Theaetetus,* where he refers to his discomfort and lack of ability to engage in Socratic conversation, an act he compares to wrestling (169a6ff). He was also upset at the need to criticize his old friend Protagoras (162a4ff). But since the Stranger does not wish to wrestle with him, Theodorus can enjoy listening to his conversation with young men on topics that are not of central importance to him. He can concentrate on the technical nature of the Stranger's use of diaeresis.

The Stranger is not fatigued; no doubt he enjoys displaying his wisdom. In any event, he underlines the necessity of continuing the discussion but suggests that he shift from Theaetetus to the young man's *sungumnastēs* or fellow-exerciser (257c2–8). Theodorus authorizes the shift in interlocutors: "since they are young, they will more easily bear the entire burden if they are given a rest" (257c9–10). This exchange reminds us that the Stranger does not claim merely to be displaying the Eleatic teaching but to be training his interlocutors, and through them his adult audience, in method.

So too in the *Parmenides* (135d3ff), the old philosopher refers to his interrogation of Socrates as a kind of gymnastics. We should bear in mind that doctrinal exposition and methodological gymnastics are not necessarily compatible, unless the method is the doctrine. Again, the choice of interlocutor is based not upon his individual nature but upon the desire to avoid fatigue.

Socrates then endorses Theodorus's recommendation while transforming its basis. This is also his last speech in the dialogue (257d1–258a6). He is indeed interested in observing the respective natures of the two youths. One looks like him and the other bears his name, which fact, Socrates ironically adds, suggests a certain relationship. The point is that we need to know whether the young men resemble Socrates' soul. If he is present only in name or only through a physical resemblance, then he is not present at all. We are reminded of the invisible presence of Plato in his *Republic* through the personae of his brothers, Glaucon and Adeimantus, whose differing natures make an important contribution to the substance of the conversation. Although the issue could be verified only by a close analysis of the responses of the two youths, it does not appear from the *Sophist* and the *Statesman* that the differences between Theaetetus and the Young Socrates play a significant role. The mode of training employed by the Stranger abstracts from these differences, just as mathematics abstracts from human life.

This being so, one may well wonder what Socrates learns from the two conversations conducted by the Stranger. He did not after all say that he was interested in hearing the Stranger's doctrine, but only that one should strive to become acquainted with one's "relatives" (*sungenneis*) through discourse (258a2–3). Perhaps he was disappointed by what he heard yesterday concerning the nature of the sophist. However this may be, Socrates, despite his portrait of the philosopher in the *Theaetetus*, does not abstract from human life; at least he does not do so as a teacher. In the *Theaetetus*, Socrates spoke with the young mathematician, and in the *Sophist* he listened to his interrogation by the Stranger. In the *Statesman*, he will listen to the interrogation of Young Socrates, whom he does not know at all, by the Stranger, and suggests that he will interrogate Young Socrates later (258a6). We may wonder what will be the topic of this proposed conversation.

If the pattern established by the three dialogues of our trilogy is to be continued, not only must Socrates interrogate Young Socrates, but it is unclear with whom the Stranger will expound the nature of the philosopher. Presumably it is of no interest to the Stranger with whom he discusses this topic. But it is never suggested that he do so with the old Socrates. In short, not only is the last discussion not presented, but it is entirely unclear who could have presented it, given the dramatic structure of the trilogy. The shift in interlocutors is agreeable to both the Stranger and Young Socrates. The Stranger then decides to discuss the statesman rather than the philosopher, and we are ready for the main conversation (258a7–b3).

CHAPTER TWO

The Diaereses

The Method

AT the beginning of the *Sophist*, Socrates asks whether the residents of Elea believe the sophist, the statesman, and the philosopher to be one, two, or rather three in *genos* as they are in name (217a2–8). The Stranger replies that his countrymen consider these to be three, but "it is no small or simple task to define clearly in each case what it is" (*ti pot'estin:* 217b1–3). As Theodorus testifies, the Stranger is thoroughly familiar with what we may call with some hesitation the Eleatic doctrine on the nature of the three human types (217b4–8).

We hesitate for the following reason. The Stranger never explicitly states that the definitions he is about to present are due to Parmenides or to some identifiable school of his followers. Later in the dialogue, when introducing the topic of nonbeing, the Stranger says that he will have to put to the torture the command of "father Parmenides" against saying that nonbeing is (241d5–7). Whether or not a parricide occurs (and the Stranger indicates that he should not be accused of this crime: 241d3), the crux of the Stranger's doctrine is plainly a modification of the Eleatic teaching. More precisely, the Stranger introduces a new way of considering nonbeing that has obviously been devised by Plato himself.

We have no historical account of the Eleatic doctrine of the statesman, but it would seem to follow from the extant fragments of Parmenides' poem that politics falls within the domain of "the opinions of mortals, in which there is no secure truth" (*Diels*, B 1, 30). Furthermore, the Stranger applies the method of diaeresis, which is associated in the Platonic corpus with Socrates, to the task of answering the typically Socratic question "what is it?" with respect to the sophist and the philosopher. Even the accommodation of his discourse to the format of question-and-answer is probably a deviation from the Eleatic procedure, although Socrates, in an obvious allusion to the *Parmenides,* says that he was once present as a young man when Parmenides employed questioning to utter splendid speeches (217c4–7).

If the Stranger has come from Elea in order to continue the punitive education of the old Socrates, it is certainly not to introduce a new method or a new question. What he does is rather to extend the application of the Socratic method of diaeresis from formal structure to the task of defining two of the three most ambiguous human types. As we shall see, the Stranger attempts to punish Socrates by showing him that the method of diaeresis applies to the human as well as to the divine realm. This is as much a modification of Parmenides' teaching as is the Stranger's solution to the problem of speech about nonbeing. The Stranger, in other words, is neither simply an Eleatic nor a Socratic. He extends the Socratic method to human affairs in the attempt to acquire technical knowledge of what has hitherto been the realm of human opinion.

In so doing, the Stranger necessarily deviates from the Socratic procedure of connecting the method of diaeresis to discourse about the Platonic Ideas, whether these are separate from the domain of genesis, as in the *Phaedrus,* or accessible within the intelligible structure of generated particulars, as in the *Philebus.* The units of division in the Stranger's diaereses are no longer restricted to natural elements of Ideas; instead, they classify human activities, paramount among them the arts and sciences, in accord with the ad hoc intention of the investigator. These activities may be differently classified in different inquiries; as we shall see, in his pursuit of the statesman, the Stranger classifies some arts in a way opposite to that selected for the same arts in the pursuit of the sophist. The Stranger modifies diaeresis from a method for exhibiting pure formal structure to a method of what we today call concept-construction.

It is in no sense an anachronism to suggest that the Stranger is a Platonic anticipation of certain aspects of the Cartesian attempt to master nature by *technē,* including the *technē* of a *mathēsis universalis.* This is of course not to suggest that the Stranger is a Cartesian, but rather that traditional accounts of the difference between ancient and modern thought are oversimplifications. Just as the biologist finds traces of human physiology in previous or nonhuman species, so the historian of philosophy detects anticipations of later doctrines in earlier thinkers. If *homo sapiens* is descended from the chimpanzee, it does not follow that human beings are chimpanzees. Plato is no doubt separated from the modern epoch not only by the fact of modern mathematical and experimental science, but by how he would have evaluated the human significance of these activities. Nevertheless, the *Statesman* leaves us in no doubt that Plato at least experimented with the conception of politics as the technical application of *technē* to the task of defending human beings against the hazards of nature. In so doing, he discovered the problem of constructivism.

In his explicit statements about the method of diaeresis, the Stranger stays fairly close to descriptions offered by Socrates elsewhere in the dialogues. There are two important methodological comments in the *Sophist*. The first is at 227a7ff. The Stranger refers here to "the method of the reasonings" (*logōn*) and emphasizes the need to abstract from considerations of honor while regarding as relevant only family relations (*to sungenes kai to mē sungenes*). The second reference is at 253c7ff, where Theaetetus agrees to the Stranger's suggestion that "the division in accord with genera" and the avoidance of confusion between same and other belong to the science of the free man or philosopher (compare *Theaetetus* 172d1), namely, dialectic (*dialektikē*). To this could perhaps be added 267d6, where the Stranger speaks of a carelessness on the part of earlier thinkers concerning the division of genera in accordance with kinds (*tēs tōn genōn kat' eidē diaireseōs*). The passage about the science of free men is not a technical clarification of the method itself.

The term *dialektikē* does not appear in the *Statesman*, although the comparative adjective *dialektikōteros* occurs twice, at 285d6 and 287a3. In the second occurrence, to be *dialektikōteros* is associated with greater ingenuity at making clear the beings by *logos*. The Stranger comments more extensively on the nature of method in the *Statesman* than in the *Sophist*. As a preliminary example, we may consider 285b4ff. While introducing the topic of measurement (*metrētikē*), the Stranger says that most people fail to distinguish the essential components of the art of measurement because they are not accustomed to dividing in accordance with kinds (*kat' eidē*). He then says that the correct procedure consists in two parts: (1) do not abstract what is common to many things until you have established the eidetic differences; (2) do not be intimidated by differences until you have "bound up" (*herksas*) all entities related in their being (*ousia*) in a single family (*genos*).

One could understand this passage to correspond to Socrates' description of dialectic in the *Phaedrus* (266b4ff). He says there that diaeresis, like collection (*sunagōgē*), is a part of dialectic. It should also be noted that in the *Republic* (VI. 511b3–c2 and VII. 532b4ff), Socrates defines pure philosophy as dialectic in a quite different sense, namely, as reasoning from Ideas via Ideas to other Ideas. There is no reference in the *Sophist* and *Statesman* to the doctrine of Ideas as discussed by Socrates in the *Republic*. The *eidē* or kinds by which diaeresis establishes families or genera in these dialogues are not detached from their instances, and they are much more heterogeneous than the Ideas in the *Republic*. Even the "greatest genera" of being, same, other, rest, and change in their instances as letters inhere in syllables. And kinds like the sophist, the statesman, or, more amusingly, hornless land animals are obviously not the pure eidetic elements of the *Republic*.

The passage in the *Phaedrus* comes closer to the Stranger's procedure, since Socrates speaks there of the division and collection of kinds of madness and love. But we should also notice that Socrates compares the division of kinds to the carving of meat at the natural joints (265e1ff); this metaphor suggests the extraction of what we today call "concepts" from a dead rather than a living animal, or in other words indicates the difference between understanding the speeches and deeds of human life (upon which the philosophical rhetoric of accommodation to natural types is based) and the analytical understanding of formal structure. In sum: despite the official Socratic description of diaeresis as the method of pure formal analysis, the *Phaedrus* passage allows for a rapprochement between him and the Stranger. It remains true, however, that the classification of madness and love is not carried out by a full-fledged application of diaeresis, and that Socrates never engages in such exercises but only describes in general terms how they are to be conducted with respect to Ideas, as in the *Philebus* (16c1–17a5).

Diaeresis, and so presumably dialectic, as understood by the Stranger, has no clearly demarcated subject matter. That is to say, it applies generally to *eidē* or looks that are not mere parts of a larger whole or heterogeneous collections of individuals, as the Stranger asserts in the course of the diaeresis. For the moment we need say about this only that the looks actually employed by the Stranger in his diaereses are frequently arbitrary and, as noted above, can be classified in opposite ways, depending upon the intention of the investigator. Items of the same look are not necessarily "natural kinds" in the Stranger's divisions, in the sense of following a natural eidetic structure independent of human intentions or interpretations. The divisions are "natural" in the sense that they arise by cutting "through the middle" or, as we say today, by the construction of complementary classes. It is important to note that cutting through the middle is not the same as cutting at the natural joints.

The Stranger certainly implies that the cuts are natural in a more fundamental sense, but he never arrives at the point of explaining clearly and precisely what he means by this. To anticipate, one could hardly say that the *eidos* of the art of nurturing land-dwelling herds corresponds to a Platonic Idea or to a Socratic *eidos*. It seems to be compatible with the Stranger's procedure for us to infer that *eidē* or common looks can be constructed as well as discovered. The sense of an *eidos* is thus as it were methodological rather than (as the Stranger sometimes claims) natural. If this is so, then diaeresis can be employed to elicit the structure of any set of phenomena whatsoever. From this standpoint, diaeresis is a prototype of the Cartesian *mathēsis universalis*.

At the same time, it is important to emphasize that the method is not a formal one in the modern mathematical sense of the expression. Whereas one might formalize any particular instance of diaeresis, and so present an abstract schematism of the method in general, it is obvious that these formalizations make sense, if at all, only a posteriori. The actual application of the method depends on seeing and defining the concrete forms of the entities under analysis. The looks to which we attend are often ambiguous and subject to shifts in their conceptual location. If diaeresis is useful at all, it can be only as a patient analysis of the details of human experience and not as a formalization of general properties or relations of those details.

The Longer Way

Step 1. We are now ready to consider in detail the diaeresis, or rather the two diaereses of the statesman. The Stranger begins at 258b3 with what will later be called the longer way to the royal art of the statesman. The first step could arguably be called the 0 step because it is the basis for, rather than a part of, diaeresis. Since 0 is not a number for the Greeks, and because the number of steps plays a small but interesting role in the economy of the dialogue, I will speak here of step 1. As is true throughout the dialogue, what looks like numerical exactness is almost invariably ambiguous upon closer inspection, and one cannot establish the number of parts of any division with precision. This too is part of the teaching of the dialogue. The mathematical setting is somehow inappropriate to the main topic of investigation.

The Stranger begins somewhat abruptly with the assertion that they must look for the statesman after the sophist. He then establishes that the sciences cannot be divided in the same way that was employed in the previous investigation (258b2–10). This makes it clear from the outset that there is no natural—in the sense of unique and unchanging—diaeresis of *epistēmē* and *technē*. The division of the sciences is relative to what we intend to define. Whereas we divide in accord with *eidē* or looks, the looks change; the sciences look different from differing standpoints.

"Should we place the statesman among the epistemonic men or not?" Young Socrates replies in the affirmative. In the *Sophist*, the Stranger began by dividing powers or capacities (*dunameis*) into two kinds, technical and nontechnical. Here he starts instead with human beings who possess knowledge of some sort. An *epistēmōn* is one who is knowing, wise, or prudent; the term need not carry the sense of precise scientific knowledge. Having made this initial cut between persons, however, the Stranger shifts immediately to the sciences (*tas epistēmas*). In fact, the identification of the statesman as an *epistēmōn* is not part of, but the precondition for, the diaeresis. The Stranger assumes that the epistemic property of the statesman is appropriate for the exercise of defining this type by diaeresis. In other words, it is a premethodological decision to define the type by its *technē*. We could have approached the statesman in some other way, had our intentions been different, and still employed the method of diaeresis.

Step 2. The difference between the present diaeresis and its predecessors will consist in the order of the classification of the sciences. The Stranger shifts almost immediately from knowers and non-knowers, or types of human beings, to the sciences themselves. Throughout the diaeresis, there will be some confusion about whether we are dividing persons or their professional activities. The Stranger then makes a methodological remark that underlines what I have called the constructive dimension of diaeresis. Once we have found the path leading to the statesman "we must separate it apart from the others and stamp it with one form" (*idean autēi mian episphragisasthai:* 258c4–5). The same verb is used at *Philebus* 26d1 for making one genus by stamping the more and the less onto the unlimited. *Episphragizō* means to ratify or impose, but also to put a seal onto wax or to make coins (see also *Phaedo* 75d2 and *Laws* IX. 855e7). In both cases, the sense is one of production. After this, we must stamp one single form (*hen allo eidos episēmēnamenous*) on all the other sciences. The verb here has approximately the same sense as *episphragizō;* the two terms occur in the same context in the *Philebus* (25a4–26d1), during Socrates' identification of the *genē* or *ideai* of the limit, unlimited, mixed, and cause (but not, interestingly enough, in his preliminary account of eidetic arithmetic or diaeresis).

This terminology certainly indicates that there is a dimension of production within the articulation of classes, whether by diaeresis or some similar method. But the stamping or producing is by way of a *genos* or *idea* that is not necessarily produced (although it may be). We are engaged in the construction of cognitive artifacts by which to secure a grip on our prey; to "grip together" multiple instances of a given kind is to "conceive" or to prepare a concept, but one that follows and expresses the kind rather than creating it ex nihilo.

The two forms or looks by which the sciences are to be divided are introduced by the examples of arithmetic on the one hand and carpentry and the handicrafts on the other. The latter arts are employed by the craftsmen to bring into being bodies that did not previously exist. The arts represented by arithmetic are "stripped of practical application" (*psilai tōn prakseōn*). The Stranger names these two looks *praktikē* and *gnōstikē* respectively (258c6–e5). As was previously noted, there is no distinction between practice and production in the Platonic classification of the sciences; *praktikē* should therefore be translated as "practico-production."

Not every *technē* is productive; for example, arithmetic and geometry do not produce artifacts but enable us to discover the natural properties of numbers and figures. The political *technē* would seem to be a mixture of discovery and production; just as the art of weaving produces a web from threads that are themselves modifications of plants and animal hairs, so the statesman weaves together a city from modified versions of differing human natures. This seems at least initially plausible, but what is not yet evident is whether every nonproductive art is theoretical.

Consider the example of the art of hunting, which the Stranger himself uses as a metaphor for diaeresis. It is true that the hunter employs manufactured tools like hooks, nets, and spears. But this is not what defines the art; hunting is the tracking down of an animal, that is, of a natural being of a determinate look or form. It is neither the art of defining the looks of the prey nor of manufacturing the implements with which they are caught. This example has two quite distinct implications. On the one hand, there seem to be human activities that are neither purely theoretical nor productive in the sense defined by the Stranger; they do not bring into being previously nonexistent bodies. On the other hand, the hunter must discern the look of the animal as it is in order to pursue it, and so must usually make use of implements in order to capture it. Everything seems to depend here upon how we choose to divide the respective activities of looking, pursuing, and tool-using.

The Stranger abandons practico-production and turns immediately to gnostics or theory in his search for the sophist. As we shall see shortly, he will locate the political art in the commanding branch of gnostics; yet he will develop the analysis of the art of politics with images of production, in particular, with the image of weaving. There is a central confusion in the analysis of the art of politics in the *Statesman,* whether or not intended by Plato. This confusion will also become visible within the diaeresis, but for the moment we can say simply that whereas the diaeresis locates the statesman within the class of those who know but do not produce, the actual discussion of politics makes it plain that the statesman is also a producer. This confusion is justified but not removed as soon as we recognize that the separation between gnostics and practico-production is inadequate. By this I mean not simply that Aristotle was wise to distinguish practice from production, but more fundamentally that there is a productive element within cognition, as is evident from the metaphors of stamping or sealing in the act of determining the look of the divisions of science.

Prologue to Step 3. There is a brief prologue to the third step, in which the Stranger establishes an important point about the political art, again independently of diaeresis (258e8–259c5). The Stranger asks whether the statesman, king, despot, and head of a household are all one *technē* or four. In order to assist Young Socrates in his answer, the Stranger asks a second question: is the statesman defined by holding office or by knowledge? This question is posed by means of a comparison with medicine. In his analogy, the Stranger establishes that a private citizen with a knowledge of medicine is as much a physician as an officeholder with the same knowledge. This is intended to substantiate the inference that a private citizen with the requisite knowledge to advise a king possesses the knowledge that the king himself requires.

But this is not really persuasive. Even in the case of medicine, one can easily imagine that a sick person would prefer to consult with the officially designated specialist. As a justification for this preference, it is reasonable to suppose that the official physician has more experience in treating patients. This of course has no bearing on the actual knowledge possessed by the private consultant. But one may possess a theoretical knowledge of medicine without knowing how to apply this knowledge to the particular case, as Aristotle points out at the beginning of the *Metaphysics* (A.1. 981a12ff). In the case of politics, it seems reasonable to maintain that experience in ruling is part of the knowledge of ruling, or that, unlike the case of medicine, there is no purely theoretical knowledge of statesmanship.

It seems to be a defect of the Stranger's purely theoretical approach that he overlooks the importance of experience in exaggerating the importance of a theoretical knowledge of politics. And there is a difficulty with the assimilation of household management to kingship or ruling. The deficiency is already obvious from the fact that household management and despotism are tacitly subordinated to, rather than assimilated into, the art of the statesman. It is the king who gives his name to that art, not the householder or the despot. We think here of Aristotle's criticism of this point in the *Politics* (I. 1252a7ff).

The Stranger's assumption would be quickly exposed as erroneous if we were to speak of the art of household management instead of its presumed synonym, the royal art. Again the problem lies in a kind of abstractness that is inappropriate to the subject matter. To mention nothing else, the Eros of the family is quite different from the Eros of the city; nor is the sexual Eros enough to bring out the role of spiritedness or the love of honor, which conflicts with concern for one's own family. Although this is not the only way in which to formulate the problem, we can say that the Stranger treats human beings as herd animals who must breed and be nurtured, but he abstracts from Eros or maintains a purely theoretical or methodological approach to these features of human existence.

Continuing with the prologue to step 3, the Stranger explains why he is placing the statesman, who has already been identified as the king, in the gnostic branch of the original division (259c6–d5). This is because the king is much less able to acquire rule with his hands and his entire body than with the intelligence and the strength of his soul. The Stranger assumes that the actions of the body are practical. We can see here exactly why Aristotle found it necessary to distinguish between *praxis* and *poiēsis*. Using the Stranger's terminology, we cannot bring out the fact that some practice is productive and some is not. Furthermore, nonproductive practice is not the same as theory or pure *gnōsis*. Let us see whether step 3 attends to this distinction.

Step 3. The Stranger now asks Young Socrates to turn his attention to gnostics and to apprehend (*katanoein*) a "natural division" (*diaphuē*) in it (259d9–10). This last term refers to the distinction between *kritikē*, the art of separating or judging, and *epitaktikē*, the art of commanding. Note that we are ourselves engaged in a *gnōsis* or knowing of knowing, presumably for "critical" rather than for "epitactic" reasons. This form of judgment divides at the natural joints. *Kritikē* is of special importance to the Stranger because it includes among its procedures the method of diaeresis. In order to translate *kritikē* properly, one must refer both to separation or division and judgment.

In the *Sophist*, *kritikē* appears in the fifth diaeresis; its paradigm-case consists in household tasks. In the *Statesman*, the paradigm-case is *logistikē*, calculation, which the Stranger glosses here as number theory (259e1–7). Logistics discovers the properties of numbers and judges them in the sense of asserting what these properties are. It does not pass judgment in the sense of attributing more or less honor to the discovered properties. The paradigm for the art of epitactics is the architect who is like the number theoretician in not producing, but unlike him in ruling or commanding the production of workmen like the carpenter or the stonemason. The architect therefore belongs to the gnostic branch, whereas the workmen themselves belong to the branch of practice (which, the reader will recall, is practico-productive). This raises a delicate question.

The number theoretician may do his work independently of all practical activity. But this is not true of the architect, and hence of the epitactic branch of gnostics. In epitactics, gnostics and practice come together for the sake of a production. The judgment of the architect is a case of what we call "applied" science; he transmits what is useful or proper (*to prosphoron*) for the productive activity of the workmen. This seems to be different in kind from the purely theoretical activity of the number theoretician. Whereas the architect must know arithmetic, this is not the defining mark of his art. He must of course know the nature of a house, but because a house is an artifact, the term *nature* cannot have the same meaning here as in the case of properties of numbers.

One could perhaps speak of a purely theoretical knowledge of artifacts, but this would not hold good for the architect as commander. In short, epitactics seems to unite gnostics and production rather than to fit comfortably within gnostics alone. The diaeresis is ambiguous at this point; it proceeds by way of a decision or judgment that is not simply critical but depends upon a prediaeretical decision by the Stranger. This decision is itself a blend of *kritikē* and *epitaktikē*. This helps us to see that diaeresis is not like number theory but is rather an instrument of human intentions.

The Stranger and Young Socrates agree that, in bisecting gnostics into epitactics and *kritikē*, they have spoken "tunefully" or "harmoniously" (*emmelōs*), not only with respect to the nature of the sciences but also with respect to one another. They have acted in common; their intellects are united (*homonoein*) because they have agreed upon what they perceive. They thus have the same belief or judgment (*doksa*), and so they can disregard the beliefs of others. This is an important and elaborate passage (260a9–c12). The Stranger insists upon the tunefulness of their agreement as if to acknowledge silently the delicacy of the judgment. The *homonoia* or unity of judgment is as much political as it is epistemic, because mere agreement as to the nature of the division is not in itself enough to certify the truth of their belief. On the other hand, the same tunefulness is essential for the existence of the city and the patriotic judgment that one's own customs and laws are superior to those of other cities.

Politics is certainly not like number theory, but it also differs from architecture in the following crucial sense. The *doksa* of the architect about the construction of a house must be true and not simply a matter of agreement, whether with other architects or the prospective householders; otherwise the house will be unlivable. But one can live under political regimes that are constructed contrary to the knowledge of the genuine statesman. This difference is not suppressed by saying that one cannot live well in a badly constructed city; to live well politically is not the same as living comfortably in a house. Finally, it is not the architect who builds the city but the handworker. In the case of the statesman, however, knowledge is applied in the formula-

tion of laws, written or unwritten, and not in commanding others to carry
them out. This process of legislation is then productive in the direct sense of
the term; commanding is a secondary element in the art of the architect but it
is primary in the art of the statesman.

The Stranger asks Young Socrates whether the king is a sort of spectator
(*tina theatēn*) like the judge or a commander. Young Socrates affirms that the
king is plainly a commander (260c1–5). A *theatēs* is a member of the audience
at the theater; the term can also refer to one who contemplates. This reminds
us that the distinction between the judge and the commander is also ambiguous with respect to the judge. The judge does not simply observe the
speeches and deeds of others; his decision is also a command that is sustained
by the law. Here as elsewhere one could not say that the divisions are simply
false; but they are radical oversimplifications that do not do justice to the
intricacy of human experience. This will cause us to make mistakes, despite
the *homonoia* or agreement that marks each stage in the divisions.

Step 4. "Once more we must look at (*theateon*) the epitactic art to see if it
is in any way divisible" (260c6–7). The Stranger implies that the diaeretician
is himself a *theatēs* or pure theoretician who discerns natural properties. He
thus abstracts from the controversial element in the activity of judging. But
the present step shows that decisions concerning the classification of human
activities, even of the arts and sciences, are inevitably controversial in a way
that mathematical proofs are not. The Stranger divides epitactics into an
unnamed part, of which the paradigm is "the art of retail merchants," that is,
the selling of goods that one has not oneself made, and *autepitaktikē*, or the
art of delivering one's own orders. Heralds are an example of the first art,
whereas the king belongs to the second type (260c6–d2). There are two
major difficulties here that should be examined separately.

First, it seems initially odd to suggest that retailing is a paradigm for a
branch of gnostics. One can see that by selling products made by others, the
retailer resembles a herald who communicates the orders of a king or some
other high official. But neither the herald nor the retailer needs to understand
anything of the theoretical nature of the products being sold. If we abstract
from the earning of wages, the function of selling is neither gnostic nor
productive, and besides, the herald could hardly be said to sell the orders he
transmits. Heraldry is thus another example of a practical art that is neither
productive nor theoretical. In the *Sophist*, retailing (*kapēlikē*) is introduced in
contrast to wholesaling in the sense of selling what one has made oneself
(*autopōlikē*). The wholesaler is here a producer as well as a seller who belongs
to both gnostics and practice. The retailer, because he does not produce,
must therefore be in the gnostic half of the diaeresis. But this is clearly absurd.

Second, the Stranger separates the royal race (*genos*) from the race of heralds. I repeat that whereas heralds transmit the commands of kings, they neither buy nor sell these commands. Nor does the shoemaker impose, or act as the agent of one who imposes, his shoes onto the purchaser. But there is another difficulty here. Shoemakers are producers, not commanders. If kings are commanders, then they are not wholesalers in the same sense as the term is employed in the *Sophist*. The Stranger thus varies his use of terms from diaeresis to diaeresis. So too the class opposed to autepitactics has no name and includes interpreters, coxswains, and prophets as well as heralds, each of whom might be differently classified in a diaeresis employed for some other purpose (260d11–e2). We therefore make a class by producing a likeness (*eikazomen, pareikasōmen*) or an image that reflects all of these arts in one name (260e3–4).

Step 5. Now let us see whether autepitactics will yield to another cut (261a5–6). We "appear to have" (261a8) such a cut, inasmuch as those whom we consider (*dianoēthōmen*) to be rulers all give commands "for the sake of some genesis" (*geneseōs tinos heneka:* 261a11–b2), namely, of un-souled or lifeless beings on the one hand and ensouled or living beings on the other (261b7–8). We note first that the Stranger replaces commanders by rulers, which seems to be an unjustified generalization. More important, however, is the consequence that the commands of the statesman issue in the genesis of not previously existing citizens. It is accordingly difficult to see how ruling belongs to the gnostic division of the arts. In other words, as was stated above, the epitactic or commanding branch of the gnostic arts already implicates the defining characteristic of the practico-productive arts.

Step 6. We are now ready to abandon the genesis of soulless beings, and with it the paradigm of the architect. Interestingly enough, Young Socrates is perplexed at this point; he does not know in which segment of autepitactics to look for the statesman. In other words, he is unclear about the distinction between souled and unsouled generation. There is also an important point to observe about the shift in paradigms. The architect was the paradigm of the epitactic or commanding class. One might expect him to remain as a para-digm for a subclass of that class, but this does not happen. There is no transmission downward of paradigms. But there is transmission downward of the antecedent class properties. Subclasses of gnostics are themselves gnostic; all subclasses of commanding are themselves commanding arts, and so on.

The Stranger says that the royal science is nobler (*gennaioteron*) than the science of architecture (261c9). This is a violation of his instructions in the *Sophist* (227a1ff) to pay no attention to the more or less honorable or august but to look exclusively at family relation with respect to function. One cannot speak accurately about politics without recourse to terms like noble, honorable, and the like. It is also not entirely accurate to say, as does the Stranger, that the statesman commands living beings only, since he must from time to time issue orders about such lifeless things as public buildings, temples, weapons, and so on.

The Stranger prepares to divide the art of commanding living beings into two parts. He notes initially that in some cases the genesis and nurture (*genesin kai trophēn*) of the children is of the individual animal, whereas sometimes it is the concern (*epimeleia*) for a herd (261d3–5). At this point we must look ahead for a moment to 263e8, where the Stranger refers to the division we are currently studying in what is a very puzzling manner. I restrict myself here to the observation that he speaks of animal-nurturing commanding, and in particular of herd animals (*agelaiōn zōōn*). He then goes on to say that "at this point the animals as a whole had been divided already into tame (*tōi tithasōi*) and wild."

To return to 261d3ff, the distinction is here between human beings who take care of single animals, like the tender of a single ox or the groom of a single horse, and those who care for herds (*tais agelais*). There is thus no reference to wild animals, whether solitaries or those who travel in herds. Nor could there be a reference to wild animals, because they are not referred to in the class of knowing how to command living beings. The division between tame and wild took place, but not as part of the diaeresis. Instead, wild animals were tacitly excluded by virtue of our concern with the royal art of the statesman. But there is an art of attending to wild animals, namely, hunting, which the Stranger uses to characterize the method of diaeresis.

As soon as we realize that the statesman is analogous to the shepherd, who is not himself a member of the herd that he tends, it becomes evident that either there is a defect in the diaeresis, or else the statesman is a "wild" animal in the sense that he does not belong to the herd and is not subject to its laws. In fact, the Stranger will subsequently identify this defect as the reason why he has introduced his myth of the reversed cosmos (275b1ff). But I regard it as not impossible that Plato wishes us to think about human beings who live in herds but who are nevertheless wild in the sense that they cannot be genuinely governed through commands of the statesman.

One should also consider here *Laws* VI. 766a1ff, where the Athenian Stranger says that human beings are tame but immediately qualifies this judgment as follows. They are the tamest of animals if they receive a correct education and possess a fortunate nature; if they are not sufficiently or nobly nurtured (*traphen*), however, they are the wildest being that grows from the earth. As we shall later, the Eleatic Stranger regards all actual cities as corrupt or sick; we may therefore assume that he shares the Athenian Stranger's views on the distinction between tame and wild human beings. But he does not confirm our assumption in the present passage.

Our present distinction is between types of caring for tame animals, whether individually or in herds. Whereas he spoke initially of genesis and nurture, the Stranger shifts almost immediately to nurture alone at 261e1. It is obviously easier to command with respect to nurture, but if the narrowing of responsibility is taken seriously, the diaeresis will be destroyed, because we are concerned with those who command for the sake of the genesis of ensouled beings. Reflection upon the distinction between genesis and nurture leads us to the deeper question of whether the statesman's commands should be understood as producing citizens, and so whether politics is practico-productive, or whether these commands merely nurture what is produced by nature.

The Stranger goes on to ask Young Socrates whether the care of many animals should be called *agelaiotrophikē* (herd nurture) or *koinotrophikē* (common nurture). The young man replies: "whichever occurs in the discussion." This moves the Stranger to praise him for the first time in the dialogue (*kalōs ge:* "very nobly put"). He adds that if Young Socrates guards against disputing about names, he will be revealed in his old age as richer in wisdom (*phronēsis:* 261e1–7). There is an echo here of the Stranger's remark in the *Sophist* (218c1ff) to the effect that we must agree about the thing (*ergon* and *pragma* are both used) through reasoning rather than simply about the name. As it happens, however, the difference between "herd" and "community" is not trivial. If a city is simply a herd, the common link uniting the individual members is merely physical well-being. These nuances disappear in the application of diaeresis.

After praising his interlocutor, the Stranger asks him if he sees a way to reduce what is double by half (261e7–262a2). This is a cumbersome way in which to emphasize the mathematical aspect of diaeresis. Young Socrates, who is a gifted mathematician, is about to commit an error of division; his mistake, as the Stranger will interpret it, is not mathematical but almost the opposite. It arises from human prejudice, or a love of one's own rather than of truth understood as formal structure. The youth suggests that we divide the art of nurturing herds into the nurturing of human beings, on the one hand, and beasts, on the other (263a3–4). There follows what the Stranger subsequently (263c3) refers to as a digression, namely, the discussion of Young Socrates' mistake.

Digression. Young Socrates addressed himself to the division of herd animals with extreme zealousness and bravery (262a5–6). He was, in other

words, too precipitate, and we must in the future make every effort not to
repeat his mistake, which is to take a single small part (*meros*) and oppose it to
many great parts instead of determining whether the part is an *eidos*. We have
already considered this point, which, roughly stated, is that things that have
the same look are *sungenes* or belong to the same family (*genos*). In the case of
animals, this sameness allows them to breed together. The Stranger uses the
term *eidos* as though its meaning were self-evident but in the course of
explaining the error, shifts to *ideais* (262b7).

Young Socrates mistook a part for an *eidos* because he saw that the diaeresis was heading toward human beings and wished to save time by separating them at once from other animals. But it is not safe to cut off small parts:
"it is safer to cut by going through the middles (*dia mesōn*), for thus one will
more likely encounter *ideais*" (262a8–b7). This is the first time that the
Stranger offers any explanation of the principle underlying diaeresis; there
will be another such clarification at 285b4ff, which we have already noticed.
Young Socrates does not understand the initial clarification, and the Stranger
says that he will try to speak more clearly (262c2–4).

At this point in the text, the reader should not think of *eidos* and *idea* as
referring to the so-called doctrine of Platonic Ideas. Young Socrates has
almost certainly never heard of this doctrine, and in any case there is no
reason to attribute it to an associate of Parmenides. The young man was,
however, present during yesterday's interrogation of Theaetetus, in which
words like *eidos, genos,* and *idea* were used with some frequency. We know
from the *Theaetetus* that Young Socrates is very intelligent. Yet he does not
seem to have assimilated the Stranger's terminology from the preceding
discussion.

It may seem odd to the contemporary reader that the Stranger never gives
a definition of the key terms *eidos* and *genos,* which are used interchangeably
throughout the diaereses. He begins by relying simply upon the notion of
sameness of look, in the sense of belonging to the same family or race. But
Young Socrates ostensibly makes a mistake by relying on this ordinary sense
of the terms; he correctly discerns that the statesman commands or cares for
the race of human beings, yet this correct inference from ordinary knowledge
of language and experience leads him into methodological error. Or is it in
fact an error? This depends on the truth of the assertion that looks of the kind
sought for by the Stranger will be more likely to appear if we cut down the
middle. But what does this mean? Why is the analysis of formal structure like
the repeated bisection of a line? Is there any connection between geometry
and diaeresis or philosophy? Do natural kinds—or as we now say, classes—
always exist in complementary pairs, like even and odd numbers?

In fact, we must distinguish between classes and natural kinds. A class is a logical concept, not a natural kind. The complement of a class *A* is the collection of everything that is not a member of *A*. On the other hand, if we employ a Socratic metaphor and cut at the natural joints, then in dissecting a human body, for example, we cannot find the *eidē* by cutting it down the middle. To do this is to destroy the natural structure of the body, not to exhibit it. As already noted, part of the difficulty in understanding the Stranger's method is that, despite his stated intention of finding parts that are like families or races, he seems frequently to deviate from this intention toward what looks very much like the logical analysis of classes.

Later, during the discussion of the so-called shorter way of reaching our goal by diaeresis, it will become clearer that Young Socrates' distinction between humans and brutes is substantively correct. In the present passage, if Young Socrates were an Aristotelian, he could defend himself by saying that *eidos* means "species form" and that the species of human beings derives from its look, not from its body or from the ability to breed but from the specific difference of possessing reason, which is as it were visible on the face of our experience with human and nonhuman animals.

It is worth noting that this is also the claim of most contemporary biologists, who distinguish species initially (although they do not define them) by the looks (phenotypes) of individual animals and not by their demonstrated ability to breed together. In this case, the cut between humans and brutes is formally correct; the forms in question are defined by the possession or lack of possession of the specific difference. But this is to say that Aristotle would never accept as *eidē* or *genē* collections like "herd animals" or "animals that walk on land." The Stranger's method is not that of Aristotelian division by genus, species, and difference. But it is not consistently logical analysis of complementary classes, although something like this notion clearly plays a part in his methodological exposition. What then is it?

For my part, I think that it is a mistake to try to assimilate the Stranger's method into any procedure that is defined exclusively and consistently on formal criteria. In the *Sophist* and *Statesman,* we are not sorting out pure formal elements of a single unifying form but rather classifying human types and forms of knowledge on the basis of frequently shifting purposes that themselves define what will count as a correct division and what will not. Nevertheless, it will rightly be objected, the Stranger seems to take his method quite seriously, and he is rebuking Young Socrates for having made a formal mistake. It is precisely for this reason that I am taking the diaeresis with equal seriousness and studying it in detail, exactly as one would do with any claim to have discovered a comprehensive method of analysis.

This is also the reason that I referred a moment ago to Aristotle. On formal grounds, the Stranger is mistaken. Young Socrates was correct in his division of herds into human and nonhuman. It will subsequently become evident that the Stranger understands this. Meanwhile let us follow his criticism, or ostensible correction, of Young Socrates. The Stranger begins by saying that the division of herds into human and nonhuman is like dividing the human race into Greek and barbarian, as though the latter were the name of one race (*genos*), even though the barbarians are many and consist of many peoples who do not breed together or speak the same language (262c10–d6).

This analogy seems to fail immediately because humans cannot breed with brutes, whereas Greeks can breed with barbarians. The division of Young Socrates is in accord with nature, whereas the Stranger's example is based on conventional or political opinions. In addition, the division between humans and brutes rests on a sound insight into the inadequacy of the Stranger's concern with herds, an inadequacy that he will shortly acknowledge.

Greeks separate themselves from barbarians out of patriotism; the Stranger implies that Young Socrates separated humans from brutes out of philanthropy. We have now seen that this is false, or even if true, it is methodologically secondary to the fact that the division is biologically correct. And the Stranger's next analogy is equally unsuccessful. He compares the cut by Young Socrates to the separation of ten thousand numbers from all the rest on the assumption that this is a division of numbers into two looks (*kat' eidē duo*: 262d6–e3). The Stranger says that it would be nobler or more beautiful (*kallion*: another lapse from methodological neutrality) and more in accord with the looks of things (*kat' eidē*) to divide numbers into even and odd, and human beings into male and female (262e3–5). But neither of these divisions is relevant to the goal of locating the art of the statesman (which might be practiced by a female).

The Stranger's criticism is based on the fact that there are few humans compared to the great number of nonhumans. But this is politically irrelevant, nor is it of purely formal significance. One can only sympathize with Young Socrates when he asks how exactly we are to distinguish between a *genos* and a *meros* (263a2–4). The Stranger evades this request with a compliment ("best of men") but declines to enter into this difficult task because they have already wandered too far from their investigation (263a5–8). He says only that whereas every *eidos* is a part, not every part is an *eidos* (263b7–10: note the interchangeability of *genos* and *eidos* throughout). He thus fails to clarify Young Socrates' mistake, or rather he misinterprets a correct answer as an error in arithmetic, thereby himself erring or "wandering" from the point. There will be a good bit of this sort of wandering in the balance of the dialogue.

The Stranger restates his previous criticism of Young Socrates' philanthropy by observing that if the crane is indeed *phronimos* (rational), as it is held to be, it would no doubt divide animals into cranes and all others, "thereby exalting itself" (263d3–e). He again warns Young Socrates not to divide the whole class of animals, once more tacitly excluding the obvious distinction between rational and irrational (263e3–4). The implication is that the human family is not an *eidos*. If this implication is sound, then the distinction between Greek and barbarian assumes considerable importance. More generally stated, it becomes all the more difficult, and perhaps impossible, to regard politics as natural, that is, as regulated by a natural paradigm.

Our difficulties began when the Stranger divided the care of living beings according to the criterion of number: some possessors of the art of animal nurture tend single animals, and others tend many animals at once. At that point nothing was said of the distinction "tame/wild." But now the Stranger asserts that it was implicit in our concern with herds. He describes his initial procedure as follows: "the epitactic part of gnostics was a part of the zootrophic race, in particular of [the nurture of] the herd animals" (263e8–9). This description is inaccurate. It omits autepitactics (the issuing of one's own commands) and replaces "the genesis of living beings" with "the nurture of living beings." But most surprisingly, the Stranger transposes two stages in the original diaeresis: nurturing and commanding. The threads of the diaeresis are beginning to tangle.

Is the Stranger right to say that "tame/wild" is implicit in "tending solitaries/tending herds"? Obviously not, if we look at his own examples; the keeper of a single ox or the groom of a single horse is tending one tame animal, not a wild brute. The designation "wild" is fitting only for animals, whether solitaries or herds, that are not tended by human beings at all. At this point, however, the Stranger assumes that herd animals are all tame and solitaries all wild. He has erred by shifting his attention from the *technē* of tending to the number of those tended. And the assumption is mistaken. There are wild herds and tame solitaries. This directly violates the Stranger's immediately following injunction not to divide by looking at the totality.

It is worth noticing here two points made by the Stranger in the diaereses of the *Sophist*. First, at 222b6–7, in response to Theaetetus's question whether there is a hunting of tame animals, the Stranger replies, "yes, if man is a tame animal; but assume what you like." So there is some confusion—not about oxen or horses, but about human beings. Second, in the *Sophist, thera-*

peia, the care of living beings, whether plants or animals, is a branch of poetics
(219a8ff); in the *Statesman,* it falls under gnostics. The ambiguity turns upon
whether the care of human beings is also a taming, and so whether politics is a
practico-productive rather than a theoretical *technē.* This has been brought
out in a confusing way by the erroneous clarification of an ostensible error.
The "formal" properties of diaeresis have added nothing to the clarification
of politics because the *eidē* in question are not the same as the *eidē* of abstract
structure, nor do they always correspond to natural kinds. This is the genuine
teaching of the digression.

Step 7. Palin eks archēs: "once more from the beginning" (264b6). The
Stranger signals the end of the digression by using a favorite Socratic expression. The beginning in question is the art of nurturing herds, at which we
arrived by step 6. The Stranger gives examples of water-dwelling herds,
namely, the tame fish in the Nile and in the lakes belonging to the king of
Egypt. Young Socrates has not visited Egypt but has seen tame fish in Greece
(264b11–c5). The criterion of tame/wild cuts across the political division
between Greek and barbarian; but by following the former rather than the
latter, we have been plagued by errors and delays. The second example is that
of Thessalian goose and crane farms. From the biological standpoint, there is
an ambiguity here. Step 7 separates the nurture of aquatic from that of land-
dwelling herds (264d1–9); it thereby omits reference to birds, who can be
said to inhabit not only land and water but also the air.

Step 8. It is easy to see that the statesman belongs to those who nurture
land-dwelling herds. This *technē* is divisible into the nurture of flying and
walking herds; the Stranger thus ignores the fact that birds like ducks and
swans spend much time on the water (264e3–7). Again it is plain even to
those lacking in *phronēsis* that the king tends land-dwelling or pedestrian
herds (264e8–10). At this point, the Stranger introduces a crucial second
digression.

Second Digression. The Stranger sees two paths leading from pedestrian
herds to the statesman. We can take the quicker way by dividing off a small
part from a big one. The longer way continues to obey our principle of
cutting as close to the middle as possible. We are free to choose whichever
path we wish (265a1–6). The long digression in which we were warned to go
slowly by cutting down the middle is now followed by a short digression in
which we are licensed to go quickly by cutting a small part—one with fewer
members—from a large part. This is not quite the same as being guided by
number rather than *eidos,* but it is nevertheless a violation of official
methodology.

Young Socrates asks why we cannot take both paths. He apparently enjoys the multiplication of technical procedures. I note that the choice arises at the seventh step of our division of *epistēmē* (which was itself divided from the nonepistemic procedures in the first or basis step). The Stranger replies that it is easy to follow them consecutively because the balance of the diaeresis is short (265a7–b2). In other words, the longer way is at this point not much longer than the shorter way. So much for saving time. The ludicrous nature of the situation is emphasized by the Stranger's assertion that it would have been hard to take the shorter way at an earlier stage in their investigations. Since the shorter way is the same as the longer way for the first seven steps (eight including the basis step) and consists of three steps, or one less than the longer way, it is absurd to suggest that by taking it initially we should have undergone something difficult. While I am mentioning numbers, I add that if we include in each case the basis step, then the longer way has eleven steps and the shorter way has ten, which added together equal twenty-one, or three times seven.

Step 9. We begin with the longer way. The Stranger says that tame pedestrian herd animals are divided by nature into two parts, namely, those born with horns and those born hornless (265b8–12). The Stranger here distinguishes between "tame" (*hēmeros*) and "herd" as though these were two *eidē* rather than one, as he claimed in his digression. Furthermore, he speaks once more of genesis, which had disappeared from the previous three steps. This variation between genesis and nurture is not the substitution of equivalent terms for stylistic reasons but points to a conceptual confusion in the diaeresis. We have been shifting back and forth from the criterion of *technē* to that of nature, in other words, from human commanders and nurturers to the animals being commanded.

The Stranger tells Young Socrates to divide by *logos* but not to fall into unnecessary complications by attempting to give names to the parts of pezonomics. Instead, he is to refer to two kinds of science (*epistēmēs*). We can add to this that there are no names for the tending of horned or of unhorned pedestrians. Why then should there be a name for the science of tending walking animals (*pezonomikē*)? I believe the point is that we can produce any *technē* we wish. Whereas there are *technai* for the study of nature, there is no natural discovery of *technai*. The production of art is artificial; this is why there is no natural diaeresis of the arts analogous to the cutting at the natural joints.

This is also indicated as follows. Once more it is plain that the king is the tender of the herd whose horns have been "mutilated" or "cut off" (*kolobon*: 265d3–5). The metaphor suggests that human beings do not constitute a natural race or that force must be employed in taming them. No doubt this force is technical; more generally, humans are technical animals and therefore cannot be understood simply by the contemplation of nature. The Stranger then says, very fittingly, "let us now break up [*katathrausantes*] this herd" and try to assign to the king his part (265d6).

Step 10. The arbitrariness of diaeresis should now be apparent to the observant reader. The Stranger offers Young Socrates a choice of criteria for the breakup; he can use either "cloven/uncloven" or "common/private breeding" (265d6–11). This refers to the fact that horses and asses are cloven hoofed and can interbreed, whereas the other hornless animals are not cloven hoofed and cannot interbreed (265e1–6). It is worth noting that neither horses nor asses can make up a single *genos* on the basis of either of these criteria. Yet they are obviously distinct in *eidos*.

Step 11. We now have to "tear open" or "define precisely" (*diastellein*) the two parts of the ambiguous herd made up of crossbreeding cloven-hoofed land animals. The Stranger says that "just about" (*schedon*) all but two tame herd animals have already been divided, for the *genos* of dogs does not merit being included among the herd creatures (265e7–266a4). In the *Republic* (II. 376a5ff), Socrates calls the dog the philosophical animal because it is gentle with friends and barks at strangers. Dogs both travel in packs when wild and live either singly or severally with human beings when tame. They do not fit into the structure of the diaeresis because they are not tame herd animals. Perhaps this also refers to philosophers.

The Stranger says next that Young Socrates and Theaetetus ought to divide the remaining two species in their capacity as geometers. This cumbersome passage depends upon the comparison of four-footed animals to the square root of four and two-footed animals to the square root of two. The Stranger explains that the walking human being is like the diameter of a square having sides of one foot on each side, whereas the four-footed walker has sides of two feet each (266a5–b9). He does not mention it, but in this analogy, man becomes "irrational," since the square root of two is incommensurable with the unit. And there is an additional joke (*heteron au ti pros gelōta*) that he mentions but does not fully explain, no doubt because it is "one of the best known." The human being is joined by lot to, and acts together with, "the noblest and laziest race" (266b10–c6). According to some, this animal is the pig (perhaps *hustata*, "last," at 266c8 is a play on *hus*, the word for "pig").

The slowest are the last to arrive; this certainly seems to refer to practitioners of diaeresis. And the comical character of the diaeresis emerges fully at the end of the longer way, since the king is made to run side by side with (in other words, appear in the segment coordinate with that of) the swineherd

(266c10–d3). The Stranger draws a moral from this result with a reference back to the passage at *Sophist* 227a7ff. We should never be concerned with the more august; this is a point that is raised again by the Stranger at 263d3 when he says that each species is inclined to revere itself. Here he adds that we should not dishonor the smaller in comparison with the greater. The method "always continues in accord with itself in the truest way" (266d4–10). This is hardly the lesson that we have learned from our study of the longer way.

The Shorter Way

The shorter way is very short indeed. The Stranger states it in one speech with no help from Young Socrates (266d11–267a3). Beginning from step 8 in the longer way, pedestrian herds are divided into four-footed and two-footed animals, and two-footed herds into winged or feathered and wingless or bare. The shorter way takes it for granted that man is the only two-footed featherless animal; I will not dispute the point. The statesman is then identified, not as the tender or therapist of human beings but rather as the charioteer who holds the reins of the city. This suggests a comparison between human beings and horses. Furthermore, if the "horses" are the citizens and the charioteer is the statesman, to what does the chariot correspond? It cannot be the city because horses do not ride in the chariot but pull it. If the comparison with horses is rejected, then the citizens must themselves be the chariot, and this emphasizes their artifactual status.

At last the Stranger summarizes the diaeretic procedure without distinguishing between the longer and the shorter way. The summary runs as follows: gnostic episteme, commanding, giving one's own commands, nurturing animals, nurturing herds, the *nomos* of pedestrians, the nurturing *technē* of the hornless nature. From this we must plait together three parts in order to obtain one name, (1) the pastoral (*nomeutikēn*) (2) science of (3) unmixed breeders. The only division remaining is anthroponomics, the herding of two-footed animals, or what we seek—the art that is called both royal and political (267a8–c3).

The summary is marked by a number of peculiarities. It combines step 1 (the basis step) with step 2. Much more important, it omits step 7 (the nurture of land animals). The effect of this omission is to blur, or to suppress altogether, the distinction between fish and birds. This is related to the omission of the feathered/featherless distinction, which belongs to the shorter but not the longer way. There is a significant terminological shift from *technē* to *nomos*, which prepares us for a later topic; namely, the merits and demerits of laws, a topic that is in turn rooted in the difference between *phronēsis* and *technē*. I also note that four footed/two footed is the final step in the longer way but the penultimate step in the shorter way.

It is unnecessary to repeat in tabular form the various general points I have made along the way about diaeresis. The Stranger is about to offer his own criticism of its application thus far, a criticism that leads him to tell a myth in order to make good the failure of the method. We are however not yet done with diaeresis, which will make subsequent appearances in the dialogue. Presumably no great effort is required to persuade those who have followed the preceding analysis that the use of diaeresis is somehow ironical or playful. If the joke seems cumbersome, we may recall the fondness of specialists at all times for stating the obvious in a pompous nomenclature that lights up a specious appearance of scientific respectability.

But this touches on only a part of Plato's irony. The Stranger has set into motion machinery that will render progressively more inaccessible the knowledge, common to himself and to Young Socrates, of the human type from which they started. In each successive case, a step forward is subsequently revealed to be a step backward; progress is unmasked as failure; the rectification of error is by means of another error. And each step of diaeresis, although it is intended to discover or acquire an already existing feature of the natural and conceptual order, itself produces, or contributes to the production of, an artifact. Those who dislike irony and who prefer to think of the Stranger as a stalwart expression of Plato's intellectual progress must acknowledge the ironical consequence of the use of the *technē* of diaeresis to define the *technē* of politics. Philosophy is transformed into technology and the doctrine of Ideas into ideology. Platonism is then indistinguishable from the late-modern version of the Enlightenment, according to which humans make themselves.

CHAPTER THREE

The Myth of the Reversed Cosmos

The Incompleteness of the Diaeresis

IMMEDIATELY following his eccentric summary, the Stranger startles Young Socrates by suggesting to him that they have not arrived at a complete definition of the statesman (267c5–d1). The problem is as follows: in the case of each nonhuman herd, there seems to be one person who claims to nurture or care for it. But in the case of the human herd there are numerous technicians who claim to be *suntrophos* or co-nurturer with the king; examples are merchants, farmers and grain producers, gymnasts and physicians (267d2–268a3). Note that at 267d6ff, the science (*epistēmē*) of nurturing humans in common (*koinotrophikē*) is identified with the care (*epimeleia*) of the human herd. This identification was of course assumed throughout the diaeresis.

As we saw in the previous chapter, Socrates may or may not conceive of politics as a *technē*, but if he does, it is as a *technē* that cannot be taught and that is associated with knowledge of the best or the Good, and so with the whole rather than with a particular skill directed toward the care of the human animal. The multiplication of claimants to the title of king is already an indication that the assumptions underlying the use of diaeresis, if not diaeresis itself, are inadequate and misleading. Instead of division or separation, we may need addition or unification. The Stranger will ultimately arrive at this "Socratic" conclusion. But it cannot be established by his initial procedure.

In addition, the tangled and comical nature of the diaeresis has done nothing to demonstrate the nature of the ostensible *technē*. The designation of herdsman, as the Stranger will state explicitly later, is misleading because the herdsman or shepherd belongs to a race different from that of the animals he tends. It is demeaning to human beings to treat them as herd animals somehow on a par with pigs, yet the scientific study of politics has led us to conceal the distinguishing characteristics of the human race. Instead of arriving at definitions like "the political animal," we define a human being as "the featherless biped." And our diaeresis has not at all succeeded in identifying the *technē* of the herdsman, as the Stranger has just observed.

The merchant, physician, and so on, to be sure, do not each claim to be the herdsman of the human flock, but they insist that they share the task of nurturing human beings. And, in fact, their contention is sound. One way to bring out the defect of the diaeresis is by noting that we have not explained what it means to "nurture" or "care for." The emphasis is on physical nurture, as is shown by the examples of the king's rivals; there is no mention of music.

The absence of music is rectified in the Stranger's next speech, but, ironically, with respect to nonhuman animals. The shepherd of a nonhuman herd combines all of the nurturing arts in his care; he is physician, matchmaker, midwife, and he even enlivens and soothes his flock with games and music (268a5–b7). This is not possible in the human herd because of the peculiar nature of the human animal. People possess *logos*, which does not define in the sense of closing their nature but rather opens it. Human needs together with reason produce *technē*, which in turn multiplies the needs and the power of reason, thereby multiplying and refining *technē*, which leads to a proliferation of specialists, and thus to an apparently unending progression.

The same point is made in the *Republic* (II. 370b1–6) by Socrates when he introduces the division of labor as the basis of the city. In order to limit the unending progress of *technē* and rational desire, one must effect the regulation of politics by philosophy. The regulation of *technē* is obviously impossible when philosophy is itself defined as a *technē* rather than as the love of wisdom. In sum: if the shepherd is the paradigm of the statesman, then there is no actual statesman for two reasons. The shepherd is not a human being or member of the tribe he tends, whereas human cities are ruled by human beings. A city is not a herd. Second, no human being can master all the *technai* required for the care of the entire city.

The Stranger puts the problem as follows. Thus far we have produced a sketch (*schēma*) of the king. In order to complete our work with precision, we must separate or purify him from the claims of those who wish to partake of his authority (268b8–d1). We must, in other words, clarify what is meant by *epimeleia* or the properly political care; this will require us to distinguish it from nurture. It is plain that many arts contribute to the nurture of the human animal, but these are so different from one another that they could not collectively define the political art. Human beings are physicians, gymnasts, merchants, and musicians, but it does not follow from this that the king must possess all these skills or that they are a part of the political art. Concentration on the diversity of the arts, or more fundamentally on the diversity of human desires, leads us away from politics rather than toward it, because it leads to a disintegration of the city into what is today called "society." It leads not to the political *technē* but to sociology. We are searching not simply for the royal art of the statesman but for the unity of the state.

The *logos* or diaeresis was not "correct" (*orthos*: 268b8, 268c5); it did not exhibit mathematical truth but something quite different, namely, a "sketch" that has to be worked into a portrait (as is indicated by the verb *apergazomai* at 268c7). We are not merely shifting from *logos* to *poiēsis* but rather coming to recognize that our *logos* was itself an inadequate poem. But this is stated only indirectly by the Stranger; we must not bring shame to the *logos* by leaving it in its present inaccurate or impure condition (268d2–3; compare 268b8). The honor of the *logos* will be restored, not by another *logos,* but instead by a different beginning (*palin toinun eks allēs archēs*) or road (*hodon*), one that is mixed together with playfulness (*schedon paidian engkerasamenous*: 268d5–9). The first part of the dialogue was presumably not play but work, that is, exercise in diaeresis. I have given reason to believe that this work was rather another kind of play. But whether we refer to diaeresis as work or play, the Stranger's point is unmistakable. Diaeresis cannot correct or purify itself. For this, art—and, in particular, myth—is required.

We can infer the political nature of the link between myth and play by considering two passages from the *Laws* that bear directly on the myth we are about to study. In the first passage (II. 663c7ff), the Athenian Stranger asserts the need to persuade the young citizens of their new city that the life of the unjust man is not only more shameful and more wretched than that of the just man, but also less pleasant. He adds that even if this were not true, the lawgiver could do nothing more useful than to persuade the young by "daring to lie for the sake of the good." In general, young persons may be easily persuaded even of the most astonishing things by means of myth; the Stranger cites as an example the myth of the race sprung from teeth sown in the earth. It is a variation of this myth that the Eleatic Stranger is about to incorporate into his own effort to correct the diaeresis.

The second passage comes later (VII. 803b3ff); the Athenian Stranger has been discussing the role of music (song and dance) in the newly legislated city. He goes on to compare the determination of the right way of life to the task of laying down the keel in order to build a ship. To this he adds that "the affairs of human beings are not worthy of great seriousness; it is however necessary that one take them seriously, which is our bad luck." In short, "one should be serious about what is serious, and not serious about what is not; by nature god is worthy of complete blessed seriousness, but the human being, as we said previously, has been devised by god as a plaything, and this is truly the best part of it. Each man and woman must spend life in this way, playing the most noble games, and thinking about them in a way opposite to the present manner." The games in question are sacrificing, singing, and dancing. I cite this text at length because when taken in conjunction with the earlier passage, it helps us to understand the playful dimension of the philosophical founding of the city and, in particular, of the serious play of mythmaking. No expression better describes the activity of the Eleatic Stranger than "serious play." On this point, he is at one with his Athenian counterpart.

The myth that the Stranger is about to tell is very great, and we will require a large part of it; nothing is said here about cutting down the middle. "Henceforward" (*to loipon*) as before, we will separate part from part and arrive at the peak of our investigation (268d8–e3). So we are not yet finished with diaeresis but are about to engage in the effort to purge it of shame. The question will also arise later as to how we know what is the right amount of the myth to employ. There is a kind of analogue to diaeresis in such cases; stated in more general terms, the question of method is raised throughout the dialogue, but in different contexts. As Aristotle remarks at the beginning of the *Nicomachean Ethics* (I, 1094b1off), there is no single method that is appropriate to all inquiries.

We are now ready to follow the Stranger's advice to Young Socrates to "turn your attention to the myth, just like young children" (*paides*: 268e4–5). There must in other words be a willing suspension of disbelief if the myth is to amuse us. But we must also read the myth with the same care that we invested in the case of diaeresis if we are to understand it. This is because the play of adults is not in fact the same as, even though it is related to, the play of children. We are about to engage in serious play. In a previously noted passage from the *Sophist*, the Stranger objects that his predecessors have spoken to us about beings in myth, as though we were children (242c8ff). Since the life of a human being encompasses both childhood and adulthood, and since the myth purports to explain the very basis of human life, I will engage in both kinds of playfulness.

The Myth

Part One: Introduction (268e3–269c3)

The section of the text just studied may be called the prologue to the myth. As I am about to argue, the myth consists of seven parts. The first part contains a general introductory statement. The Stranger begins as follows: "Of those tales that have been recounted by the ancients (*palai*), many actually took place and will occur again, and in particular the account of the heavenly sign [*phasma*] of the strife between Atreus and Thyestes." This sign or visible manifestation, as we are about to see, is closely connected with what Nietzsche refers to as the eternal return of the same.

The story to which the Stranger refers is about two brothers who are shepherds and who fall into a dispute over kingship. The quarrel is settled by Zeus's preference for Atreus; the god changes the course of the sun and the Pleiades as a sign of his decision. The pertinence to our diaeresis of the quarrel between shepherds over accession to the throne requires no comment. That quarrel, however, is settled by Zeus, not by philosophy. This is an important indication of the relation between religion and the origin of the city, a relation upon which all the main speakers in the Platonic dialogues are agreed.

We ourselves cannot see the *phasma* or heavenly manifestation of the will of Zeus, but we can visualize it in our imaginations on the basis of the Stranger's prophetic myth. There is, however, a fundamental difference between the old story and the Stranger's version. He is uninterested in the events of the conflict between the two brothers and in the associated tale of the golden fleece. What interests him is the change in the setting and rising of the sun and the stars (268e12–269a6). In other words, the Stranger abstracts from the human perspective; his treatment of human beings in the myth will adopt the cosmological perspective. From that standpoint, the myth shares something of the deficiency of diaeresis; this will be confirmed when the telling of the tale has been concluded.

As we can also express the previous point, the Stranger abstracts from Eros. In the original myth, Thyestes seduces the wife of Atreus, but this is suppressed in the Stranger's account. At this point I need to make a terminological distinction. The Stranger generalizes Zeus's changing of the motion of the sun and the Pleiades to make it apply to the entire cosmos, which thus moves in two perpetually recurring epochs. In one epoch, namely, our own, which I shall call the *normal* epoch or cycle, the motions of the cosmos and of nature in general are as we experience them. But when this epoch runs its course, there is a sudden shift of direction, caused by the intervention of a deity other than Zeus, and the cosmos as it were repairs the damage inflicted by its decay or old age in the normal cycle by a reversal of all natural motions.

In this restorative epoch, which I shall call the *counternormal* epoch or cycle, there is no Eros. Eros functions as we know it in the normal cycle, but it is thereby associated with decadence and even destruction. Furthermore, when discussing the normal cycle, the Stranger is not explicitly interested in human relations as such, whether erotic or political, but rather in the effect on these relations of the cosmic motions and, by extension, with the presence or absence of a deity who cares for mankind. The reader should bear in mind that each epoch is "reversed" in comparison with the other.

I note the following inconsistency in the general economy of the Stranger's story. As the tale is originally told, Zeus exercises his *epimeleia* or care of human beings by interceding on Atreus's behalf; the result of this intercession is the reversal of sun and stars. In the Stranger's revised version, Zeus does not intercede during the normal cycle; when this cycle is winding down, some other, non-Olympian deity intercedes by taking the tiller of the cosmos and rewinding it in the opposite direction. The result of the god's intercession is to abolish Eros and politics entirely. In sum, the Atreus-Thyestes quarrel occurred in what would on the Stranger's reckoning be the counternormal cycle. But in the Stranger's version, no such event could have transpired in the counternormal cycle, within which all life goes backwards, that is, in a direction that is the reverse of the motions of life in the normal cycle. Otherwise put, in the traditional myth, Eros and politics characterize both cycles (nor are we told that these cycles will repeat forever, thanks to perpetual reversals).

The Stranger next indicates that he is going to mix together three elements from a multitude of stories all referring back to the same cosmic event (literally, "suffering": *pathos*): (1) the reversal of the stars; (2) the reign of Kronos; and (3) the myth of the earthborn humans who did not generate sexually from one another. These stories have become disconnected from each other and so from the single cosmic *pathos* to which they refer. The stories are traditional, but no one prior to the Stranger has ever recounted the original cause (*aition*) of the cosmic transformation that underlies these scattered traditions (269b3–c3). The Stranger will unify these fragments of tradition in a comprehensive myth that explains the art of the king by means of an explanation of how the gods rule the cosmos. Cosmological genesis replaces human Eros and spiritedness as the first principle of human existence. The Stranger's myth will explain politics as a consequence of theological physics.

Part Two: General Description of Cosmic Motion (269c4–270b2)

"At one time the god himself guides the all [*to pan*], traversing its cycle in conjunction with it. But at another time he lets go, when the periods have achieved the measure of the time appointed by him. [The cosmos] then reverses spontaneously [*automaton*] back into the opposite direction, since it is alive and has a share in *phronēsis* thanks to the one who fitted it together in the beginning" (269c4–d2).

The opening statement of the myth proper raises a number of questions. The first is that of the identity of "the god himself." It cannot be an Olympian, because the age of Zeus coincides with the normal epoch only (272b1–4). The counternormal epoch on the other hand is the age of Kronos (271c3–d6). If Kronos is also the creator-god, then he is superior to Zeus and in a sense rules even during the normal epoch through the instrumentality of the *phronēsis* with which he has endowed the cosmos. Indirect or "hands off" rule means that human beings are partly free, but not entirely so because the cosmos has as it were a mind of its own; we have not yet established what role Zeus plays in human life during the epoch of relative human freedom.

It is never said in the balance of the myth that Kronos is the *dēmiourgos* of the cosmos, and so there is room for doubt as to whether he is the guide of the counternormal epoch. In the text quoted above, it is not said that the guide and the divine maker are one and the same. Toward the end of the myth, the Stranger identifies the demiurge with the captain or co-rotator of the counternormal epoch (273d4ff). Since Kronos is mentioned only in conjunction with the human condition, this does not establish him as demiurge and co-rotator of the cosmos. I will return to this question below.

Second, according to a principle to be introduced below by the Stranger, the same god cannot move in opposite directions. This is why the captain of the counternormal epoch, Kronos or someone else, must let go the tiller as the preface to the normal epoch. The divine demiurge has endowed the cosmos with *phronēsis,* so that it may function by itself during the normal epoch. But independence is reversal or opposition to the rule of the tiller. The demiurge seems to contradict himself through the instrumentality of cosmic *phronēsis.* It would be more coherent if the maker of the cosmos were neither the tiller (and certainly not Kronos) nor Zeus, but some higher principle that arranges for their opposed reigns. But this is not the Stranger's last word.

Third, since all motion is reversed during the counternormal epoch, human beings grow younger rather than older; eventually they disappear into the earth. At 271b4ff, the Stranger says that at the beginning of the counternormal epoch, the dead who are lying in the earth are reconstituted and spring up as old men. These must be the persons who died in the usual way during the antecedent normal epoch. Their corporeal life is a process of unraveling; if this must apply to their perceptual and mental processes as well, then their perception and thought must resemble the viewing of a film that we are rewinding on our video recorders. As we shall soon discover, however, this image is not adequate to the details in the Stranger's account. But it comes close enough to justify the inference that there is no *epistēmē* and hence no astronomy in the counternormal epoch.

This will have important consequences, one of which is that it cannot be evident to unraveling mortals that they are living in what they would have to regard as a counternormal epoch if they were genuinely conscious of it. Stated more directly, whatever their mode of consciousness, it is the reverse of that in the normal epoch; hence the events of what is for us the counternormal epoch must be normal for them. Furthermore, the counternormal persons are reincarnations of ourselves. The myth is not about two distinct races, but rather about two aspects of human existence.

Fourth, when the captain of the counternormal epoch lets go the tiller, everything (*to pan*) reverses spontaneously. In other words, dissolution is natural to it because it is itself an animal and possesses a soul or intellect in addition to a body. In the counternormal epoch, the cosmic animal is growing younger, exactly like its human inhabitants. It must then be moving back toward disappearance into the void or origin-point, which is to say that it is no more able to exercise its intelligence than are its inhabitants. Why does the captain of the counternormal epoch move in this contrarational manner? The question is all the more pressing if the captain is identical to the cosmic demiurge. But in either case, there seems to be only one possible answer. Counternormal motion is required in order to repair the dissolution intrinsic to normal motion. The counternormal epoch is for the sake of the normal epoch. In theological terms, "only a god can save us."

Fifth, the cosmos is made by the demiurge to reverse perpetually at the necessary times, namely, in each case prior to cosmic destruction, whether from extreme old age or extreme youth. But the cosmos was constructed; hence there must have been a first epoch. Was this first epoch normal or counternormal? One might assume that since revitalization is required of old age, the normal epoch must have been first. But it is also tempting to say that the act of construction in a myth has no temporal significance, and that the two epochs represent two concurrent aspects of ongoing human existence.

I spoke previously of a distinction between a youthful and an adult interpretation of myth. By *youthful* I refer to the reading that gives primacy to the global significance of the myth and does not attempt to translate each of its details into an element in a rational reconstruction. The *adult* interpreter, as I am employing the term, does not overlook the global significance of the myth but argues that it cannot be found without a close consideration of the details. In our analysis, we must attempt to do justice to the logic of story-telling as well as to the tropes and modalities of persuasion.

To come back to the question, we would have to decide whether it is more likely that the divine demiurge would initially co-rotate with his artifact or stand back and watch it function on its own. It is mere speculation, but I suggest that the latter is more likely. What point would there be to creating a cosmos, if not to observe its operation as an independent result of divine ingenuity? This hypothesis receives some support from the explicit feature of the myth to the effect that counternormal motion is required to rejuvenate the aging cosmos in its normal condition. But if the creator, whether him- or herself or through the agency of the divine captain, co-rotates at the outset, then that initial epoch must be normal, and our own epoch is counternormal.

Normal and *counternormal* are of course my terms, not the Stranger's; more precisely stated, on the present hypothesis, the age of Kronos is the golden age that we cannot literally inhabit except through a reversal of consciousness as well as of bodily motion or, in other words, comprehensive forgetting. Rejuvenation is forgetting, just as wisdom is recollection. But at the same time, recollection is illness or aging. Can it be that philosophical medicine requires a forgetfulness as the basis of good health?

The Stranger next explains why reversal is innate and necessary (269d3ff). "To be always the same forever and in the same way" (the Greek is emphatic: *to kata tauta kai hōsautōs echein aei*) "belongs exclusively to the most divine of all things, and the nature of body is not of this order" (269d5–7). This terminology certainly reminds us of the Stranger's doctrine of the greatest genera, as well as of Socrates' doctrine of Ideas. The implication is evident: the gods are not the most divine of beings; not even the divine demiurge is of this order (*taksis*). There are then three orders of being: (1) that which is always the same; (2) that which is sometimes changing and sometimes not; (3) that which is always changing. The demiurge and the co-rotator, whether the same or distinct, presumably belong to the second order. We will be told that, when he is not at the helm of the cosmos, the co-rotator retires to his lookout point (*periōpē*: 272e5); it seems that he engages in pure contemplation of the heavens and does nothing. Nothing is said of activity prior to the construction of the cosmos.

It is a striking feature of the myth that what I call the first order of being is mentioned indirectly and plays no role, either in the myth itself or in the dialogue as a whole. If we try to reconcile the Stranger's teaching in the *Sophist* on the greatest genera or elements of stability and intelligibility with his teaching in the *Statesman*, grave problems arise. What cannot be denied is that the greatest genera play no role in the analysis of political existence. In the *Statesman*, the central problem is how to construct a rational ordering of human life in a changing cosmos that is largely if not entirely hostile to the stability of our existence. Apparently the perception of ontological structure is of no use in the resolution of this problem.

Otherwise put, practice is productive and depends upon the capacity to adjust our intentions to continuously changing circumstances. If there is a stable and intelligible structure that underlies and makes change possible, it contributes nothing to the productive activity by which we order change on the basis of our primarily defensive intentions. In the background of the actual discussion in the *Statesman* is the following implicit thesis: Although there is an inseparability of theory from practico-production in human life and, in particular, in the art of politics, this weaving together of theory and practico-production must be distinguished from the pure theory of the philosophical contemplation and analysis of intelligible order.

There can thus be no identity between the statesman and the philosopher but at most only a partial overlapping. The task of defining the philosopher is accordingly a separate exercise. It follows as a corollary that the application of diaeresis to the task of defining the statesman is not a political act. Unfortunately, if diaeresis is in fact the production of concepts, it is also not an exercise of pure philosophy. The science of the free man turns out to be the initiation of the process by which philosophy is transformed into the history of ideas, that is to say, of rival conceptual productions, and so of ideology.

To continue with the myth, the cosmos is always moving in one direction or another; it must therefore belong to the third order. But the Stranger clearly wishes to distinguish between the cosmos and its animal inhabitants, including human beings. The cosmos has been blessed by its creator; it is always alive and, we recall, it possesses *phronēsis*. But it also possesses a body, and therefore it cannot continue forever in uniform motion; this does not belong to its order of being. The upshot is that the cosmos moves always in a circle but reverses the direction of its motion (269d7–e4). In order to determine that the cosmos has reversed its motion, we would require an independent fixed point of vision. But such a standpoint is available only to the divine co-rotator (and the demiurge, if he is a separate deity). The Stranger has also been vouchsafed some kind of access to that lookout point, no doubt as divine gift or prophetic vision.

The Stranger continues: "To move itself forever is scarcely possible, except for that which guides all moving things" (269e5–6). To whom or to what does the exception refer? Not to the co-rotator, since he drops the tiller during the normal epoch. If the co-rotator is also the demiurge, who is taken to guide and so move together with all living things, then he seems to contradict himself in his two *personae*. But if (contrary to the Stranger's closing remarks) the demiurge is not the helmsman, is he still to be understood as guiding all moving things, and so the cosmos, during both epochs? This would make entirely impossible the attribution of independent motion to the cosmos during the normal epoch. The conclusion seems to be that nothing is able to move itself forever; or rather, if the god himself—the divine demiurge—moves himself forever, he does so in a sense that is independent of the motions of the cosmos. In sum, this principle seems to be violated by the Stranger's identification of the helmsman with the demiurge.

In fact, says the Stranger, no god can move in opposite directions; this is not *themis*, a term that presumably refers here to necessity rather than to divine decree. Therefore the same god cannot guide the cosmos during both of its two epochs. But neither must we say that the cosmos could be guided by two different gods, since then the gods would as it were contradict one another. This also sustains the inference that the demiurge cannot move the cosmos altogether and at all times. In sum: no god can move in opposing directions; no two gods can oppose each other; the cosmos cannot move in the same direction forever; the cosmos cannot move in two directions under divine guidance. The only other possibility is that the cosmos have a co-rotator in one direction or epoch and move independently in the other (269e6–270a7). It also follows, contrary to the Stranger's previously stated principle, that neither the demiurge nor the co-rotator can control the motion of the cosmos during the normal epoch by means of its innate *phronēsis*. I will return to this last inference shortly.

We must now look more closely at 270a2ff. The Stranger formulates his conclusion concerning cosmic motion as follows: "at one time [the cosmos] is guided by a separate divine cause, from which it once more derives life and receives rejuvenated deathlessness from the demiurge; at another, when it is let go, in order to move by itself, having been released at the right moment," and so on. This says either that the co-rotator and the demiurge are one and the same, or else that the co-rotator is provided with essential assistance by the demiurge. On the first alternative, it remains valid to refer to them as two distinct *personae*, or in other words to acknowledge that there is a contradiction between always moving everything on the one hand, and, on the other, sometimes moving everything and sometimes moving nothing but merely watching.

We are told later in the myth that the counternormal epoch is the age of Kronos. This raises the question, unresolved by the Stranger, whether the age of Kronos is indeed the golden age for human beings. Kronos is thus, both in the Stranger's myth and in traditional mythology, a political god in the sense that he rules the Titans and is associated with human welfare. Most important, Kronos is the father of Zeus. It seems unlikely that an inner-cosmic god (whose father is Ouranos) would be associated by the Stranger with the external cause of the cosmos. But this line of reasoning is hardly conclusive. I note finally that the Stranger says nothing about the erotic relation between Kronos and Zeus in Greek mythology. Politics is a corollary of cosmology.

Part Three: A Rational Reconstruction of Cosmic Motion (270b3–271c2)

The Stranger signals that we are shifting to a new stage in the myth when he says: "let us by calculative reason think through together [*Logisamenoi de sunnoēsōmen*] the cosmic *pathos* on the basis of what has been said previously, the *pathos* which we said to be the cause [*aition*] of all these marvels" (270b3–4). It is not quite clear whether the Stranger means to imply that we are shifting from myth to *logos*, or whether we have been using calculative reason already; certainly the careful presentation of the possible types of motion would suggest the latter alternative. In either case, there can be no doubt that the Stranger's tale is a mixture of *muthos* and *logos*, and so that we are right in our attempt to understand each detail as carefully as possible.

Since the reversal of motion is the greatest of all cosmic changes, it has the most drastic consequences for living beings, which cannot sustain a multitude of great and simultaneous alterations (270b10–c10). Most affected is the race of human beings, of which only a small part survives the reversal (270c11–12). We note that this destruction, together with many marvelous effects (*pathēmata*), takes place during the shift from the normal to the counternormal epoch. Since the cosmos is running down during this epoch, the human race is already in the process of decay, which can be halted only by the radical destruction of cosmic reversal. This is the ancestor of modern revolutionary doctrines of destructive purgation; it is also the cosmological version of Socrates' assertion of the need to rusticate everyone over the age of ten in order to begin the beautiful city with fresh material.

The greatest of the aforementioned *pathēmata* is that the aging process of all animals stops entirely; more precisely, "everything that was mortal stopped the journey toward the look of aging" (*epausato . . . epi to geraiteron idein poreuomenon:* 270d7–8). The language suggests an important distinction. There is a difference between aging and the look of aging. We have to distinguish between what I will call absolute and relative time. From the standpoint of relative time, a person who is forty years old at the moment of reversal begins to grow younger in appearance and lives as it were backwards for another forty years before disappearing into the earth. But from the standpoint of absolute time, the two periods equal eighty years. Life, however, is a matter of relative rather than absolute time; the counternormal period takes back what the normal period gives, with the result that human life adds up to nothing, even though from the absolute standpoint a normal life span is doubled by the reversal. There is then, on the one hand, a disjunction between cosmic motion and human significance or value; but, on the other hand, it is precisely this disjunction that provides a space for human autonomy.

There is another very important consequence of this stage of the myth. Since every resident of the cosmos undergoes reversal, there are so to speak two dimensions of nature that correspond to the two epochs. In the counternormal epoch, everything is in the continuous process of losing the nature it had in the normal epoch. Everything loses its look or *eidos,* just as animals cease "to look" (*idein*) as though they are aging. It follows either that there are no Platonic Ideas, or else that the Ideas of the normal period lose their efficacity and visibility in the counternormal epoch.

More important for the immediate context, if there are no looks or *eidē,* then diaeresis is impossible in the counternormal epoch. As the Stranger says, the reversal occurs "with respect to the soul and the body," so that the old become young and the young look like (*aphomoioumena*) babies (270e1–7). In the cosmos as a whole, there are no stable looks; nothing is always of the same form. There cannot be an Idea of a being that is both itself and its opposite; but if there were two Ideas, one for normal humans and the other for counternormals, then these would be two distinct species of being. In sum, during the normal epoch, nature is a "shining forth" (*ekphasis*), whereas in the counternormal epoch, it is "utter disappearance" (*eksephanizeto:* 270e8–9). A marginal comment: if the two epochs actually refer to two dimensions of human existence, then this existence is a presence and an absence. There can be no Idea of human being that corresponds to human existence.

Thus far the Stranger has spoken of the reversal of nature, but the same point holds for those who die by violence. They too wither away until their corpses shrivel up and disappear (270e9–271a1). So there is violence in the age of Kronos, presumably from natural disasters; at least it is difficult to see how unraveling animals could attack unraveling human beings, and the Stranger will identify this as an epoch of peace for the human race. But there is a deeper problem for the economy of the myth. Those who die by violence in the counternormal epoch do not correspond to anything in the normal epoch. Such victims fail to complete the life that was lived in the normal epoch. Someone who dies by violence in the normal epoch and is buried there springs up from the earth in the counternormal epoch and repeats in reverse order that portion of his or her previous existence from the moment of death backwards to the moment of birth.

This account of reversed existence leads Young Socrates to ask how the animals reproduced during the counternormal period; he understands their destruction, but not their genesis (271a2–3). There is for him still an obscurity in the Stranger's assertion that counternormal animals spring up from the earth. The Stranger replies: "it is clear that generation from one another was not a part of the nature of that time" (*en tēi tote phusēi:* 271a3–4). This is correct in itself but unsatisfactory because sexual generation must be one of the processes that are reversed in the counternormal epoch. In other words, unraveling humans must disappear, not into the earth but into their mother's wombs, where the seed and the egg will in turn be dissolved. The Stranger's version is thus at odds with itself; and this can only be due to his desire to banish Eros entirely from the counternormal epoch.

The Stranger goes on to say that the earthborn race of tradition is the one that "returned again at that time out of the earth, and it was remembered by our first ancestors who, when the previous period had been completed, were neighbors to the next time [the normal period] and so grew up in it from the beginning" (271a5–b2). In other words, the first normal generation is not born into the normal epoch but is left over from the reversal out of the counternormal epoch. Our ancestors were neighbors to the new normal epoch because they were the last survivors of the previous counternormal epoch. They thus belonged to the race of earthborn men who returned by springing up out of the earth "at that time," namely, in the counternormal epoch. The Stranger silently accounts for the obvious impossibility that the human race could have originated by sexual reproduction (since there would be no humans to initiate the race until a man and a woman had already appeared). He also attempts to account for our racial memory of the earthborn race, which could hardly be furnished to a generation originating in the normal epoch.

The Stranger next reasserts the thesis that it is natural for the reversal of epochs to resuscitate those who are dead and lying in the earth, but he forgets to explain the appearance in the counternormal epoch of those who were still alive at the end of the normal epoch. Nor does he ever suggest that the race is entirely destroyed by cosmic reversal. And there is another break in the cycle of nature; it consists in "those whom god escorts to another destiny" (271b4–c2). This cannot refer to the philosophers or other favored persons who in the normal epoch are moved by the gods to the blessed isles because as so removed, they would not appear in the counternormal epoch. Their identity is left unexplained. But the point is made that the god, who is presumably the co-rotator, can interfere with the motions that transpire within the cosmos.

To summarize: our rational calculation with respect to the reversal of motion has revealed numerous defects in the Stranger's story. This does not invalidate the general sense of the myth; on the contrary, our attempt to follow the Stranger's instructions and think through the details has both enriched our understanding of the myth and shown us that it would be extremely difficult, probably impossible, to provide a coherent analysis of the origin of human existence. For both Plato and the Stranger, a sound political foundation requires a founding myth in order to bridge the disjunction between human and cosmic nature. This means that, contrary to the first impression produced by the Stranger, diaeresis is insufficient for an exposition of political life. Diaeresis, as the process of classification by looks, abstracts from the difference between the noble and the base. It is therefore unable to distinguish between noble and base lies.

The Stranger's pedagogical method has been taken by some to have led him to begin with diaeresis as a way of attracting the interest of young mathematicians and to show them by example its insufficiency. There is something in this suggestion, but it hardly explains the recurrence of diaeresis throughout the dialogue or the overall intention of the Stranger to produce a conceptual articulation of the structure of the *technai* together with a technical model of political existence. In another formulation, the adoption and revision of Socratic procedures is not a sign of the Stranger's implicit Socraticism, but rather of his attempt to assimilate Socrates into what could be called a theory of practics or practico-production. We must not fail to see that in an important respect, one which also connects him to the sophists, the Stranger is a distant ancestor of Descartes, although of course it would be absurd to refer to him *tout court* as a Cartesian. One of the deepest contemporary problems is to find a way to reconcile the disenchantment of the scientific Enlightenment with the need for a just and reasonable political order. The myth of the Enlightenment has itself failed; we are today not in a strong position to repudiate the Stranger's approach as irrational.

Part Four: The Problem of Kronos (271c3–272b1)

Let me first recall a passage from Hesiod's *Works and Days* (109ff). "The deathless ones who dwell on Olympus first made the golden race [*genos*] of articulate human beings. These belonged to the time of Kronos, when he was king in heaven. They lived like gods with a careless spirit [*thumon*], far from pains and misery. Nor did miserable old age approach them." For these residents of the golden age, death was like falling asleep. They did no work; all goods were theirs by nature's bounty. This race was followed by the silver race who enjoyed a childhood of one hundred years, followed by a brief adulthood marked by crime and an absence of divine worship. They were destroyed by Zeus. The third race, produced by Zeus, is that of bronze and consists of warriors. The heroes make up the fourth race, and we ourselves are the fifth race who inhabit the age of iron.

In this part of the myth, which is distinguished from its predecessor by a question from Young Socrates, the counternormal mortals resemble the residents of the golden age in certain ways. Young Socrates is thinking of this age when he asks the Stranger, "In which cycle does the life occur whose nature [*dunamis*] you say derives from Kronos?" (271c3). He offers as a reason for his uncertainty the fact that the change in the motion of the stars and the sun occurs in both epochs (271c4–7). According to the Stranger, the reign of Kronos and the earthborn race are both associated with the heavenly reversal. On astronomical grounds, either epoch could be the golden age, but the Stranger has clearly placed the earthborn race in the counternormal epoch. Apparently Young Socrates is not convinced that this race is capable of blessedness. As we shall see, this is a reasonable doubt.

The Eleatic Stranger evidently agrees; he praises Young Socrates for having "followed the *logos* nobly" (271c8). The word *logos* can mean either "story" or "rational account." It is therefore not at all impossible that the Stranger is using the term as a virtual synonym for *muthos*. But I believe it to be more likely that *logos* here points back to *logisamenoi* at 270b3. In either case, by shifting terms, the Stranger renders ambiguous the distinction between *muthos* and the *logos* of the diaeresis, which we are attempting to purge of shame (268d2–3). The Stranger then goes on to say, "that which you ask about, the springing up spontaneously of all things for mortals, belongs not at all to the presently established course, but it belongs also to the previous one" (271c8–d3). "Also" must refer here to the mode of genesis of the earthborn race. The Stranger takes Young Socrates' question about the golden age—the question of blessedness—to refer to the spontaneous production from the earth of all means of human subsistence. He will shortly say that the question can be answered only on the basis of the presence or absence of philosophy. At this moment, however, there is no reason to assume that any but corporeal factors are involved.

In sum, to the question "which is the age of Kronos?" the Stranger answers obliquely that so far as Young Socrates is concerned, namely, with respect to the science of natural or bodily motions, the criterion for the golden age refers to the counternormal epoch. But he does not actually say that the counternormal epoch is, or contains, the golden age. In that epoch, at the beginning, "the god ruled and took care of the whole" (*ērchen epimeloumenos holēs ho theos:* 271d3). "In the beginning" (*autēs prōton*) seems to refer to the beginning of that epoch, rather than to the making of the cosmos by the divine demiurge. If the expression *epi Kronou*, "during [the time or reign] of Kronos," which appears at 272b1, is intended to refer to the counternormal epoch altogether—and not just to the human experience of it—then obviously Kronos is the co-rotator. But in this case, he must also be the demiurge or god who rules the whole.

Those who, like me, find this puzzling if not extremely unlikely will be attracted to the thesis that Kronos represents only the human experience of the rule of the demiurge as co-rotator. In other words, the Stranger's own account of the principles of motion, as well as of the various divine powers, is ambiguous and requires us to interpret his theology rather than merely to repeat or summarize it. My interpretation is that the ambiguities arise because the Stranger is forced to give differing identities to his supreme deities in order to avoid divine contradiction, but this effort is seen to fail as soon as we "calculate" about, rather than merely accept as rhetorical ornamentation, the roles assigned in his myth to the demiurge, co-rotator, Kronos, and Zeus. If we merely summarize the main or most explicit teaching of the myth, the demiurge, co-rotator, and Kronos are one and the same god. But in this case the god who makes, and so moves, everything is also the god who abstains from moving the cosmos during one-half of its existence. Or else the god moves everything always, functioning during the normal epoch through the implantation of memory, in which case the difference for human beings between the two epochs is merely illusory.

The ambiguous nature of the Stranger's reference to the demiurge, or as I have expressed this, to the two *personae* of the deity who governs during the counternormal epoch, leaves a space for the following hypothesis. Zeus and Kronos are coordinate and reciprocal expressions of the two dimensions of human existence; both are subordinate to, or applied expressions of, the demiurge who does not only rule but who has made the whole. Human freedom is therefore, if not entirely illusory, highly problematic. In the age of Zeus, we are free to understand that our existence is conditioned by cosmic motion, the necessities of the body, and the arbitrariness of fate as represented mythically by the Olympian gods. This is certainly reminiscent of Spinoza's definition of freedom as knowledge of necessity. For a Platonic commentary, the reader should consult *Laws,* I. 644d7ff. The Athenian Stranger says there that human beings are puppets of the gods, dangling from cords and manipulated by them, whether for their play or for a serious purpose we do not know; but we must strive to assist the effects of the golden cord of calculative reason (*logismos*), which is the "common *nomos* of the city."

To continue with our own myth, the Stranger goes on to say that the cosmos is divided into spheres or regions (*topous*), each of which is assigned to the rule of a separate deity (271d4–6). If the division is carried out by Kronos in his identity as divine helmsman, then he must keep the rule of humans for himself. The animals (*ta zōa*) are divided by races and herds and distributed to the autarchic authority of daimons who rule "like divine shepherds" (271d6–e1). But "animals" must refer here to nonhumans or brutes because a few lines later the Stranger says of human beings that "God himself was their shepherd and superintended them, just as now human beings, who are a different and more divine animal [*zōon on heteron theioteron*], shepherd the other animals that are inferior to them" (271e5–7).

The shepherd of the human herd is then certainly Kronos. This passage is reminiscent of Socrates' myth in the *Phaedrus* (246d6ff) in which Zeus is said to "order and care for everything" (*diakosmōn panta kai epimeloumenos*), including the distribution of the cosmos and, in particular, of types of human soul, into spheres of management by the Olympians. The main difference is that in the *Phaedrus* there is one cosmic cycle, and Zeus is the leader of the philosophical souls in addition to ruling the whole. In the counternormal cycle of our myth, Kronos rules mankind, and the Stranger leaves it an open question whether philosophy occurs in it.

Since every herd of animals has a daimonic shepherd, all are tame and do not trouble human beings; furthermore, there is no meat eating in the counternormal epoch, no war, and no sedition (*stasis:* 271e1–2). This reinforces my previous remarks about discontinuity in the internal logic of the myth and shows that counternormal existence cannot be simply like the rewinding of a video tape. Each epoch has certain events that do not occur in reversed order in the other; furthermore, even though human beings are growing younger in the counternormal epoch, they eat fruit. A comprehensive reversal of the normal epoch would make this impossible; instead of ingesting food, counternormal humans would be expelling it. It is obvious that, in order to make his point, the Stranger requires us to allow a kind of "normal" existence to counternormal humans. We allow him this as the prerogative of the mythmaker, without surrendering our privilege of thinking through the consequences of the limitations that are intrinsic to his tale.

In the counternormal epoch, as is now evident, humans do not simply rewind or unravel. In some not fully specified sense, they exist or live a quasi-human life. There is a discontinuity between cosmic and human reversal; this is hardly surprising, since there is also a discontinuity between cosmic motion and human existence in the normal epoch. The difference between the two discontinuities is as follows: in the normal epoch, cosmic motion, as transmitted to us through our bodies, brings war, disease, old age, and death; in the counternormal epoch, war, disease, and old age are absent, and death is transformed into a careless return to infancy. Under the supervision of Kronos, people are *carefree;* under the supervision of Zeus, human existence, because it is not fully governed by a divine shepherd, is full of cares. The *epimeleia* of self-caring is associated with hardship, debility, and sorrow. This is the dark side of human freedom, and the same shadow is cast over the philosopher, so long as he or she remains a member of the human herd and is not transported by the gods to the blessed isles.

The carelessness of the autochthonous race extends from the absence of political life to that of the family because there is no possession of women and children; equally important, "they were all born from the earth, nor did they remember their previous lives" (271e8–272a2). In this epoch, the earthborn humans are like plants, with one certain and one possible exception: they eat fruit, and they may have the capacity of speech—a point that the Stranger is about to address. Again we see that the details of counternormal existence are not at all a reversal of normal existence but something quite different. Biological reversal is not only joined to the absence of city and family: more fundamentally, there is neither Eros nor spiritedness in the counternormal epoch. One is therefore led to doubt that there can be any intelligence; as to desire, if it exists at all, it must be radically different from the desire of erotic human beings. It looks very much as if counternormal humans have no souls; certainly they lack at a minimum two-thirds of the soul as it is described in the *Republic.*

Part Five: Knowledge and Speech (272b1–d4)

So much for life in the age of Kronos; as to life in the present age, Young Socrates knows this from his own direct experience. The Stranger indicates that a new part of the myth has begun by asking him whether he is able and willing to judge in which age life is more blessed. The youth replies in the negative. The Stranger offers to make "some kind of judgment" on his behalf, and Young Socrates agrees (272b1–7). This conversation serves as an interlude between parts four and five. The interposition of question and answer within the myth suggests another reason why it is also referred to as a *logos.*

The Stranger says that "if those who are nurtured by Kronos, having so much leisure and capacity [*dunamis*] to become acquainted, not only with human beings, but also with the brutes through discourse [*dia logōn*], used these altogether for the sake of philosophy, conversing with the beasts and with each other and learning by inquiry about every nature whether, by possessing some peculiar capacity, it perceives something different from everyone else for the collection of *phronēsis*, it will be a good judgment that the humans of that epoch are ten thousand times superior to us with respect to blessedness" (272b8–c5).

The passage just quoted is one-half of a long double conditional. The Stranger does not attribute speech to the counternormal humans but employs the genitive absolute to state a corollary of his general conditional (*parousēs autois*). He is thus saying that if they can speak and use this ability to philosophize with each other and the animals, then they can be said in effect to live in the golden age. Nothing he has said about life in the epoch of Kronos gives us any reason to affirm the antecedent of this first half of the conditional sentence. The absence of initial memories rules out any version of the doctrine of recollection; the absence of Eros, desire, and the subsequent need to work mitigates against the accumulation of experience. Nor was anything said about speech or any other activity of the soul in the part of the myth devoted to life in the counternormal epoch. Even granting a certain stability or normal existence within the counternormal cosmos, this existence is vegetative, not reflective or contemplative. And finally, since there are no stable looks, there cannot be diaeresis, the so-called art of the philosopher.

The second half of the conditional falls within the scope of the corollary condition in the genitive absolute; if, in other words, the counternormal humans possess the ability to speak to the brutes as well as to themselves but do not use this capacity to philosophize, "but if, filling up on food and drink, they told each other and the animals myths" (restoring *muthous,* which Burnet follows Wohlrab in deleting) "such as those that are now told about them, as it seems to me [literally, "to my opinion"], it would again be very easy to judge" (272c5–d2). So the Stranger does not judge the matter as he offered to do; he simply states the criterion on which one might judge. Burnet presumably deletes *muthous* because its presence makes the sentence sound as though it applies to the Stranger's own tale. But this is typical of Plato's sense of humor; one must always resist the efforts of nineteenth-century philologists to smooth out the text when there is no syntactical reason for doing so. We must also note that the word may refer to traditional tales, not to the Stranger's corrected synthesis.

Just as the Stranger attributed *phronēsis* to the cosmos, so too he picks out *phronēsis*, or rather the increase in *phronēsis*, as the condition for blessedness. The cosmos exercises *phronēsis* in the same epoch that philosophy actually occurs. There is thus some kind of harmony between the motions of the cosmos and those of human thinking; this harmony is obviously lacking in the counternormal epoch, and the absence of such harmony is connected to the direct management by Kronos of cosmic rotation. It would therefore be misleading to speak of the aforementioned harmony as a kind of natural teleology, except in the possible case that the golden age is in fact situated within the normal epoch but inhabited exclusively by philosophers. For everyone else, and for the philosophers in their identity as human beings, the harmony is associated with neediness or care, war, sedition, old age, and consciousness of death. One could almost say that philosophy is a product of decadence and that it flourishes as a kind of transcending excrescence of decay.

The Stranger concludes part five as follows: "nevertheless, let us leave these matters until someone who brings us information [from the counternormal epoch] casts sufficient light for us on whether those who lived then had the desires for the sciences and the use of speeches" (*tēs tōn logōn chreias*: 272d2–4). We are therefore required to infer for ourselves from the tangled web of the Stranger's discourse whether such desire and its necessary medium, *logos,* is conceivable as the defining mark of life in the age of Kronos. Neither does the Stranger explain why he offered to pass judgment on this point but has failed to do so. The pervasive ambiguity of his story is that it is a mixture of *muthos* and *logos,* of allusiveness and explanation. No one expects a myth or a fairy tale to make rational sense, but there must be a mythical coherence for the tale to convey its poetical or rhetorical function of illumination. The Stranger intermittently explains his story *as he tells it,* thereby transcending it even as he invites us to enter within its fabulous dimension. But his explanations are as obscure as the myths he has employed.

As for myself, I infer from the Stranger's tale that if philosophy is present at all in the counternormal age, it can only be as *phronēsis,* which is distinct from *diaeresis* or articulate speech. This point will be taken up in a different way later in the dialogue, when the Stranger distinguishes between rule by *phronēsis* and rule by *nomos.* But he will make clear at that time that in order to rule, *phronēsis* must speak and in so doing divide the better from the worse, or the fitting from the unfitting. The possibility of philosophy in the counternormal age rests finally upon our decision as to whether judgment and speech are possible in the absence of stable looks. In my opinion, this is not possible.

Part Six: From Counternormal to Normal (272d5–273e4)

So much for Kronos; the Stranger now says that he will give the reason why he has collected together parts of traditional stories into a myth

(272d5–6). We find a similar statement at 268d2–3, where we were told that the purpose of the myth is to rescue the *logos* from disgrace. No doubt this is why the Stranger shifts back from *logos* to *muthos* in referring to this section of the dialogue. Instead of repeating that reason or giving another, however, the Stranger launches into a detailed account of the shift from the counternormal to the normal epoch. Just as in the previous part, the Stranger announces that he will do one thing and then does something else.

He begins as follows: "when the time had been completed and the change had to take place, and the earthborn race had been entirely used up through the return by each soul of all of its ordained births as seed falling into the ground" (272d6–e3). The plantlike nature of counternormal life is stressed; in addition, we learn that there are epicycles within the epochal cycle, of which no mention has been hitherto made. Presumably these correspond to the transmigration or reincarnation of the soul in the normal epoch. Continuing: "then the governor [= pilot or co-rotator] as if dropping the handle of the rudder, withdrew to his lookout, and fate and innate desire made the cosmos reverse again" (272e3–6). Whoever the co-rotator may be, he does no work during either the reversal or the normal stage itself. Instead, he views the heavens, thereby resembling a divine paradigm of the astronomer or theoretical life rather than of the shepherd or statesman. And this is appropriate for the age in which philosophy occurs. But it suggests a split between the theoretical and the practical life that is not entirely compatible with the subsequent discussion of the royal *technē*.

The distinction between fate and innate desire must refer to necessity on the one hand and the construction of the cosmos on the other. Previously we were told that the demiurge gave *phronēsis* to the cosmos so that it could govern itself during the normal epoch. The innate desire to reverse is apparently something different from *phronēsis* and represents its precondition. The cosmos is so made that it desires to reverse at the moment that the helmsman lets go the tiller. Why are things arranged in this way rather than having the helmsman himself reverse the cosmos at the appropriate moment and then drop the tiller? We recall that the cosmos has no innate desire to reverse from the normal to the counternormal state, but it must be rescued by the captain's return to the tiller. No doubt it is exhausted by old age and lacks the innate strength for such a self-transformation. At the end of the counternormal stage, however, the fated rejuvenation has been completed, and the instinct for life that marks the very young is now able to reassert itself.

At this moment, "all the gods who govern the regions with the great daimon, knowing what is about to occur, let go the parts of the cosmos

under their care" (272e6–273a1). Earlier the chief helmsman was called a
god and his subordinates were designated as daimons; here the Stranger
reverses his terminology. Normally when a daimon is contrasted with gods,
it refers to a divine power in contrast to personal gods. During the reversal
itself, there is another destruction of all kinds of animals; after a time the
violence ceases and the cosmos orders itself into its accustomed (*eiōthota*)
motion, exercising "care and rule" (*epimeleian kai kratos*) "over the things
inside it as well as over itself, remembering as much as possible the teaching
of the demiurge and father" (273a4–b2).

This passage reminds us that human beings are not entirely free during
the age of Zeus. Apart from the role played in human life by the Olympians,
we are also subject to the power of the cosmos, and through that power to
the will of the demiurge, and finally, to the same fate or necessity that
governs the gods themselves. What precisely is the teaching of the demiurge
that the cosmos remembers? Surely the implication is that this refers to the
various kinds of corporeal motion. As we have already seen, there is no
political life among counternormal humans and very little, if any, psychic
experience. But during the normal epoch, the cosmos is moving in a way
that reverses the motions of the counternormal epoch. The memory in
question must therefore be of the original act of genesis; again we note the
strong likelihood that our age is the original condition.

The cosmic memory is more precise at the beginning of the normal cycle
and more blurred toward the end (273b2–3). Nothing is said about cosmic
memory in the counternormal epoch, nor would any be required given the
regulative function of the co-rotator. The memory is weakened by the
"corporeal nature" (*sōmatoeides*) of the cosmic mixture, which is the con-
genital property of nature as it was prior to the origination of the cosmos (*to
tēs palai pote phuseōs suntrophon*). This passage explains why Plato would
reject a doctrine of creation *ex nihilo;* it makes the deity responsible for the
disorderliness of matter, or as Plato would express this, of the bodily *eidos* of
"the present cosmos" (*to nun kosmon*), which refers here to both epochs,
counternormal as well as normal. The cosmos can receive "all noble things
from its constructor." It follows that baseness is eternal and intrinsic to the
nature of cosmic existence; the Stranger mentions harshness and un-
righteousness as heavenly in origin (273b2–c2).

So long as the captain is at the tiller, there is little bad and much that is
good in the lives of the animals. When he lets go, the cosmos carries on
initially in a most noble manner, but with the passage of time, its memory
deteriorates and the old disorderly condition progressively reasserts itself.
"Thereupon the god who had fashioned the cosmos, seeing it to be in

aporia and concerned [*kēdomenos*] lest, storm-bound, it might dissolve from the shaking and sink into the boundless sea of unlikeness, once more sat down at the rudders, reversing the sickness and dissolution from the period when the cosmos was on its own; he orders and sets it straight, thereby making it deathless and ageless" (273d4–e4).

This passage makes it unmistakable that demiurge and co-rotator are one and the same. I have already stated at length the difficulties this raises and will not repeat them. The deterioration of its memory leads the cosmos away from the original intention and control of the demiurge. The memory, in other words, is an expression of the limitations as well as of the power of the demiurge. This raises an important question that we have not yet sufficiently considered. Why does the demiurge in his persona as co-rotator let go the tiller in the counternormal epoch? The Stranger refers to this event three times in his myth. At 269c5–6, he says that the suitable number of periods in the counternormal cycle are completed. At 270a3–5, the release follows the rejuvenation of the cosmos, which has now reacquired life and deathlessness. At 272d6, the Stranger says that the release comes when the time has been completed and the change was necessary and the earthborn race had been used up.

The following inference seems to be compatible with and, indeed, to follow from these three explanations. The purpose of the counternormal epoch is to restore the vitality of the cosmos, which is in turn necessary to rescue normal human beings from extreme decadence and, finally, extinction. This in turn supports my hypothesis that the original status of the cosmos was a normal epoch which, despite the good intentions of the demiurge, deteriorated because of the intrinsic disorderliness of the bodily *eidos*. It was therefore the intention of the demiurge that the cosmos move on its own, guided by an innate memory of the divine impetus. This being so, the demiurge, *qua* co-rotator—if we take him as a paradigm of the royal art of the statesman—is like a benevolent despot who rules directly by guiding every motion in the human herd, just as the co-rotator guides, either personally or by daimonic surrogates, every motion in the cosmos. This will become directly relevant in the last part of the dialogue when the Stranger considers the superiority of *phronēsis* to political laws. For the time being, I note only that human beings are like plants or at best monkeys during the rule of Kronos. To be genuinely human, in other words, is to be detached to some unspecifiable degree from the gods, but not to be completely sundered from them. And politics arise from the detachment, even though, interestingly enough, the detachment must itself be covered over by the statesman through the use of noble lies.

It is therefore false, despite occasional appearances to the contrary, that the sense of the myth is to depict the counternormal epoch as a golden age from which our own, normal epoch is a fall. To the contrary, ours is the golden age, as is evident from the presence of *logos* and philosophy. In other words, gold and iron are inseparable in human existence. Philosophy is the sister of decadence. The rejuvenative function of the counternormal epoch is inseparable from a temporary suspension of our humanity; it is a period of forgetting and silence. If we can speak to the brutes during this period, it is because we ourselves have become brutes. The god lets go the tiller so that we may become human beings; he takes up the tiller to restore us to this condition. And the continuous reversal is necessary or fated by the innate disorderliness of the body in all its forms, cosmic and animal.

Part Seven: The Myth as Paradigm (273e4–274e3)

"This is the completion of the whole story. But for the exhibition [*apodeiksin*] of the king, it will suffice for us to grasp the previous part of the story" (273e4–6). Why then did the Stranger tell the entire myth? And what exactly does the Stranger mean by "previous part" as opposed to "whole"? He begins to speak about the reversal "to the present road of genesis" (273e7), but this was never described in the myth, which was also silent about the details of existence in the normal epoch, with which Young Socrates would be familiar from his own life (272b2–3). The Stranger says that the counternormal motion of aging ceases and new motions, opposite to the old ones, begin. These motions, animal and cosmic, "imitate and follow along with the affection of the all" (*tōi panti*); in other words, the local motions of animal genesis are in accord, as far as possible, with the normal motions of the "autocratic" cosmos (273e7–274b1).

At 269c7, the Stranger says that when the co-rotator lets go the tiller, the cosmos reverses "spontaneously" (*automaton*) into the normal period because it possesses life and intelligence. The same term is employed at 271d1 and e4–5 to refer to the life of the earthborn race that "grows out of the earth" (271c1) like the plants that nourish it. Obviously the counternormal animals are not autocratic. There are then two kinds of spontaneity, one of which refers to counternormal motions independent of human intention or work, and the other to natural motions, cosmic and human, that are at least proximately caused by memory and intelligence. Only the second of these two senses could have political significance: hence the term "autocrat" (*autokratora*: 274a5). The Stranger emphasizes that human generation is also now, like the cosmos, arranged to be as autocratic as possible. It is therefore obvious that the normal epoch provides us with the paradigm for political life; but it is not at all obvious that the paradigm implies an equivalence between the art of the statesman and that of the king.

The paradigm of the king is exhibited by the account of the demiurge and co-rotator, which belongs properly to the discussion of the counternormal epoch. This discussion was plainly necessary in order to bring out the point of the political significance of the autocratic nature of the normal cosmos. There is obviously a conceptual relation between autocracy and monarchy, but all that follows from the discussion of the normal epoch is that humankind is sufficiently independent of the very natural processes that give it bodily existence to allow the human race to produce cities and to modify biological by political existence. The myth of the counternormal, on the contrary, in effect identifies the statesman with the demiurgic god in his persona as co-rotator; the term *autocratic* could apply here only to the god and in no way to humankind. This part of the myth thus continues with the implication of the diaeresis that the king is a shepherd who differs by nature or race from the animals in his herd. It also follows the longer way by reducing the stature of human beings to that of the brutes, or even goes beyond this in transforming human beings into plants.

"We are now at the point for which the entire *logos* was launched" (274b1–2). The Stranger shifts back without comment from "part" to "whole." Much more could be said about the animals; speech about human beings is shorter and more fitting (274b2–5). The Stranger in effect admits that he has been excessively garrulous in recounting his myth. He also reminds us that the extensive "punishment" applied to Young Socrates for quickly separating animals into human and nonhuman was certainly misapplied; that is, it had some other purpose than to bring out a useful diaeresis. Each part of the dialogue is on the one hand both too long and insufficiently ordered, but on the other hand designed to teach us that it is impossible to speak clearly and succinctly about politics.

At 273c4–6, the Stranger said that at the beginning of the normal epoch, "everything proceeds most nobly" because the cosmic memory of the co-rotator's design is still fresh. But now (274b5ff) we are told that life for human beings in the initial stages of the normal period (*kata tous prōtous chronous*) is dangerous and harsh, since they lack experience (*mēchanē*) and *technē* and must now protect themselves against fierce beasts and produce their own food, which is no longer spontaneous (274b5–c4; for the Athenian Stranger's version of the initial stage, see *Laws* III. 677e6ff). Once more we note that there is a discontinuity between cosmic and human nature. Spontaneity is replaced by "the necessity of need" (274c3–4). Humankind is from the outset "in aporia," which can be resolved only by divine assistance. "For which reason the old stories about the gifts of the gods were given to us with the necessary teaching and education" (274c5–7).

The old stories about Prometheus, Hephaestus, Athena, and so on, to whom we ostensibly owe the use of fire, *technē,* agriculture, and the other arts, seem to contradict the theme of human autonomy during the normal epoch. And in fact, the Stranger's own account is puzzling because he says next, immediately after having referred to the gifts of the gods: "and everything that jointly organizes human life has arisen from these [gifts], since the care [*epimeleia*] of the gods, as I said already, was taken away from humans, and they were required to provide the guidance and *epimeleia* for themselves from their own efforts, just like the whole cosmos, which we imitate and follow throughout all of time, now in this way, whereas then we live and grow in the former manner" (274d2–e1).

This passage implies that the paradigm is not the demiurgic god but the cosmos. Political existence arises from the harshness and neediness of our (normal) origins. The actual significance of the origins is that the gods do not care for us. To be sure, we invent myths assigning the discovery of the arts to the generosity of Prometheus, an ambiguous remainder from the age of the Titans, and to the Olympian gods. But the Stranger himself entirely ignores the gods immediately after referring to them and emphasizes that their care is absent in the present epoch; we must care for ourselves, like the cosmos. The Stranger gives no explanation—not even a mythical or quasi-logical one—of the nature and role of the Olympian gods in the age of Zeus. By referring to them, and by his invocation of a divine demiurge and co-rotator of the counternormal epoch, he avoids the charge of impiety. Camouflaged as it were by this bow to piety, the Stranger rather bluntly states that the gods play no role in human affairs.

"Let this be an end to the myth. We will make use of it in order to see how much we erred in presenting the royal and the political art in the previous *logos*" (274e1–4).

Summary

Let me now present in outline form some of the pervasive features of the Stranger's ambiguous mixture of myth and *logos.* I will refer to it for convenience as a myth, unless the mixed nature is directly relevant.

I. The myth has a prologue and seven parts that exhibit a pattern of interrelationship. I list the parts together with a brief reminder of the main theme of each:

Prologue. 268d5–e7: A new *archē* is required because of the error in the diaeresis.

  1. 268e8–269c3: General description of the three main themes (reversed cosmos, age of Kronos, earthborn race).

  2. 269c4–270b2: Explanation of the existence of and need for two epochs.

  3. 270b3–271c2: Rational analysis of cosmic and human reversal.

  4. 271c3–272b1: The age of Kronos.

  5. 272b1–d4: The (unresolved) question of the identity of the golden age.

  6. 272d5–273e4: The shift from the counternormal to the normal epoch.

  7. 273e4–274e3: The purpose of the myth.

The themes are interrelated as follows. The prologue corresponds to part 7; parts 1, 2, and 3 correspond to parts 4, 5, and 6, respectively.

  II. The Stranger makes seven statements concerning the reason for telling the myth, two of which occur just after the point we have reached in our analysis:

  1. 268b5–c2: It is required to expiate the shame of the *logos* (= diaeresis), which failed to distinguish the king from the other nurturers of the human race.

  2. 272d5: The Stranger says that we may tell the purpose of the myth but instead explains the shift from the counternormal to the normal epoch.

  3. 273e5: For the exhibition of the king, it will be enough to return to the early part of the myth.

  4. 274b1: We have now arrived at the purpose of the whole myth (to explain the political significance of the human relation to the cosmos).

  5. 274e1: We told the myth because it was useful for understanding the error we made in diaeresis (this statement extends to 275a7).

  6. 275b1: The myth was introduced in order to clarify the art of nurturing the herd.

  7. 277b1ff: The myth was introduced to illustrate an error in diaeresis, but erred itself in being too long and employing too much content.

These statements are by no means inconsistent with one another; they are rather excessive, constituting thereby a direct reflection of the excessiveness of the myth itself.

  III. According to Brandwood and my own check, the noun "error" (*hamartēma*) occurs once at the very beginning of the dialogue, in a statement by Theodorus (257b7), and seven times in the balance of the dialogue between the Eleatic Stranger and Young Socrates. Since the question of error arises initially in connection with the relation of the myth to diaeresis, I list the passages here: 274e5; 277b3; 296b9; 296c4; 297a6; 297d1; 300b4. In the last passage, the Stranger says that whoever persuades the people to violate the laws "multiplies a mistake many times itself," as Benardete translates it. And there are seven distinct references to errors committed within the diaeresis and the myth: 262a3ff; 268a4–d5; 274e1ff (two errors are noted); 276c3ff (again two errors are noted); 277a1–6).

There is a brief exchange immediately following the completion of the myth that is devoted to the topic of the errors that have been committed to this point. It runs from 274e5 to 275c8, and it will be convenient to discuss it here. Young Socrates wants to know "in what way and how much" we erred. The Stranger replies that we made a smaller (*brachuteron*) and a greater (*meizon*) error (274e5–8). This echoes the distinction between the longer and the shorter way in the diaeresis section, a distinction, we recall, that came to one step (265a1ff); there is also a reference at 266d7–e2 to the fact that diaeresis does not honor the greater ahead of the smaller (an assertion that is rendered ambiguous because the Stranger goes on directly to attach greater importance to the greater of two errors: 266e7ff).

We come back now to the Stranger's answer to Young Socrates' question. The greater error was that although our concern lay with the king and statesman of the current, normal epoch, we spoke of the divine shepherd of the human flock instead. The smaller error was that we did not say in what way the king rules the entire city (274e10–275a6). The second mistake is evidently about *technē*. Taken together, the two mistakes involve the two types of division—namely, of herds and of arts—that became confused in the diaeresis. The diaeresis failed to distinguish between human and divine. The myth made this distinction but pursued the wrong branch and so established the wrong paradigm. It seems inconceivable that the Stranger would not have discovered and expunged these errors in advance, especially since at the beginning of the *Sophist*, Theodorus says that they have just been discussing a question very similar to that of the nature of sophist, statesman, and philosopher; the Stranger is supposed to be recounting Eleatic doctrine, and he has just had a dress rehearsal (*Sophist* 217a6ff).

Making every allowance for the variations that are a natural part of every fresh discussion of old topics, we cannot reasonably doubt that the most obvious errors, repetitions, and confusions must have been intended by the Stranger. They are themselves part of the teaching. I believe that this is so in two ways. First, the Stranger, and behind him, Plato, illustrates how tangled is the web of political analysis and reflection. Abstract structures, mathematically precise methods, and unequivocal terminologies are altogether out of place in this context. Second, the errors, false starts, duplications, lists, even the arithmetical structure of the various parts of the dialogue are all part of Plato's teaching on the themes of the dialogue. We must understand these in addition to the so-called explicit argument of the dialogue. Even further, there is no explicit argument of the dialogue but instead a series of ambiguous treatments, not always clearly related and each filled with asides and obscure discontinuities, mistakes, repetitions, and the like. Otherwise stated, the explicit argument of the dialogue is the dialogue itself in its entirety. Those who attempt to extract an academic argument from the literary ornamentation of the dialogue will inevitably understand nothing of the dialogue because they do not understand the most obvious features of Plato's manner of writing: most important, they entirely lack Plato's sense of humor, which in the *Statesman* gives a baroque costume to his usual irony.

If we fall victim to the heavy sonorities of the Stranger's discursive style, then we shall be forced to conclude that he is incompetent, since he has botched entirely the construction of the myth that was intended to save the diaeresis from shame. In one of his seven references to the purpose of the myth, the Stranger follows his account of the two errors by stating that we need to define the manner (*tropos*) of the king. "And this is why we told the myth," namely, to show the various contestants for the title of statesman, whom we thereby point out in accord with the paradigm of the shepherd and herdsman (275a8–b7). Despite Young Socrates' approving "correct," we entirely failed to accomplish the stated intentions. The schema of the divine herdsman exceeds that of the normal human statesmen who are "much more like the natures of those being ruled" (275b8–c4). Much more, but not entirely. In any event, we have to start again.

CHAPTER FOUR

Correcting the Diaeresis

THUS far we have identified three major parts of the *Statesman*. The prologue is very brief, running from 257a1 to 258a10. There follow two very long sections, the diaeresis (258b1–268d4) and the myth (268d5–275c8). We now begin the fourth part, which is again quite short (275c3–276c2) and is devoted to the topic of correcting the errors of the diaeresis. The Stranger signals that we are in a new part by saying "Let us then go back" (*palin epanelthōmen*) to the part of the epitactic art that nurtures herds (275c9–d2). We erred, he says, somewhere in this division by failing to grasp and name the statesman, "who escaped our notice by fleeing into our terminology" (*onomasia:* 275d4–6). Instead of capturing the prey by collecting him together with his herd, our technical language has concealed the statesman among the nurturers of the human race. We failed to notice that, unlike the other herdsmen, the king does not nurture (*trephein*) his flock (275d8–e1).

Let us pause for a moment to consider the Stranger's terminology at this point. He has introduced two main terms to refer to the art of the herdsman: "nurturing" (*trophikē*) and "caring" (*epimeleia*). Nurture includes feeding and rearing; this refers in principle to the tending or serving (*therapeia*) of the body. "Caring" (*epimeleia*), as we have seen, has been used carelessly, in such a way as to apply directly to the art of politics, whether practiced by mortals or gods, but at the same time as a virtual synonym for "nurturing." One could explain this terminological carelessness as due to a failure to distinguish between care of the body and care of the soul. In the entire diaeresis section, the word "soul" occurs only twice as applied to human beings rather than to animals, at 258c7, where it refers to the intellectual capacity of the Stranger and Young Socrates to grasp the forms of knowledge, and shortly thereafter at 259c8, where we are told that the intelligence and strength of the king's soul is much more efficacious in maintaining office than are his hands or his entire body. The Stranger distinguishes between "unsouled" or nonliving and "souled" or living things at 261b4ff, but this fails to differentiate human from nonhuman souls, a failure that leads to great confusion.

The reference to the king at 259c8 is part of the reasoning by which his art is classified under gnostics rather than under the practico-productive arts. Yet there is no further mention of the soul until the myth. In the diaeresis, attention shifts from the arts as knowledge to the practical arts of breeding, feeding, and rearing. This is closely connected to the Stranger's mistaken criticism of Young Socrates for attempting too quickly to distinguish between human and nonhuman animals. At the root of this problem, I believe, is the ambiguity in the nature of the political art, which seems to be both gnostic and practico-productive. More immediately, however, the Stranger has forgotten the soul in his pursuit of the statesman by way of diaeresis. As we shall see in detail, and as can be represented in advance by reference to the central metaphor of politics as weaving, there is an unmistakable tendency in the *Statesman* to consider politics from the standpoint of the body, at least up to the concluding discussion of politics as the art of weaving together opposite types of soul (306a1ff). Even here, however, the soul is treated as if it were a body, or as material for the construction of an artifact.

Returning to 275e3, the Stranger says that therapy is common to all herdsmen and is not defined by nurturing or any other activity (*pragmateias*). *Therapeia* is serving in all senses and so includes breeding, feeding, tending, healing, and so on. It is not so clear, however, that it includes the political *epimeleia*. We do, of course, refer to statesmen as "servants of the people," but one might well regard this as a euphemism. Is not the statesman, and in particular the king, the Stranger's paradigm, a master rather than a servant? Or does the Stranger wish to say that masters are also servants? Contrary to the situation in Hegel's dialectic of master and servant, there is no inversion of roles in the age of Kronos. But what of the age of Zeus? Is not even the philosopher-king a servant of the people to the extent that he or she must turn away from philosophy because of the legal compulsion to rule the city?

Perhaps the simplest formulation of the main point is that political existence is mutual caring by humans for one another; this is so regardless of the form of the regime. In other words, the statesman, whether one or many, exemplifies the duality of human nature; we are all of us both masters and servants, and in a multiplicity of senses. This would be one way of glossing Aristotle's definition of man as the political animal. But there is no such definition in Plato, who tends to understand politics in terms of a hierarchy within the soul, and so of the souls of individual human beings. There is for

Plato a master element in the soul, called *nous, dianoia,* and *phronēsis* in different contexts, which ought to rule by nature over the other elements (in the *Republic, thumos* and *epithumia:* spiritedness and desire). "Ought to": one cannot avoid this Kantian-sounding expression when speaking of Plato, because in fact the intellect, or intelligence, does not rule, or rules rarely, in the case of the individual, and, by Plato's own account, it never rules in actual or historical cities.

Man is for Plato the animal who is "by nature" sick, and this extends to human cities. The Athenian Stranger refers in the *Laws* (VI. 782e6ff) to the three human sicknesses—hunger, thirst, and Eros—of which the last is the greatest. The philosopher is the physician of the soul, literally, the psychiatrist who must heal human beings by reinstituting the rule of reason, not simply or explicitly, but through surrogates. This is more obviously true for Socrates than for the Eleatic Stranger, as we can easily see by consulting *Republic* IV. 445d1 to V. 449a5. Or again, at *Gorgias* 478d6, Socrates says that righteousness (*dikē*) is the medicine of psychic wickedness. But that the Stranger believes essentially the same thing is strongly suggested by the continuous comparison between politics and medicine in the *Statesman* from 293b1 almost to the end of the dialogue, as well as by his very Socratic distinction between the one genuine city or ruler and all actual regimes at 301c6ff.

The Stranger is more impressed by the need to make self-defense primary in view of the hostility of nature, and so with every allowance for the salutary rhetoric of his peroration, he is driven to give priority to the body over the soul in the domain of politics. This is true even when he speaks of the soul as primary, since it is treated as an ingredient in the construction of the stable because harmonious city, in other words, the city that resists the steady dissolution of cosmic or natural motion as much as possible.

In the Socratic teaching, the city is for the sake of philosophy, just as the body is for the sake of the soul, and this is conveyed by Socrates' concern for "the best" in the sense of the best way of life. This in turn is made possible by the Ideas, which are not themselves citizens and which direct the soul of the potential philosopher beyond the city. And this is the only way the soul can be healed of its natural illness. The nonphilosophers must be treated constantly, as if in a never-ending psychoanalysis, with myths that incorporate as much rationality as possible—as much as the patient will bear. The surrogates of reason or techniques of philosophical psychiatry can be expressed in a variety of metaphors, but underlying them all is the central notion of practico-production. The statesman, as a genuine practitioner of the *technē,* may be said in one sense to follow nature, because he or she attempts to reinstitute the rule of reason. But this is done through "medical" artifacts. The citizen is accordingly an artifact of political medicine. More precisely, the citizen is the simulacrum of the philosopher: the false image of the rational human being.

The Stranger is in agreement with Socrates about the manner of treatment for nonphilosophers. But I believe that he extends the same type of treatment to the philosopher qua citizen. There is, in other words, no extrapolitical life for the philosopher in the Stranger's teaching. Philosophy as the science of the free person is diaeresis, or the division in accordance with kinds (*Sophist*, 253c6ff). Diaeresis is said to be a part of dialectic; the other part is presumably the intellectual perception of the greatest genera. Grasping the elements of intelligibility and classifying in accord with looks are the two parts of philosophy, which is entirely nonpolitical. If it were possible to define the statesman by means of diaeresis, that would not be a political act. Politics begins with the founding of a regime and the institution of laws, and these acts are determined fundamentally by the body. This also explains why there is a closer tie between politics and *technē* for the Stranger than for Socrates.

Nothing that I have said on this point should be taken to imply that Plato has a clear and distinct preference for Socrates over the Stranger. The question of Plato's relation to his two dramatic personae cannot be established by drawing up lists of contrasting textual passages, and certainly not by the simplistic assumption of historical development. We are forced to think for ourselves about the significance of the Platonic writings in the context of our own understanding of the nature of philosophy and politics. The situation is complicated by the fact that the Stranger seems to be simultaneously incompetent and a master of philosophical pedagogy. There is good reason to suppose that he is punishing or correcting Socrates, but also that he is forced to accommodate his own views to those of Socrates even as he administers that punishment. What Plato wishes to convey, then, is not a clear-cut superiority of one thinker over the other, but a kind of dialectical give-and-take in which both parties to the dispute have something of value to contribute. Stated with the greatest possible concision, Socrates is superior to the Stranger in his understanding of the human soul. But the Stranger has a more articulated grasp of genesis. Thus the confusions in his presentation of politics are in a way more useful than are Socrates' more lucidly because more single-mindedly "idealistic" presentations of the defects of actual political life and of the means by which they may be removed.

For example, in my opinion the confusion in the Stranger's terminology between ruling and serving is intrinsic to politics; it cannot be extirpated by an ostensibly precise methodology of differences and similarities. But neither is it "sublated" (in Hegel's terminology) by the inversion of masters and servants. Servants who become masters continue to be servants. Marx's dream of a race of independent masters is a peculiar distortion of the Platonic dream of the mastery of reason. Unlike Marx, Plato does not stay continuously at the level of dreams in his treatment of politics, but the shadow of the dream is discernible everywhere in that treatment, and particularly in the *Republic*, whereas it is not so visible in Aristotle's political writings. Aristotle writes about politics in the light of common sense; the shadow of Platonism is discernible only in Book Ten of the *Nicomachean Ethics*, in the discussion of the two forms of happy life, theoretical and practical. After this necessary digression, let us return to the text.

Our intention is to distinguish politics from nurturing. It might seem that the simplest way in which to do this would be to return to step 6 of the diaeresis and to rename "herd nurturing" as "herd serving." We could then divide the art of serving herds into the nurturing and caring arts. But the problem here is that "caring" is undefined; it seems to include nurturing as well as politics, or to be indistinguishable from serving or tending. In other words, we cannot divide in such a way as to arrive easily at the political art because we do not know in advance and with precision the defining marks of that art. These defining marks cannot be discovered by diaeresis, which depends at each stage on our knowledge of what we are looking for. In the early stages, there is no problem, so long as we have a very general knowledge of our prey. As we move farther down the diaeresis, however, our lack of advance knowledge works against us and leads to endless confusion.

When the Stranger says that the statesman does not nurture (feed or rear) the members of the human herd, he is still relying on general or everyday, pretechnical understanding. Unlike the case of herd animals, human beings once they reach a certain age can feed themselves, and when they are too young to do so, they are fed by parents or servants. Marie Antoinette said "let them eat cake," but it did not occur to her to go through the city distributing pastries to her subjects. Nor would any sane person confuse the wholesaler or retailer of nourishment with the king. Otherwise put, something went wrong with the diaeresis at step 5, the division of the art of delivering one's own commands into the genesis of unsouled and ensouled beings. In arriving at the class of ensouled beings, we failed to distinguish between nonhuman and human souls.

At 275e3ff, the Stranger suggests that we change the name of herd nurture (*agelaiotrophikē*) to something like the tending, serving, or caring for herds in order "to wrap round with a covering" (*perikaluptein*), or in other words, to classify together all those who serve (*therapeuein*) herds. This striking image calls our attention to the fact that the king or statesman will accordingly be "concealed" by the covering that includes all servants. In other words, the Stranger's terminological carelessness is entirely transparent in this passage. But he cannot be more careful because he has not yet established what he means by political care.

I must allude once more at this point to the diaeresis in the *Sophist*. At 219a10, the Stranger divides the poetic arts into therapy and mimesis, where therapy includes farming and whatever pertains to the service of the entire mortal body. This accentuates the subterranean connection between politics and the care of the body in the Stranger's teaching. To continue with the *Statesman*, the Stranger says next that we should proceed as we did before, "dividing the nurture of herds into pedestrians and flyers, as well as the unmixed [breeders] and the hornless" (276a3–5). In fact, however, we divided herd nurture into the nurturing of water and land herds; the Stranger omits this step and inverts the original divisions of pedestrians and hornless herds. Most striking, he omits the final division between four-footed and two-footed herd animals. In other words, he omits any mention here of the two-footed land animal known as the human being.

But this is only the beginning of what is on the face of things an unintelligible correction of the error of the original diaeresis. The Stranger goes on to say that we should divide the art of tending herds (*agelaiokomikē*) just as before but now include in the generic term the kings of this epoch as well as of the age of Kronos (276a5–7). But why should we extend the reference of "herd nurturing" in such a way as to include gods with mortals when we were told at 274e10ff that our big mistake was to take a god as paradigm for the human king? The shift from nurturing to tending, just negotiated, leaves room in the broader class for kings who feed and those who do not feed their herds. These will presumably be separated in subsequent steps of the corrected diaeresis, but the entire procedure is cumbersome and unnecessary. More important, it entirely ignores the proposed correction of our previous error.

The Stranger confirms that "herd tending" is broader than "herd nurturing"; he implicitly equates it with "herd caring" (*epimeleia*). Had we begun with tending, in other words, we could have arrived by division at a caring that is not nurturing or feeding. By beginning with nurturing or feeding, we are open to the objection that kings are carers who do not nurture or feed their herds (276a9–b6). But there is a serious defect in the Stranger's suggestion. If we follow it, then we make every subsegment of this branch of the division an *eidos* of tending in the sense of caring (*epimeleia*). In this case, we still fail to identify the art of the statesman. And the Stranger adds that nurturing (feeding) is not a *technē;* the web of diaeresis from step 5 downward is hopelessly tangled.

That the Stranger prefers *epimeleia* throughout as the term for political tending, namely, caring, is once more made evident at 276b7ff: it is the first word in the Greek sentence with which the Stranger asserts that care of the entire human community (*koinōnia* replaces *agelē* or herd) is the art having the strongest claim to be called the *technē* of the king and ruler of all human beings. He speaks here as if we know what is meant by *epimeleia,* but the assertion is a circle. Care is the royal art; the royal art is care.

I remind the reader of the two errors we were said to have committed, one bigger and one smaller. The bigger error was that we used a god instead of a human being as the paradigm for the statesman. The smaller error was that we failed to state precisely what the king does as ruler of the city. It is obvious that the smaller error is not only bigger than the bigger error, but that it is the key to the entire dialogue. The Stranger makes this switch in his measurement of the relative importance of the errors, but without calling attention to the fact. He asks Young Socrates whether he sees that they made a large (*suchnon*) error at the very end of the diaeresis. They should not have assumed immediately that the art of nurturing two-footed herds is the royal art of politics but should have changed the name "nurture" (*threptikē*) to "care" (*epimeleia*) and then looked for further, nontrivial subdivisions (276c3–d3).

This statement must refer to the longer way. In the shorter diaeresis, "two-footed land tribes" includes the feathered and the featherless races; no assumption about politics was made in advance of this division. In the summary of the entire diaeresis (267a4ff), there is no reference to the distinction between two-footed and four-footed. In the longer way, the last step is that of the division of two-footed from four-footed herds. But even in this case, the Stranger does not say where we should have changed *threptikē* into *epimeleia.* The latter term is used with respect to the royal art at 265e7; as to *threptikē,* it is replaced by the suffix *nomikē* (the art of pasturage) after step 7, where the nurturing of herds that dwell on the land is separated from those who dwell on the water. It was at this point that the question of how to divide the class of birds arose; it is here that the Stranger raises the possibility of a shorter way.

The notions of caring, shepherding, breeding, and feeding have all been confused together throughout much of the diaeresis section. This confusion is implicated in the failure to divide off birds from human beings (recall the Stranger's reference to the intelligent cranes) in step 7. All these confusions may be summarized as follows: the correct procedure would have been to separate immediately the care of humans from the shepherding or nurturing of nonhumans. Young Socrates was criticized for making a very similar division of the nurturing of herds; he used "nurture," however, rather than "care," in keeping with the Stranger's immediately antecedent terminology (261e8). Just before this, the Stranger introduced the confusion by interchanging freely "nurture," "breeding," and "care" (261d3–e3).

In contemporary language, the Stranger fails to separate biology, technology, and politics from one another. Hence shepherding and the various arts of nurturing nonhumans are falsely employed in the attempt to define the art of politics. It is extremely important to note that this error is inseparable from the previously identified bigger error of using a god as the paradigm of politics instead of a human being. If we start from the nurture of herds, we arrive at a distinction between ruler and ruled that is analogous to that between gods and human beings. From the standpoint of a divine demiurge, it might well be difficult to distinguish between birds like cranes and human beings.

We have now sorted out the main lines of the diversions or errors introduced by the Stranger's procedures in the diaereses and the myth. Whether we identify these as diversions or as errors will depend upon whether we regard them as intentional or not. If they are unintentional on the part of the Stranger, then he is surely incompetent; this leaves open the question whether Plato is incompetent as well. I regard both these alternatives as absurd, not because Plato is beyond error but because the construction of the errors and the spinning of the web of confusions are both too intricate and too intelligible to be fortuitous. But there is a difference between incompetence and being caught up in the inconsistencies and oversights that are the inevitable consequences of excessive theoretical ambition, or the attempt to capture human life in the grid of diaeresis. The Stranger is not just educating Young Socrates or punishing old Socrates. He is educating and punishing himself.

The Stranger himself formulates what should have been done in a way that partially alleviates the confusion. We should have divided the *epimeleia* of two-footed herds in such a way as to separate the divine shepherd from the human curator (*ton anthrōpinon epimelētēn*: 276d5–6). This is not quite right, since it uses *epimeleia* to refer to birds as well as human beings, but it points in the right direction. All "care" of herds by a being superior to those constituting the herd is to be excluded from the political art. But this requires that we separate a community (*koinōnia*: see 276b7) of human beings from a herd of brutes. Or at least this is required if we wish to study human beings from the human rather than the divine perspective. In different but not unrelated terms, we cannot understand politics adequately by technical methods such as diaeresis that are designed for the articulation of formal structure. What we require eventually is an adequate diaeresis of *technē* that is not itself formal or too abstract to capture the relevant distinctions.

The Stranger continues his rectification of past errors by saying that we should have divided *epimelētikē* (the art of caring for human beings) into two parts: by force and voluntarily (276d8–11). He introduces this statement with the term *palin*, "once more," which, when it occurs in the expression *palin eks archēs* ("once more from the beginning") or some equivalent, normally signifies a new section in a Platonic dialogue. I believe that the term here calls our attention to the fact that this is a new distinction, one that did not appear hitherto in the diaereses. So long as our attention is focused on herds rather than communities, the distinction does not arise because all herds must be cared for by the use of force: the act of taming is already an imposition of force. It would be interesting to determine whether the human animal is also wild in what later thinkers called the state of nature. If so, then the Stranger may be taken to exclude the taming of the human animal from the category of properly political acts. Political life in the proper sense of the term begins, according to his new distinction, when human beings voluntarily accept the care of the statesman. They must then voluntarily accept punishment and other forceful restrictions imposed by the law.

The Stranger does not raise this line of questioning; he repeats that their error occurred more or less (*pou*) when they put together the king and the tyrant, even though they and their manner of rule are "most unlike" (*anomoiotatous ontas*: 276e1–4; cf. 273d8). Young Socrates replies: "true," but this must refer to the last part of the Stranger's statement because in fact there was no previous mention of the tyrant. At 258e8ff, the Stranger asks whether we should not establish by a single name the statesman, king, despot (*despotēn*), and householder, using the sole criterion of knowledge (*epistēmē*). A *despotēs* is a master, whether in the sense of an absolute ruler or the head of a household. The Stranger makes clear, however, that he is using the word in the latter sense at 259b7: "and indeed, *oikonomos* and *despotēs* are the same." If the big error now being discussed refers to the nurturing of tribes at step 6, then the Stranger seems once more to be confused, or else to be confusing Young Socrates.

The correction in effect amounts to a shortening of the longer way that differs from the original shorter way. We now have what amounts to a third diaeresis. Herd nurture is changed to herd care, which is then divided into divine shepherding and human curatorship or management. The latter is in turn divided into forceful and voluntary care. Care by force is called "something like tyranny" (*pou . . . turannikēn*) and "the voluntary herd-tending [*agelaiokomikē*] of willing two-footed animals" is called the political art. We will then call the possessor of this art of *epimeleia* "the genuine [*ontōs onta*] king and statesman" (276e6–13). Just as a failure to distinguish between the king and the tyrant must plunge us into "the sea of dissimilarity" that is intrinsic to the bodily nature of the cosmos, so too by making this distinction we are following a line of reasoning that establishes a similarity between the human race and the cosmos during the normal period of the Stranger's myth, which "itself possesses care and mastery over itself" (273a7–b1).

We should not fail to note that the Stranger now requires willingness on the part of the statesman as well as from his subjects. This would seem to exclude the philosopher-king of the *Republic* who is constrained to rule by his obligation to the city. More important for us is the fact that the crucial term *epimeleia* did not appear as a result of diaeresis; it was instead inserted into the corrected diaeresis by a reflection on terminology. Young Socrates now assumes that the exhibition (*apodeiksis*) of the statesman has been completed (277a1–2), but the Eleatic Stranger disagrees; there is no community yet in their discussion. He makes a long and important statement about the defectiveness of their procedure, in the course of which he introduces a new mistake.

The schema of the king has not yet been completed; we have proceeded like sculptors who sometimes hurry and add too much to, sometimes delay and remove the excess from the figure they are creating: in short, we have proceeded *para kairon,* in deviation from what is appropriate, and so employed too many kinds and too great a quantity of material (277a3–b1). "In order to make clear the error of the previous exposition quickly and magnificently [*megaloprepōs*], and believing that it was suitable to the king that we make large paradigms [*megala paradeigmata poieisthai*], we took up a wonderful mass of myth and were forced to make use of a greater part of it than was required. Therefore we have made the exhibition [*apodeiksis*] too large, and we have not established a comprehensive conclusion for the myth" (277b1–7).

The Stranger implies that he and Young Socrates were carried away by a kind of artistic or (as we would say today) creative enthusiasm. Are we to attribute this to the Stranger's inexperience with political affairs, as might be suspected of an Eleatic metaphysician? Has he unintentionally made use of the wrong methods? Or did he intentionally entangle Young Socrates in a web of confusion for pedagogical reasons? But if the latter, who is being educated? And for what? If the purpose of the discussion is to acquire training in dialectic, is this the best manner in which to proceed? Why does the Stranger present doctrines that are not radically different from those expressed or implied by Socrates in other dialogues, but in an extraordinarily cumbersome and apparently inappropriate manner? Can we infer from the silence of Socrates that the Stranger is attempting to demonstrate his methodological superiority to the dialectic of question and answer and succeeding only in discrediting his ostensible improvement of the Socratic procedures?

I have now indicated in broad terms my general response to this cluster of related questions. Plato is neither the Stranger nor Socrates, but both and more. The two men represent finally irreconcilable aspects of the philosophical nature. In order not to repeat what has gone before, I will express this difference here as follows. Neither Socrates nor the Stranger is interested primarily in politics but rather in philosophy. But the Stranger attempts to conceptualize politics, or to modify human experience by *technē*, whereas Socrates normally tries to rescue the potential philosopher from politics. On the one occasion when Socrates seems to be offering a philosophical account of the city, namely, in the *Republic,* what he in fact shows is that there is no theoretical resolution of the political sickness, that the rule of philosophers could be established only by radical injustice and brutality, in particular, by the murder of everyone over the age of ten and by forcing the philosopher to govern by means of a garrison of guardians, noble or medicinal lies, and the complete regulation of the beliefs and activities of the soldiers in that garrison.

In addition, rather than being allowed to pass his life in contemplation, the philosopher is forced to rule or to choose a worse instead of a better life on the grounds of obligation to the city that has produced him. But this obligation cannot apply to the founder of the city. As to the philosophers who have ostensibly been produced within the city, it is easy to see that they are figments of Socrates' imagination. The explicit argument in the *Republic* rests upon the premise that the rule of philosophers is in fact the rule of wise men and women, namely, those who possess the science of genuine dialectic. Since according to Socrates' testimony elsewhere, there are no wise human beings but only lovers of wisdom, the city in the *Republic* is certainly a dream, an idea in the modern sense of the term.

The Stranger's daydreams are of quite another kind. He represents the sober attempt to slow down if not to master the hostility of nature toward mankind. This attempt requires the application of theoretical techniques to the understanding and modification of genesis. Since pure philosophy is incapable of such an application, the Stranger must discover a practico-productive imitation of theory. Ironically enough, it is Socrates who has discovered the prototype of this imitation: the method of diaeresis. The Stranger's task is then to bridge the gap between theory and practice by an appropriate adaptation of theoretical diaeresis. He fulfills this task by the invention of applied diaeresis or what I will call the method of concept-construction. The gap between theory and practice is thus filled by production. From this standpoint, the Stranger is a link between the sophists and the modern scientific Enlightenment. He reconceptualizes the nature of political activity without entirely departing from the Socratic dimension of Platonism.

I underline the importance of the regular recurrence of metaphors from the arts of painting, sculpting, stamping with seals, and so on. Socrates employs the same metaphors in analogous investigations, but not within the same theoretical matrix. For Socrates, there is no self-defense except philosophy, whereas for the Stranger, the philosopher can defend himself only as a citizen. The science of the free person leads to the loss of freedom unless it is extended to practical tasks; and this extension transforms the philosopher's science into a kind of practice. We are no longer contemplating or gazing at eternal forms or discovering a natural teleology of human existence. We are in the process of producing an interpretation of political existence that is in some imprecise sense regulated by nature but not simply dictated by it. This is not merely to say, with Aristotle, that art completes nature, although it does not go so far as to say that art is man's nature. But we must not overlook the fact that what the Stranger is producing is the paradigm of the statesman, not some local application of it.

We can now return to the text. Our portrait of the living statesman is thus far satisfactory in its outlines, but the clarity of inner detail derived from the colors of life is not yet visible (277b5–c3). To this the Stranger adds immediately: "it is more fitting to make evident every animal by speech and rational discourse than by drawing and all of handicraft, for those who are able to follow; but for others it is better to do it via the handicrafts (*dia cheirourgiōn*: 277c3–6). The most immediate inference from this statement is that the complications and mistakes of our investigation have been due to the necessity of accommodating to Young Socrates' inability to follow a more fitting exposition. But this is not very likely in view of his mathematical talent, if "more fitting" means "more technical" in the sense of "more precise." The inference becomes more plausible if the Stranger means instead that he has been forced to employ technical procedures that are suitable for a mathematician but not fully appropriate to the subject matter. But it still fails to explain the shift from diaeresis to myth, nor will it account for the topics that the Stranger is going to introduce in the remainder of the dialogue.

The Stranger summarizes his own statement as follows: "It is difficult, you daimonic fellow [*ō daimonie*], to point out any of the greater things without making sufficient use of paradigms" (277d1–2). The word *pa-*

radeigma can be translated either as "model" or "example." The two translations can be combined by noting that a model is an example selected or constructed because it seems to illuminate all members of a single class. As soon as we find an example that contradicts the model, we must reject or modify it. At 277b4 the Stranger said that the "large paradigms" constructed in the myth were mistaken. In the present context, the word *paradigm* refers to a picture rather than to a scientific model. But a picture of a general type is clearly inadequate for exhibiting the characteristics common to all instances of that type. We could not explain precisely what a flower is by painting a single flower, which would have to be a rose or a pansy, but not flowers as such, and not even roses or pansies as such.

But even less is there a picture of the statesman; a portrait of Napoleon is not a portrait of all statesmen, nor is it even a portrait of Napoleon's art of statesmanship. Obviously enough, the metaphors of painting and sculpting are themselves too imprecise to convey the desired point. We need a verbal portrait, not a copy of the body of this or that statesman but a *logos* of what it is to be a statesman. We need an answer to the question "what is a statesman?" It might seem that for a Platonist, this question could be answered with precision if and only if there were an Idea of the statesman. It could be answered if and only if the paradigm is a Platonic form. If so, the Stranger is not a Platonist; there is no reason to suppose that he accepts the doctrine of Ideas in the required sense. Certainly we cannot derive an Idea of a statesman from the *megista genē* or greatest kinds of the *Sophist*. Even if the Stranger did accept the doctrine of phenomenological forms, however, there is no reason to assume, either from our own experience or on the basis of what has transpired to this point in the dialogue, that there is an Idea of the statesman.

A picture is like a silent image or dream of a *logos*. The Stranger implies this when he says that "it seems that each of us knows everything as if in a dream but when awake we are ignorant of everything" (277d2–4). The difference between waking and dreaming is somehow suggestive of the difference between the normal and the counternormal epochs in the Stranger's myth. A myth is more like a dream or prophetic vision than a discursive analysis. Just as the divine demiurge silently constructs a silent cosmos, so we construct our paintings or statues, the silent expression of the significance of our lives. Just as we are rejuvenated in silence by the counternormal motion of the cosmos, so is our speech refreshed by the waking visions of philosophical prophecy.

The Stranger prepares us for the transition to a new stage in the conversation by his comparison between dreaming and knowledge. Previously the Stranger employed diaeresis and myth to construct paradigms of the statesman. These procedures have proven to be radically deficient, at least as

employed by the Stranger. We will therefore attempt to progress by attacking
the problem of paradigms directly. Yet we cannot be completely direct; it is
not possible to start with a scientific description of the nature or essence of
paradigms. This is of course because we cannot step outside of our limited
human perspective in order to see everything fully and precisely. A paradigm
is an expression of our finitude or of the fact that we see things whole only in
dreams; the more closely or precisely we look, the more the whole is obscured
by the details. We must therefore proceed in a reciprocal manner, from
dreams or visions to concrete details, and then back again to dreams and
visions. In the middle of each of these continuous cycles, we construct a
model that exemplifies our dream of the whole, as suggested by our mastery
of the details of a finite number of examples, which examination was in turn
conducted in the light of an antecedent dream or vision.

We have gradually shifted to the topic of paradigms, but this cannot be
discussed directly. Instead, we require a paradigm of paradigms, and this in
turn will depend upon a more careful analysis of the difference between
models and examples (277d5–e1). I will attempt such an analysis in the next
chapter.

CHAPTER FIVE

Paradigms

Introductory Remarks

THE Stranger signals the shift to a new section in his next remark to Young Socrates: "One must speak, since you are prepared to follow. We know that children [*paides*], when they are just becoming experienced with letters—" (277e2–4). At 268d5, the Stranger began his presentation of the myth as follows: "Once more . . . from another beginning" and then admonished Young Socrates to attend to the myth "just like children" (*kathaper hoi paides:* 268e5). In both cases, the Stranger takes Young Socrates back to his childhood, but in two quite different ways. In the myth, his pupil is required to undergo a willing suspension of disbelief and so to grow young again, or to accept the fabulous story of the counternormal epoch without becoming a resident of that age. In the present discussion, Young Socrates will engage in a discursive analysis of the elements of discourse, not so much for its own sake as for the light it casts on the nature of paradigms. Spelling, he is told, is a paradigm of paradigms.

The first step is to determine what the Stranger means by a paradigm (*paradeigma*). As I noted in the previous chapter, a paradigm can be understood very generally as either a model or an example. It is very difficult, perhaps even impossible, to preserve a sharp difference between these two senses. Yet we do make the distinction in ordinary language. The distinction and its difficulties can be brought out quite easily by considering some examples. And note that we illustrate general points with examples, not models. Models clarify examples. To begin with, a human being is an example of the race of mammals, but a model of that race would be a representation of those properties that define what it is to be a mammal. We would never say that a human being is a model of mammals, so there is certainly some difference in how we understand the words *model* and *example*.

We can get at this difference from another angle. Whereas an existing human being is an example of a mammal, an existing mammal—say a horse or a dog—is not a model of human beings. The model is some kind of abstract entity or conceptual construction that allows us to understand the individual animal as a mammal. There could then also be a model of what it is to be a human being. Although a human being is a mammal, it does not follow that a model of the race of mammals is also a model of the race of human beings. If our purpose were merely to determine to which race of animals human beings belong, then the model of mammals might suffice. But that model would cast no light on our political nature, to take only the example that is most pertinent to the *Statesman*. What counts as a model is thus relative to our intentions or, more precisely, to what we intend to understand or explain.

Here is another simple example. An architect's blueprint or scaled-down replica in wood or plastic of a design for a house is a model of all those houses that are built in accord with the given blueprint or in strict keeping with the proportions of the scaled-down model. But there are many houses that could be built in accord with the model. Some could be of brick and stone, others of wood (unless the material is specified in the model itself); some could be of cedar, others of pine; some could be painted white, others could be brown, and so on. This or that house, then, is an example of the model on the blueprint, but the converse is not the case.

At first glance it might seem that models are originals of which examples are copies. But a moment's reflection shows that this cannot be true in all cases. A model gentleman is an example of a perfect gentleman; he is not the model itself but some close approximation of it. If the model is exemplified by some man, however, his capacity to serve as an example derives from the presence and visibility within him of what it is to be a gentleman. But we certainly do not mean by this that there is another man, namely, the perfect gentleman, who is both inside and also visible within the person we perceive to be a model gentleman. No doubt what the model gentleman exemplifies is our concept of a perfect gentleman. But even if that concept could be fully articulated, it is hard to see how a man could be a copy of a concept.

Expressions like "model gentleman" are ambiguous because the word *model* seems to modify directly the gentleman in question, whereas it actually refers to that which the gentleman exemplifies. Here is another example that also illustrates the ambiguity of the word *copy*. A model airplane is in some sense a copy of an original airplane. If I look at a model of a 747, I recognize the original type of plane, which is also called a model, but not the individual plane that served as the model of the copy. "Model" is used in this sentence in three different senses. The first model is a copy of an original; the second use refers to the type of airplane; the third use is that of an original that was copied by the model in the first sense of the term. Furthermore, the model in the first sense does not actually copy the model in the second or third senses; for if it did, it would be another full-sized airplane of the same sort. In this case, both planes would be examples of something else, let us say a set of specifications or a blueprint, which stands to the two airplanes as do two gentlemen to the concept of a gentleman.

No doubt many more difficulties could be propounded in order to illustrate that we use the words *model* and *example* in ordinary language in two ways, depending upon the circumstances. Sometimes we distinguish the two and speak of examples of models. But sometimes there is no difference between the two words; they may be used interchangeably. When we distinguish between the two words, "model" conveys the sense either of an original that is copied by something else, as for example when we say that the model for a fictional character is some actual person, or else we use it to refer to a standard, rule, or some other conceptual entity, such as the definition of a perfect gentleman.

So much for ordinary English usage. But what about Greek and, in particular, what about the Stranger's assertion that "the paradigm is itself in need of a paradigm" (*paradeigmatos . . . kai to paradeigma auto dedeēken:* 277d9–10)? Do we need to distinguish between models and examples when translating this expression? Liddell and Scott give both "model" and "example" as separate meanings for *paradeigma,* so that does not take us very far in understanding the sense of the passage. But the following reflection seems to me to be decisive. The Stranger has just introduced the general case of paradigms, namely, bridges between dreaming and waking knowledge, such as the use of the figures of the shepherd in the diaeresis and the divine helmsman in the immediately preceding mythical presentation. These were not merely examples of the nature of the king but were intended to illustrate the essential nature of the royal art. As I understand him, the Stranger is now saying that we require a model of what it is to be a paradigm or archetype in order to see what went wrong with our models of the king. We require not merely an example of a paradigm but a paradigmatic example. Not all examples of models fulfill this function. The stranger implies that the model he is about to introduce does indeed fulfill the paradigmatic function. We shall have to see whether he is right.

One might wish to take this passage in a much weaker sense and to understand the Stranger as saying nothing more than that his previous reference to examples requires another example. But what would be the point of such an example? The Stranger's intention is this section of the dialogue is not to replace one example with another, but to clarify the nature of examples altogether. Such a clarification is itself a model of examples. A model of this kind exhibits what it is to be an example, and that is to say it shows how the example exhibits the general structure of a set of instances of the same kind. For this reason, in showing what it is to be an example, the model of examples shows what it is to be a model (assuming, of course, that it is possible to begin with). It thus achieves the status of a model of models. The "example" (to use the weaker translation) of examples in general (the bridge or mediation between dreaming and wakeful knowledge) that he is about to introduce, namely, spelling, is intended to exhibit the general structure of all examples. It is intended as a model example. We should therefore be able to determine by its use how examples serve as models and how some, like that of the divine tiller, fail. In this sense, the example of spelling is intended as a model of models. That this is so will be confirmed below when we come to 278e4–10, a passage in which the Stranger announces his intention to apply our "knowledge of the nature of paradigm altogether" to the smaller and partial paradigm of weaving. It is his discussion of the art of spelling that the Stranger relies on to make that transition.

I call to the reader's attention two points that may cause confusion in the present inquiry. First, let us assume that spelling is indeed the model of models. It remains true that we have to provide an interpretation of the model of models in every attempt to apply it to an example of a possible model. We have to say something like this: "the model of models applies to candidate *m* as follows . . . " and then list the ways in which the candidate fulfills the essential qualifications for being a model. We cannot simply wave the model of models over the candidate like a magic wand, as though their proximity were sufficient to establish the genuineness of the candidacy in question. Second, each model is an example of a model, but not a model of models. In particular, the captain of a ship is a model of the statesman, but not of a fireman or a baseball player. If there is a model of models, it will also be the model of all examples of models, but not of all examples *tout court*. Napoleon is an example of a statesman and Joe Di Maggio is an example of a baseball player. But the model of models is not the model of Napoleon or Joe Di Maggio.

The term *model* has a contemporary technical use in mathematics and the natural sciences that should be briefly noticed. This will prevent us from mistaking the Stranger's investigation for a crude anticipation of what is today called model theory. At the same time, it will help us to identify points of similarity between the two procedures. I quote from Ronald Giere, *Explaining Science* (Chicago, 1990, p. 47): "Imagine some axioms formulated in a simple first-order language *L*. A *structure* for *L* is a set of objects, *O*, and a function that assigns subsets of *O* to one-place predicates of *L*, ordered pairs of objects to two-place relations, and so on. A *model* of a theory *T*, expressed as axioms in *L*, is any structure in which the axioms are true. The concept of a model, being defined in terms of truth, is therefore a semantic, as opposed to a syntactic, concept." For a more elaborate discussion, one can consult *Foundations of Set Theory*, 2d rev. ed., by Fraenkel, et al. (Amsterdam, 1973, chap. 5, par. 3.)

A mathematical model in the sense just described is an *interpretation* of a scientific theory. There can be more than one interpretation of a given theory; mathematical models thus differ from architectural blueprints in at least the following way. Whereas there is just one blueprint or set of specifications for a single design of a house, but many houses that exemplify it, for any individual theory there are many possible models. A Platonic Idea in the traditional interpretation would be like a blueprint rather than a mathematical model, insofar as there is just one Idea for each family of examples or instances of the formal properties codifed forever in the Idea itself. The Stranger does not refer to Platonic Ideas, but his sense of a model is closer to a Platonic Idea than it is to a mathematical model. More precisely, if we take each Platonic Idea to be a model or archetype, then the model of models (to use the full expression) is the Idea of Ideas.

The differences between the Stranger's concern and those of contemporary model theory are not hard to spot. I will mention three of the more important differences. We can start with how models fail. The Stranger's initial attempts to construct a model of the statesman fail because they are contradicted by facts that everyone, or every citizen of normal intelligence and education, already knows. There is no question here of falsified predictions or the discovery by the process of deduction of a logical contradiction that was not previously seen to be implied by the model.

Second, as was just noted, it is also assumed in model theory that there are an indefinite number of possible models for any given aspect of behavior of empirical objects. The Stranger, in contrast, assumes (or seems to assume) that there is just one true account of the art of the statesman, or one model, despite his failure up to this point to have constructed it.

Third, in the natural sciences—if not in mathematics—we begin with ordinary or perceptual experience rather than with formalized entities. But in these cases it is assumed that the objects of perceptual experience can be described by means of formal languages that abstract from subjective or contingent properties and relations in such a way as to arrive at precise descriptions of one aspect or another of the behavior of those objects. The

Stranger does not move from ordinary experience to a formalization, nor would there be any point in his doing so. One might formalize the method of diaeresis, but the method is not the model of models.

This last point should be stated more fully. The attempted models are quite different from their modern scientific descendants in that they are not themselves formal objects. Even the definition of the statesman as determined by diaeresis, "person who nurtures the two-footed herd of land animals," or its corrected version, "curator of communities of human beings," cannot be formalized in any meaningful sense without losing precisely what we were looking for in the first place. The definitions just given are of course shorthand for a fuller definition, assuming one to be possible. In order to grasp the nature of the *technē* of politics we have to become more concrete, not less so. This is why, with all of its defects, a painting or a statue of the statesman would be better than a mathematical model because it would at least exhibit the fact that a statesman is a human being. It goes without saying that this in itself is not enough, but it is essential. It puts us on the right track.

In his attempt to instruct Young Socrates about the art of the statesman, the Stranger moves from diaeresis to myth to further uses of diaeresis. The initial diaeresis is the Stranger's analogue of the modern process of formalization; it fails to do its job, and the Stranger turns to myth (as it happens, unsuccessfully) to repair the damage. But a myth is more like a painting or a statue than a mathematical formalization. Let me call it a discursive picture, the pedagogical function of which is to make the diaeresis more vivid and concrete. The fact that the myth fails is not due to an error in assessing its function, but rather to the construction of the wrong myth. This forces the Stranger to explain his mistake by interpreting the myth still more discursively, or in other words, by eliminating its pictorial nature. The explanation makes it unnecessary for him to tell another, accurate myth. He is now in a position to attempt to progress further by means of a new model of the statesman's art, namely, the art of weaving woolen clothing. Subsequent employment of diaeresis is subordinated to, or regulated by, the interpretation of this model.

I wish to infer here from this sequence of events only that the crucial step in preventing the investigation from collapsing is the interpretation of the myth. Neither the use of the quasi-formal procedure of diaeresis nor recourse to prosaic accounts of ordinary or pretechnical political experience suffices to explain the art of the statesman. This is because the significance of political experience depends upon issues such as the origin of the city, the attitude of the gods toward mankind, patriotism, and the foundations of justice, which are vitiated rather than clarified or preserved by scientific or conceptual analysis. Stated concisely, the demystification of politics renders nugatory the difference between human beings and other animals. One may well suspect that a purely scientific or technical analysis of politics leads to the disappearance of the art of the statesman or to its redefinition as a branch of biology. But this was not the Stranger's intention, despite the fact that his opening diaeresis abstracts from the difference between humans and brutes, or treats cities as herds. He explicitly identifies this result as an error.

In the present context I want to concentrate on the nature of models and, in particular, on the search for the model of models. I therefore disregard the question of the Stranger's apparent incompetence in applying his own principles, a question that I have analyzed and attempted to answer in previous chapters. What is pertinent here is that the attempt to define the model of models is occasioned by the failure of the two models constructed thus far, namely, shepherd and captain. The model of models, if there is such an entity, is not a model of the art of the statesman but of models per se. The investigation of the model of models is different from and more abstract than the search for the model of the art of the statesman.

One could call this episode in the dialogue an essay in model theory, provided one bears in mind all the differences between the Stranger's investigation and that of late modern or contemporary model theoreticians. At the same time, we cannot fully appreciate the significance of the Stranger's theorizing unless we see that he is already taking what may be called the Cartesian turn toward the conceptual reconstruction of everyday experience. This is evident from the central model of weaving. If politics is like weaving clothing, then citizens are artifacts; in an equivalent formulation, the city is constructed to defend the human body against nature. And the souls of the citizens are themselves treated as warp and woof, in other words, as elements in a defensive construction.

One way to state the point I have been making in the last several paragraphs is that myths are like mathematical models in the sense that both require interpretations. But the interpretations are quite different in the two cases. An interpretation of a mathematical model is itself a mathematical artifact. When scientists attempt to describe for the layman the sense of a scientific theory in discursive or nontechnical prose, they engage in something like mythmaking, but in a way that falsifies or fails to do justice to the sense of the theory itself. An interpretation of a myth, in contrast, is not itself another myth, and certainly not a a set of mathematical equations.

Poets or mystics may claim that it is impossible to provide adequate discursive or prose interpretations of myths; but the Stranger is neither a mystic nor a poet. He rather holds that political philosophy requires myth to supplement diaeresis or conceptual analysis, but also that myth requires the pretechnical understanding of everyday political life. Myth is thus the link between everyday life and conceptual analysis. The ultimate question is whether myth is capable of preserving the regulative function of everyday life or whether conceptual analysis triumphs over both, thereby initiating the age of production or, as it is now called, theory-construction. But this question takes us beyond the boundaries of the immediate inquiry.

So much, then, for general preliminaries. Now let us turn to the Stranger's paradigm of paradigms.

Spelling

Young Socrates interrupts the Stranger's opening statement about children who are just beginning to acquire experience in spelling (277e2–5). This is the only instance of such an interruption in the dialogue, and it goes counter to the decorum of the occasion. We interrupt others when we are excited or impatient, either because we are highly pleased or because we are irritated if not in fact angry. In either case, we give way to emotion and so act rudely, or in a way that would count as rudeness in someone old enough to understand polite behavior. For one moment, Young Socrates has relapsed into childishness. This is a curious ornament to the beginning of the discussion of paradigms. It is obviously related to the association between spelling and childhood, but also to Young Socrates' impatience with the turn to so elementary a *technē*. Also important is the word *empeiroi,* possessing a knack, being familiar with how to do something through practice, being experienced but not yet possessing the relevant *technē*. This is one type of the knowledge that is required in order to construct myths.

The Stranger introduced the example of spelling in the *Sophist* to illustrate the theme of the smallest elements of intelligibility. Here its function is to serve as an initial paradigm of paradigms, which I have argued should be translated "model of models." The underlying notion is quite simple. Once they have acquired some experience with letters, children discern them well enough in the shortest and easiest syllables; but in turning to other syllables, which are longer and harder, they become doubtful and make mistakes, both in thinking and speaking. The Stranger then suggests the best way to lead children to apprehend letters they do not yet know. As his account shows, he means to refer to letters that are sometimes identified and sometimes not. One should start with occurrences in which the letters are correctly identified and then compare these with occurrences in which they are not in order to show that the letter in question is the same in all combinations. "Being pointed out in this way, they become models" (278a1–c1).

The Stranger then defines the genesis of a model as occurring "whenever something that is the same in a second, unconnected thing is correctly opined and brought together with the first so that we end up with one true opinion about both together" (278c3–7). In other words, the letter *a* in "at" is seen to be the same as the letter *a* in "that," assuming that the former is first correctly identified and used as the basis for identifying the same letter in the second occurrence. This cannot be understood to mean that the physical manifestation *a* is the model underlying such an identification. We teach a child the identity of the letter *a* in all of its manifestations by means of the concept "the letter *a* as first letter in the English alphabet," even though we do not mention that concept to the child at the beginning of our instruction. But this is what it means to say to someone, "this is the letter *a*."

In this context we can reaffirm the difference between a model and an example. In order to understand what it means to say that a certain symbol is an example of the letter *a*, we have to know the letter *a*. We may learn this inductively on the basis of two or three encounters with examples of that letter, during which we are informed on each occasion that the letter is called "a." But when we grasp what is common to the examples, it is not just their exemplary function that we have grasped but the model of which they are examples, namely, the letter *a*.

I will return to this refinement shortly. Meanwhile it is enough to see that every occurrence of the letter *a* is formally the same. Since the letter could be written in different scripts, the form in question cannot be the physical shape or *morphē* alone, but we recognize the *logos* or intelligible form by conventions that define the sense of the physical symbol. This cannot be said of the divine helmsman or the human shepherd on the one hand and the statesman on the other. Not all helmsmen share the same shape, nor is the sense of their shape defined by the *logos* of the art.

But furthermore, helmsmen do not look like statesmen. In the case of the myth, we are presented with something that is different from the statesman even though the two possess some common property. This community does not make one true conception or opinion (*doksa*) out of a captain or shepherd on the one hand and the statesman on the other in the way that our conception of *a* is one and the same in "at" and "that." What is the same in the former case is the conception of the property that the captain or shepherd and the statesman share; and even here, there is not sameness but similarity. A captain "rules" or "commands" his ship, and a shepherd his flock, in a way that is quite different from the way in which the statesman rules or commands the city.

We need not object to the claim that spelling is an example of a model. But we must object that spelling is unable to do the job assigned to it, namely, to serve as the model of all models. Two distinctions will make this obvious. First, we must distinguish between spelling as the recognition of individual letters and spelling as the concatenation of letters into words. The Stranger alludes to both of these operations as though they were part of the same model, but he is mistaken to do so. Statesmen in particular are concatenators, not recognizers, as the model of weaving itself makes clear. The second distinction is between two modes of recognition: (1) we recognize tokens of types, for example, symbolic representations of the letter *a* or the identity of a particular cow by way of the Platonic Idea of the cow; and (2) we recognize one thing by analogy with another, for example, statesmen by way of the analogy with shepherds, captains, or weavers.

The simplest formulation of the difficulty faced by the Stranger is that the model of models must exhibit not only recognizing and concatenating but also the two types of recognition. Spelling qualifies on the first count, but not on the second. But there is a still more serious difficulty with respect to the model of spelling. It is anything but evident that all models are contained in the disjunction between recognition and concatenation. To give only the most important example, this disjunction does not seem to cover the method of diaeresis. Diaeresis is both collection and analysis in accordance with kind. Recognition of the kind or form is obviously a case of recognizing, but neither collecting nor analyzing seems to be a case of concatenating. My ability to combine the letters *c, a,* and *t* into the word "cat" may depend on prior acts of recognizing individual letters, separating them by kind, and so collecting instances of the same kind. But the capacity to make a word out of individual letters goes beyond these and is different from either.

The synthetic act of producing a meaningful word out of meaningless elements is neither an act of collecting meaningless elements nor of separating them. A collection of meaningless elements is meaningless without an additional synthesis. And the separating out of implied or constituent meanings from a more general meaning is also not the production of meanings but is more like dividing "hat rack" into "hat" and "rack." We are now faced with an alternative. We can agree that the production of meanings is an aspect of spelling, in which case the latter is too broad to be a model of diaeresis; it imputes to diaeresis an essential function that the method as such does not exercise. Or we can deny that spelling is itself the production of new meanings, in which case we have identified an activity of crucial importance for which a model is required. Either alternative leads to the rejection of spelling as the model of models.

One might want to defend the Stranger by choosing the first alternative and arguing that the model of models can and must be richer than any single model; otherwise, it could not cover them all. But this would be like arguing that the Idea of Platonic Ideas is that of a collection of the forms of every entity in the world to which an Idea corresponds. If there is an Idea of Ideas, it must express what is common to every Idea as an Idea, not as the form of a cow or a horse and so on. The form or look of a cow has nothing in common with the form or look of justice. In order to arrive at the Idea of Ideas, we would have to abstract from the particular look in each case and to concentrate on what it is to be a look. So too, in order to arrive at the model of models, we would have to abstract from everything in each particular model that distinguishes it from any other model. The residue would be what every model must possess in order to be a model; it would be the same in every model. This residue, and nothing other than this residue, must be exhibited by the model of models.

To come back now to spelling, if we assume that it includes the production of new meanings, then to identify it as the model of models is to claim that every example of a model is a model of the production of new meanings, among other things. But that is not true, as I have claimed with respect to the method of diaeresis, which can itself serve as a model as easily as the art of weaving. No one can employ the method of diaeresis who does not know in advance, at each step, what is to be divided and how. One could say of diaeresis what others have said of the syllogism, that it does not discover new truths but organizes or analyzes truths discovered by some other means. In so doing, diaeresis may produce new concepts, but these are intelligible only on the basis of knowledge antecedent to diaeresis. The contemporary expression "the myth of the given" illustrates nicely the Platonic understanding of the dependence of diaeresis, or more broadly, of rational analysis, on myth.

My discussion of the candidacy of spelling for the title of model of models has been based on the working assumption that recognizing, concatenating, and producing meanings are the only activities that a model must exhibit. This assumption was made for the sake of simplicity, not because I think that it is true. In fact I have no idea of the number of activities that would have to be exhibited by the model of models. To know this would be to know everything or to be wise rather than merely a lover of wisdom, and this, as I have previously observed, is a difference between Socrates and the Stranger. Socrates says regularly that he is not wise but a lover of wisdom. The Stranger, despite an occasional remark about the fragility of human knowledge, is in effect claiming to be wise. This at least is the consequence of the claim to identify spelling as the model of models.

I want to consider briefly now the problem arising from the fact that there are two kinds of recognition: perception of the same look, and recognition by way of analogy. In the art of spelling, we recognize letters because they have a certain look that is the same in all tokens of the same type. Every example of the letter *a* exhibits the look "a," which is unique and distinguishable from the look of every other letter. There is no question here of perceiving a meaning, sense, or definition that is common to instances of the letter *a*; they just look alike. But captains and shepherds do not "just look like" statesmen any more than all statesmen resemble each other physically. Nor is there a conceptual identity in this case; the definition of the art of navigation is not identical to the definition of the art of shepherding, and neither is identical to the definition of the art of the statesman.

We can go farther than this; the Stranger himself tells us that captains and shepherds are incorrect models for the statesman. Nevertheless, they illustrate an important point. There must be some analogy between these two arts and the art of the statesman, which suggested them to the Stranger in the first place and which has led us to employ them for millennia when discussing politics. Whether the analogy is complete or partial is irrelevant to the fact that it assists us in recognizing the statesman; and it is especially significant that a partially incorrect analogy can play the same role as a correct one. It may be true that every analogy has the same look *qua* analogy, or that there is an Idea of analogies, like the hypothetical Idea of Ideas, that abstracts from the particular properties of each individual analogy and exhibits their common essence, but nothing more. If so, however, the Idea of analogies would be useful to us only in identifying analogies as analogies. It would take an additional act of intellection to recognize the analogy between the captain and the statesman. If there is a sameness of look between the Idea of analogies and any analogy in particular, it is not the identity of the look between the captain and the statesman. And indeed, there is no such identity.

Let us now apply this result to the problem of the model of models, which for the sake of convenience I will also refer to as the archetype. The archetype is itself a model; it must be stated discursively, just as the Stranger describes the function of navigation, shepherding, spelling, weaving, and so on. Let us further assume that models are of three kinds, depending on the mode of recognition that each incorporates. Some models are based on recognition of the sameness of the look, some recognize by analogy, and some employ both. If the archetype employs both, then it is not a model of models that employ only one or the other. Conversely, if the archetype employs one or the other, then it does not employ both; the disjunction is exclusive because otherwise it would be indistinguishable from joint employment.

The problem I have in mind is this. An archetype is also an example of a model. Therefore it must embody one of the three modes of recognition. But whichever it embodies will disqualify it from being the archetype of models that embody the other two modes. Again the objection can be made that the archetype may be rich enough to allow for models of every kind, but this will not help the Stranger because he means by archetype the sameness of one thing to another: to repeat, he says that "there is a genesis of a paradigm, whenever something that is the same in a second, unconnected thing is correctly opined and brought together with the first [instance] so that we end up with one opinion about both together" (278c3–6). Less awkwardly, a model is the conception of the sameness of two distinct instances. As the example of spelling shows, the Stranger has in mind sameness of look or form. His approach to models, and so to the archetype or model of models, thus precludes his accounting for analogies like that between the captain and the statesman, where there is no question of sameness of look. One does not avoid the difficulty by understanding "sameness" here to refer to sameness of definition. The definition of the captain is not the same as that of the states-man, and furthermore, even though the analogy is defective, it still works. There is no sameness here, but only partial similarity.

Let me bring this line of reasoning to some kind of conclusion. A model of models is for the Stranger like a picture of a resemblance that requires an interpretation of the sort in which we say that the picture portrays us as looking at two things and perceiving their common form. In this sense, spelling is like a picture of pictures. The letters stand for anything at all. One could discard the picture (in this case, spelling) and simply state the inter-pretation, as the Stranger in effect did in the passage quoted a moment ago. But interestingly enough, if the Stranger had merely stated the definition, we would never have known what he meant by "sameness." The picture is thus essential to our understanding; it serves as an interpretation of the interpreta-tion. Both are necessary, and they are related reciprocally; we need a picture to illustrate the discursive interpretation, but we also need a discursive inter-pretation in order to understand the point of the picture.

It seems to me that this procedure is required regardless of the examples chosen to illustrate models and the model of models. Even if some way could be found to circumvent all of my objections to the adequacy of the Stranger's argument, the result would be to arrive at a statement so general and so abstract that it would be intelligible only by way of interpretations and pic-tures. This point can be restated in such a way as to make an additional and important claim. What is a model from one point of view is an example from another. Even a model of everything is itself an example of a model and so must have some determinate structure, which will inevitably give it a particu-lar identity and so prevent it from being a model of everything.

Human cognition is both discursive and pictorial. This is why in the *Philebus,* Socrates refers to two demiurges in the human soul—a writer and a painter. It is also why he speaks in the *Republic* of the Idea of Ideas as the Idea of the Good, which he illustrates by the image of the sun. This is not simply, as Socrates implies, an accommodation to the intellectual limitations of Glaucon, his interlocutor. We require examples in order to understand definitions; the more abstract or comprehensive the definition, the more we need examples. This is the way in which Socrates proceeds, and it is rather unfair of him to chastise Theaetetus in the dialogue of that name for offering examples of knowledge initially, instead of a definition of knowledge. How else could we get to a definition of knowledge but by inspecting individual examples of what we already take to be knowing? Is this procedure circular? Yes, of course it is; but so what? That is how human beings think: in circles.

The Stranger defines a model as arriving at "one true opinion" or belief with respect to the sameness of two separate occurrences of something. This is a slovenly definition, but the point seems to be clear, given his example of identifying letters. But the form that we think as the same, although it is of course "present" or "visible" in each occurrence, must be separate from either, in the way that the letter *a* is separate from any two instances of "a." We can modify the Stranger's definition accordingly by saying that a model is the exhibition of sameness and otherness. But this is unacceptable because it is too general, too abstract. *Everything is an exhibition of sameness and otherness.* On the basis of this definition, everything can function as a model.

We could modify the definition again by noting that it is the exhibition per se to which we refer, rather than to the being or entity in which the exhibition is present. But the generality remains. We still have to explain what it is to be an exhibition per se. To state only the most salient question: Are these concepts or Platonic Ideas? And could anyone on the basis of the definition explain how anything, whether a concept or a Platonic Idea, can be exhibited in something that is other than a concept or Idea? If the exhibitor is other than the concept or Idea, it is other than its form or look, in which case it must be some *other* form or look, and so an exhibition of some other concept or Idea. But if it is the same form or look, then is it not indistinguishable from, and so the same as but other than, the concept or Idea? Let this suffice as an indication of the problem.

No definition of models is satisfactory unless it contains the core conception of the exhibition of sameness and otherness. Since everything is such an exhibition, everything can function as a model; alternatively stated, everything is either a model or example, depending upon how we look at it. This being so, in my opinion, we arrive at the following conclusion. The world, or the cosmos, or the whole, or whatever one wishes to call our experience is articulated into an intelligible structure of sameness and otherness, similarity and difference, archetype and image, in such a way that we can distinguish model from example, but only with respect to an intention or purpose. The whole exhibits an independent ontological structure, but there is no univocal definition or articulation of that structure. This is how one may reconcile objectivity and perspectivism.

Sameness in Otherness

The Stranger may not have intended to convey the conclusion that I have just reached, but it is compatible with the language of his definition at 278c3ff. Let us look at it more closely. "Have we then sufficiently comprehended [seized, grasped, collected: *suneilēphamen*] that there occurs the genesis of a paradigm whenever the same thing occurring [on] in another separated instance [*hopotan on tauton en heterō diespasmenō*], it is correctly judged [opined, believed: *doksazomenon*] and united [*sunachthen*] with the original [the first of the two cases: *peri hekateron*] so that the two together accomplish [*apotelei*] one true judgment" [opinion, belief: *doksa*]. Whereas the two instances that are brought together may not be generated, the act of bringing them together is the genesis of a paradigm, which comes into existence in accord with the human intention underlying the act of bringing together what is separate. Therefore the Stranger speaks of a single true *doksa*, not a *logos*. The Stranger's language could be taken to refer exclusively to paradigms of type 1, but it is also possible to read his statement as referring to the taking together of two instances of the same property that occurs in two distinct entities such as a captain and a statesman.

To see the same form, property, or element in another is to see the same in the other, or sameness in otherness. This is the essential nature of the paradigm. The Stranger continues at 278c8ff: "ought we to marvel, then, that our soul, since it is naturally affected in the same way with respect to the elements [letters: *stoicheia*] of all things, is at times certain about [brought to a stand by] the truth concerning each aspect of certain cases, but at other times is reduced to confusion about every aspect of other cases, and so that it somehow or another judges correctly about some mixtures, but that when the same [elements of correctly judged mixtures] are transferred into the big and difficult syllables of things [*pragmatōn*], the soul once more becomes ignorant of those same [elements]?"

In general, the soul grasps the elements of the things, acts, or events (*pragmata*) when they occur in simple compounds or mixtures, but it is reduced to confusion when these same elements occur in more complex combinations. The Stranger thereby implies, in a way that is again compatible with my previous conclusion, that the all or whole is intelligible with respect to its constituent elements, and so that the confusion of particular cases is at least in principle open to amelioration or dissipation by a proper analysis of the formal structure of the complex mixture in question. In contemporary terms, we can say that the Stranger certainly endorses analysis, but that he insists upon the priority of intellectual or sensuous perception in the knower, and so too upon the priority of synthesis to analysis in the *pragmata* themselves. We can also say that the procedure of analysis here indicated is more or less the same in principle as the method of analysis of formal structure or eidetic arithmetic described in the *Philebus* by Socrates. I say "more or less" because the Stranger makes no reference to *eidē* or *ideai*. In neither case, incidentally, is there any reference to a transcendent or separate world of Platonic Ideas.

Even further, and contrary to his procedure in the *Sophist,* the Stranger is not concerned with the letters as such, or with the ultimate elements of things, but with letters that recur in different syllables or words, and so with the process of grasping the sameness within otherness. Since spelling proceeds by rules, which can be taught to others, it is a *technē,* even though it is rooted in the capacity of the speller to perceive looks, and so to discern sameness within otherness. The written word, considered as a product of spelling, is an artifact. It may be a sign of some natural being, but it is not itself natural in the way that we say that thunder and lightning are signs of rain.

All of this corresponds to my independent analysis, according to which concatenation is production, whether with natural or artificial elements. To anticipate, the two main examples of concatenation or "spelling" in the balance of the dialogue are the weaving of clothing from the warp and the woof, and the weaving of cities from gentle and spirited human beings. There is no clothing by nature, no warp and woof until the threads are prepared from, say, the wool of sheep. But there are also no citizens by nature because the city does not exist by nature: it must be woven together through commands that are addressed to elements of diverse natures. Human beings are the natural "threads" from which the city is woven in accord with the *technē* of the statesman.

In the last interchange of this part of the dialogue, it is established that if we begin from false *doksa,* we cannot arrive at even a small part of truth or acquire *phronēsis* (278d8–e3). An incorrect identification of or ignorance about the elements, or in other words a failure of sensuous or intellectual perception, makes knowledge about the web of existence impossible. Nor can we arrive at these elements by analysis alone. I have to perceive that this *a* is the same as that *a*. The analysis may assist me to isolate the two *a*'s, but it does not show me that each is the same as the other. If all this is so by nature (278e4), then, suggests the Stranger, we ought to attempt "to see the nature of paradigms per se [*holou paradeigmatos idein tēn phusin*] in a smaller and partial example [*paradeigmati*] and to try afterwards, by transferring the same *eidos* from the lesser things to the greatest case of the king, to cognize technically the therapy of the city, in order that it become for us wakefulness rather than dreaming" (278e4–10).

Our need for a smaller example arises from the fact that the paradigm of paradigms, here represented by spelling, is too general. In my terms, it shows us that paradigms exhibit sameness within otherness. The example that we are going to study is weaving. Weaving is like spelling in that it is a kind of concatenating process that makes artifacts. The artifacts of spelling could be said somewhat poetically to "clothe" the intellect, whereas the artifacts of weaving may be said quite prosaically to clothe the body. Since the body is more visible than the soul or intellect, perhaps the example of weaving will be more illuminating than the ostensible paradigm of paradigms altogether.

CHAPTER SIX

Weaving

A Diaeresis of Weaving

"WE have to go back again to the previous *logos*" (279a1). So the Stranger signals the beginning of a new section in the usual manner. We do not simply move forward, but we make progress by revising something that we have already accomplished. Just as the cosmos in the myth moves back and forth from normal to counternormal epochs, so the conversation in the dialogue goes back and forth, rejuvenating itself by recognizing its mistakes and attempting to rectify them with the introduction of new methods or topics for analysis. Obviously the similarity to the continuous cosmic reversal is only partial; nothing new enters into the picture in each fulfillment of dual reversal. With respect to the comprehensive motion of the cosmos, there is no progress; there is no history in the modern sense of the term. With certain rare exceptions, consisting of those who are translated elsewhere by the gods, the cast of characters in each phase of the double cosmic cycle is exactly the same because the dead persons of the normal epoch furnish the births of the counternormal epoch, and vice versa.

It is now necessary for us to return to the myriads who dispute with the royal family about the curatorship (*epimeleia*) of cities (279a1–3). This is the sixth part in the dialogue, and our point of return is the sixth step in the longer version of diaeresis. The reader will recall that in the original division we referred to "the nurturing of herds" (*agelaiotrophikē*), which was corrected subsequently to "caring for human herds" as distinguished from caring for nonhuman herds. Now we also change "herds" to "cities." The purely biological standpoint of the original diaeresis has been entirely replaced by a properly political standpoint. There is a dispute among human practitioners of various arts as to which of these count as political. This dispute will not be settled by further distinctions of anatomy, natural habitat, and the like. In order to divide properly, we must bring into play our antecedently acquired political knowledge. We do this by choosing an appropriate paradigm of the king.

If the term *paradeigma* means here "model," then we would have to state without any further examples the nature of the royal art. As contemporary scientists put it, we would have to produce a theory of political rule. Instead, however, we are about to study politics via an example: weaving. Presumably the previous discussion of the nature of models has prepared us to construct an example of a model of statesmanship. But it has not prepared us to discover the single correct model of that art because there is no such model. This confirms indirectly my previous assertion that we cannot proceed without examples.

The Stranger must know in advance that the details of his example are going to cast light on the difference between characteristically political and nonpolitical arts of caring. Why is he unable to state this difference directly and to define politics from the outset in the manner of a contemporary political theorist? As a matter of fact, there is no reason to suppose that he could not do this. But as it turns out, his main intention is not to define the political art; it is to exercise Young Socrates, and old Socrates as well, to become *dialektikōteros*, a better dialectician, with respect to any topic whatsoever (285d4ff). If the Stranger's detours, revisions, mistakes and rectifications, and choice of puzzling examples developed in tedious detail are all intentional, then the exercise he has in mind is quite different from the exercises employed, for example, by mathematical logicians or experts in scientific method who are training a new generation of practitioners of these arts.

One could say, and I as well as others have said, that the complications just noticed are all explained by the recalcitrance of politics to rational analysis and formal methodologies. But this is no answer to the question why the Stranger should have chosen so recalcitrant an example. It merely pushes the question back one step to say that he has been assigned this example by Socrates and Theodorus, who want to know how the Eleatics define the sophist, statesman, and philosopher. Why would Plato have the Stranger provide training in dialectic with two such odd topics as the natures of the sophist and the statesman? And why is there no portrait of the Stranger's exposition of the philosopher?

In my opinion, at least part of the answer to the present question is that Plato wishes to show, with or without the agreement of the Stranger, that if it is appropriate to refer to dialectic as the method for studying the natures of sophistry and statesmanship (to say nothing of philosophy), then the term has to be employed in quite a different and expanded sense from the one associated with diaeresis or with the dialectic of pure Ideas mentioned in the *Republic*. It is certainly not true that diaeresis is useless in these studies. All thinking, even the contemplation of pure form, includes diaeresis or the separation of kinds with respect to like and unlike. It should also be evident that the use of paradigms, or procedures for exhibiting sameness within otherness, is central to such an operation. The fundamental question raised by the *Statesman* is then not at all that of the nature of the royal art, but rather the nature of dialectic. But this amounts to the assertion that the fundamental theme of the *Statesman* is the question of the nature of philosophy and so, by extension, of the philosopher.

I do not mean by this that the *Statesman* and only the *Statesman* addresses itself to this question. To the contrary, the question is fundamental to every Platonic dialogue. But the specific question of philosophical method is much more visible, and I believe that it is also much deeper, in the *Statesman* than it is in almost any other dialogue. Perhaps only the *Sophist* and the *Parmenides* are from this standpoint at the same level as the *Statesman*. It is obviously not by chance that Plato assigns this topic to someone other than Socrates, whose own treatments of method are restricted in scope and couched largely in metaphors or sketches that function as promissory notes for some future and more adequate account. As an example of a metaphorical discussion of philosophical method by Socrates, I cite the account of erotic ascent in the *Symposium;* the *Republic* and *Philebus* will do nicely as examples of presentations of promissory notes instead of complete, or even reasonably detailed, discussions of the nature of dialectic.

These preliminary remarks were intended to motivate what follows, and to guard against what might strike some readers as tedious and over-ingenious if they did not bear firmly in view our goal. We propose to understand everything that we can extract from the *Statesman* about the central question of philosophical method or dialectic. The only way to do this is by studying the *Statesman* as Plato wrote it, not as it is imagined or as it is viewed through the lens of some contemporary philosophical doctrine. The Stranger himself will warn us later that no one with any intellect (*nous*) would study weaving for its own sake (285d8). Nevertheless, he discusses it in excruciating detail. I will therefore follow his discussion with equally excruciating detail. To borrow a Greek proverb from another but not unrelated domain, *chalepa ta kala* (the noble is hard).

The Stranger introduces the example of weaving as follows: "If we don't have anything else ready to hand, would you like it, by Zeus, if we choose weaving?" (279a7). A stylistic note: this is the first oath in the discussion between the Stranger and Young Socrates; we recall that Theodorus swears at 257b5 when he is embarrassed by Socrates. I believe that the present oath is related to the interruption of the Stranger by Young Socrates at 277c4–5. There is a slight but discernible raising of the emotional level, which hitherto had been extremely formal. The oath signals a recognition of the initial oddity of the example of weaving. Weaving is a concatenation like spelling; it is like politics in caring for the body through the production of artifacts. More precisely, weaving produces covers or protections against nature. It has the same *pragmateia* or activity as politics; this term is not synonymous with *gnōstikē* or *epistēmē* but conveys the notion of diligence in business or practice. Whereas study is required, it is applied study; we are halfway between *gnōstikē* and *praktikē*, contrary to the sharp bifurcation of the original diaeresis.

We are not, however, going to dispense with diaeresis itself. The art of weaving will be divided so as to prepare a diaeresis of woolweaving, and this as quickly as possible, in order to arrive again (*palin ēlthomen*) at what is now useful, namely, the *pragmateia* common to weaving and statesmanship (279a7–c3). As the word *palin* indicates, this is a return in addition to an advance, or a modification of the significance of reversal in the myth.

Step 1. Contrary to the Stranger's initial indication, we do not begin with the art of weaving wool but instead will arrive at it through the analysis of a much broader class. The actual diaeresis, which runs from 279c7 to 280a7, is of the general class of "all things that we make for ourselves and acquire." In the *Sophist*, we began with making (*poiētikē*) and acquiring (*ktētikē*) as two distinct branches of the arts, with theoretical or gnostic science under the latter heading. Here, making and acquiring go together and, as step 1 will show, are to be understood as the collection of things employed in active or defensive practico-production. They are accordingly separated implicitly from gnostics or theory.

Step 2. We now divide the basis step of making and acquiring into the class of things "for doing something" (*ta men heneka tou poiein ti*) and the class of things "for defense against suffering something" (*ta de tou mē paschein am-untēria*: 279c7–9). I remind the reader that in the *Sophist* therapy falls under production, whereas in the *Statesman* it is closely associated with political caring and falls under gnostics in the original diaeresis. Here we are concerned with a blend or web of production and gnostics. Diaeresis is itself a web that is differently spun, depending upon our intention with respect to the use of the web. The intention here is not active but passive; the web is to be used for defense of the body. If this is the same *pragmateia* as the statesman's, then his art must be used to defend the body against nature. We may infer from this once more that it is either mistaken or at best a radical oversimplification to speak of man as the political animal "by nature." In very general terms, weaving is the analogue to what the myth presents as rejuvenation through counternormal motion. But counternormal motion is from the normal standpoint unnatural.

In the *Sophist* (226d1–227c6), weaving is found in the diaeresis as a result of the division of *diakritikē* or "separation":

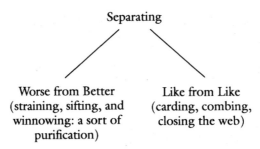

Separating

Worse from Better
(straining, sifting, and
winnowing: a sort of
purification)

Like from Like
(carding, combing,
closing the web)

In the art of diaeresis, we separate like from like, in other words, things of form *A* from things of form *B*. This also reminds us of spelling, in which instances of the letter *a* are separated from instances of the letter *b*. The separation of worse threads from better threads is presumably an auxiliary art rather than a part of weaving, but the point is moot. In general, we see the underlying similarity of diaeresis, spelling, weaving, and politics. But in the *Statesman*, weaving and politics are tacitly distinguished from diaeresis and spelling as defenses of the body against nature. It is not impossible that diaeresis and spelling are defenses of the soul or intellect against nature. The moderns, under the banner of Descartes, speak of the mastery and possession of nature. This is a radical revision of the Platonist defense against nature, but it is not totally unrelated to it, as one might assume from the traditional histories of philosophy.

Step 3. Defensive things, made or acquired, are divided into two collections: (1) divine or human antidotes or spells, and (2) protections (279c9–d1). The word used for "protections," *problēmata*, means literally "things put in front of." It can be a hindrance as well as a defense, as for example, in the form of a "problem." We should carefully note that the divine is discarded along with magic; this corresponds to the rejection of the divine shepherd as a paradigm of the statesman.

Step 4. Weapons of war (*hoplismata*), perhaps shields in this context, are separated off from screens used to defend in peace or everyday life (*phrag-*

mata: 279d2). A *phragma* is a screen that protects one from the elements or from injury in some way. This is a confusing step, although a necessary one. We must shift from war to peace in order to arrive at weaving, which is not only a defensive art but also one that is practiced in the house by women. But the art of the statesman is certainly as much concerned with war as with peace, and so with defense as well as attack. We may be intended to understand this step as an indication that the primary enemy of human beings is nature, but it is obvious that attacking human beings, even if they are soldiers of another city rather than savages or barbarians, are themselves natural beings. On balance, I believe that this step shows the weakness of diaeresis and the defect of the example of weaving. The example is of course not without value; it does bring out something important about the political art. But it is one-sided; we need something else to supplement it.

Step 5. Defensive screens are divided into (1) hangings or curtains (*para-petasmata*) and (2) protections against cold and heat (*aleksētēria:* 279d2–4). The Greek word for "protections" is interesting; it is related to *aleksētērios,* which is applied to Zeus in the sense of "able to protect." It can also mean a remedy or medicine. Here the term is applied to human production, which must replace the nonexistent efforts of the gods on our behalf.

Step 6. aleksētēria are divided into coverings attached to houses (*steg-asmata*) and those that are attached to, or make contact with, human bodies (*skepasmata:* 279d4–5). The Stranger is evidently coining words that do not occur in ordinary Greek. The exact nature of the divisions in steps 5 and 6 are ambiguous and clearly exhibit the Stranger's baroque sense of humor.

Step 7. Body shelters are divided into *hupopetasmata,* "what is spread out beneath one" or carpets, and *perikalummata,* "what is spread around one" or clothing and blankets (279d6). This word (*perikaluptein*) was used at 275e6 to describe the process of "wrapping up" the king and others who claim to care for the human herd within one family of technicians. This gives us a hint of the parallel between diaeresis, which prepares defensive coverings for the intellect (today called "concepts") and weaving, which, like politics, prepares defensive coverings for the body.

Step 8. "Wraparounds" are divided into those which are cut out in one piece (*holoschista*) and those which are compounded from separate pieces (279d6–7).

Step 9. The latter are divided into wraparounds with or without perforations (279d7–e1).

Step 10. Of the unperforated kinds, some are made from plant fibers and others from animal hair (279e1–2).

Step 11. Finally, wraparounds made from animal hair are either stuck together with liquids and pastes or fastened together by themselves (279e4–5).

The Stranger summarizes the results of the diaeresis from 279e4 to 280a7. I tabulate his main points as follows:

(1) The artifacts of step 7 are identified as *himatia*, outer garments: "to these defensive coverings produced from pieces designed to hold together by themselves we give the name of outer garments" (279e4–6). This definition includes only steps 2, 6, and 11 of the diaeresis. So once again it seems that the Stranger has used too much material in arriving at his intended result.

(2) "As to the *technē* that cares [*epimeloumenon*] for clothing, we shall call it *himatiourgikē* in accord with its work, just as previously we spoke of the political art with respect to the city" (279e6–280a3). This makes it clear that clothes stand to the body as the city stands to the citizens. In both cases the name derives not from gnostics but from practico-production, and so from manufacture. The extension of the previously derived sense of "caring" from the statesman to the weaver is quite striking. We knew that *epimeleia* is at the heart of the royal art before we learned that it has the same role with respect to weaving. So the model is itself illuminated by that which it is supposed to explain.

(3) The Stranger and Young Socrates agree that since the greatest part of the art of weaving (*huphantikē*) is the production of outer clothing (*himatiourgikē*), we may equate the former with the latter, which differ in name only, just as the royal art differed from the political art in name only (280a3–7). This amounts to a rejection of the fine distinctions introduced by the diaeresis; for political purposes, in other words, we can round off these distinctions or make use of generalizations. It also leads us to reconsider whether the art of the king is synonymous with that of the statesman or rather a generalization on the work of the statesman.

(4) I note in passing that this is the fourteenth occurrence, or twice seven, of one version or another of Young Socrates' favorite expression: "entirely correct." The interested reader may check 260a8; 261d2 and d6; 263a2; 268a4, b7, and d1; 275b8; 276b6, c2, and d7; 277c7; 278e11; 280a7 (the present occurrence); 281c6, d4, and e11; 282e10; 283a2 and a9; 284e1; 286d3; 287b9; 292c4; 295a8 (here immediately followed by an *orthōs* from the Stranger); 296a10; 300c4; 303c7; 305d5; 309a7 and d9. So responses based on the mathematician's typical word "correct" appear in thirty affirmations and two questions by Young Socrates. It is in small stylistic touches of this sort that Plato adds the last degree of perfection to his dialogues. I leave it as an exercise to the reader to compare these responses with those based on

other words and to infer from these responses shades of difference in Young Socrates' acquiescence.

Calculemus

"Now let us calculate together" (*sullogisōmetha:* 280a8); this passage is an echo of 270b3, where the Stranger tells Young Socrates that they must now "understand by calculative reason" (*logisamenoi . . . sunnoēsōmen*) the *pathos* of cosmic reversal in the myth. Someone might think that we have just carried through sufficiently our diaeresis. But such a person would not understand (*sunnoein:* again see 270b3) that weaving has not been separated from many closely connected jobs performed by people in the same line of work (*sunergoi*) as the weaver, even though that *technē* has been separated from many others of the same race (*sungenōn:* 280a8–b3). Why have we repeated the mistake made previously in the case of the king?

I see three reasons. First, emphasis is placed on the comic nature of diaeresis or, better, on the comic nature of those who apply methods like diaeresis to politics in the hope of obtaining precise conceptual results. The second reason is a corollary of the first: it is important to see in particular that diaeretic definitions of the king, or for that matter of any other art, even if they are useful, must be supplemented by the perception of similarities and differences that are blurred or ignored by diaeresis, which is too abstract to incorporate them. Third, the example of weaving has brought out with great clarity the practico-productive nature of politics, and in this way exposed the error of the initial premise of the original diaeresis, namely, that gnostics can be separated from practice in a way that is useful for defining the statesman.

In the original diaeresis we failed to divide the tending of or caring for the human herd; had we done this, we could have distinguished the various types of caring and so separated off the king from his rivals. Instead, we divided the art of the nurture of herds and so ended up with all nurturers in one family. Is there an analogous problem in the diaeresis of weaving? The Stranger claims that there is. Again, he divided the family of everything that we make or acquire in terms of the distinction between acting on others and preventing others from acting on us. By following the second fork, he divided families of defensive products (again ignoring the difference between producers and products) and so arrived at the art of making clothing (= woolweaving) as the sole representative of the care of clothes. But this fails to distinguish various ways of "caring" for clothing. Lest the point seem obscure, the reader has only to think of menders. To this I would add a much more important defect of the diaeresis that the Stranger does not mention. The example separates off attack from defense and thereby transforms politics by implication into a completely peaceful, home-centered, and *feminine* art.

The example of weaving is an important supplement to the example of the captain; in other words, neither is an example of statesmanship altogether but each illustrates a different aspect of the statesman's art. The statesman cares for the whole of the city and therefore, whether directly or indirectly, for the whole of human existence. It would not be at all unreasonable to compare him to a god from this standpoint, although of course such a comparison would have to be properly qualified. The crucial point here is that there is not and cannot be any example of the statesman that serves as a model of states-manship because of the comprehensive nature of the royal art. But therefore the method of diaeresis, which narrows down or defines by the accumulation of differences, is an entirely inappropriate method to employ in the effort to understand the political art.

Young Socrates, who lacks our opportunity to calculate the implications of the diaeresis, asks the Stranger what arts belong to the same race as weaving. The Stranger somewhat unjustly responds: "you have not followed what has been said; it seems that we must go back again (*palin*) and begin at the end" (280b5–6). This expression marks a kind of subsection of the section on weaving and refers back to the immediately preceding invocation to calculate. It also signals another reversal, this time of the diaeresis of weaving, undertaken in order to "rejuvenate" Young Socrates, who is be-coming fatigued by the discussion. The Stranger introduces the reversal with the following protasis: "If you understand kindredness" (*sunnoeis tēn oikeiotēta:* 280b6–7). This is what requires calculation: the nature of "one's own" or of family relation, one could almost say with Wittgenstein, of family resemblance. How do we collect together occupations, artifacts, races or natural kinds, or anything whatsoever?

In the previous chapter we saw that everything resembles everything else in one respect or another; hence everything is the same as and other than everything else, and so everything is a paradigm of something. This is not the same as to say that there are no natural kinds or, more generally, Platonic Ideas. It is, however, the same as to say that the task of understanding cannot be discharged by perceiving natural kinds or Platonic Ideas, assuming this to be possible. If there is an Idea of the cow, this has something essential to do with the existence of cows and our ability to perceive them, but it does not in itself explain all the ways in which cows function or can be made to function within human life. The same point applies to diaeresis. Since a king, more-over, is not a natural kind, or in other words since there is no Platonic Idea of the art of statesmanship, or for that matter of any other art, we will need multiple diaereses in order to come close to hunting him down or pinning him to the mat, just as was required in the pursuit of the sophist. I suspect that the nonexistence of the promised dialogue on the philosopher is intentional; there is no way at all in which to pin down his nature.

I will summarize the Stranger's summary for the sake of succinctness:

(1) We divided off from clothing something akin to it, namely, the synthesis of *strōmata*, by employing the distinction between placing around and placing beneath (280b6–9). This refers to steps 7, 8, and 11. So the Stranger is once more engaged in the process of tangling his own web. The word *strōmata* did not occur in the diaeresis; it means bedding and therefore includes what is spread around one (blankets), as well as what is spread underneath one (mattresses and perhaps rugs). These were separated in step 7; here they are included together as one class.

(2) We discarded the entire art (*dēmiourgia*) of making cloth from vegetable fibers (280c1–3). This is the rejected part of step 10. It is odd that the Stranger mentions this instead of the part that was retained.

(3) The Stranger continues to cite the discarded part; here it is felting (*pilētikēn*), as well as the synthesis by way of piercing and sewing, of which shoemaking is now mentioned as the outstanding example (280c3–5). Felting is the process of making cloth by compression, glueing, sewing, or plaiting. It could be classified in several ways. But piercing and sewing belong to the rejected part of step 9, namely, to making perforated cloths (used as curtains for beds that can be pulled together by cords inserted into the perforations). Felting was not previously mentioned and adds to the confusion.

(4) Here the Stranger names both parts of step 6 while adding additional terminology and using "therapy" with respect to the working of skins. In developing the separation of *skepasmata* (body shelters) from *stegasmata*, he specifies among the latter the arts of housebuilding, carpentering, making protective works against whatever flows, and all those defenses that protect against thefts and deeds of violence, such as the making of lids and covers, fitting doorways, and joining or carpentry (280c7–d5). So despite the mention of both names, the rejected part is emphasized.

(5) We separated weaponmaking (*hoplopoiikē*) and rejected it; there is no mention of the arts that were retained. This refers to step 4, in which *hoplismata*, weapons in general and perhaps here intended to refer to warscreens, were rejected (280d5–6).

(6) "At the very beginning" we divided off and rejected the whole art of magic that makes protective spells (280e1–2). This refers to step 3; the Stranger omits the distinction between divine and human and is again silent

on the part retained. And he calls this the very beginning of the diaeresis, whereas in fact there was a more general step (2), in which he divided manufacturing and possessing (1) into instances for the sake of doing something and those for the sake of preventing something from being done.

(7) The Stranger says that this leaves us with the object of our search: the art of defending against the weather by producing a protection (*problēmatos*) of wool, which art is called weaving (280e2–4). "Defending against the weather" seems to refer to step 5 and could also refer to the rejected part of step 6; the word for protection was introduced in step 3.

The Stranger gives no reason for having reversed the diaeresis, entirely apart from his alterations in the various steps; neither does he explain why he summarized the rejected parts rather than those that were retained. We could perhaps explain this last procedure as a supplementary exercise of Young Socrates' memory and technical skill, similar to proving a problem in mathematics in two complementary ways, for example, directly and by a reductio ad absurdum. But if so, why does he complicate rather than simplify his reversed summary?

In casting one more look over the diaeresis as a whole, we should perhaps note that the Stranger is here classifying what Heidegger would call the world of tools. Life consists in its everyday form of *pragmata*, not simply "things" but things we can use in our daily work. Some of these we make for ourselves; others we acquire from nature. With these tools, we can act upon others or prevent them from acting on ourselves. And here I note in passing that the Stranger has omitted to classify tools with which we do things to ourselves. Furthermore, when preventing something from being done to me, I must also do something. For example, in order to defend myself, I must take up a position behind a shield or screen of some sort. I cannot defend myself by doing nothing; this is why the Stranger refers to defensive arts. Differently stated, everyday life is productive and active even in its defensive mode; perhaps we need a category analogous to the middle voice in Greek grammar, which refers generally to acts done for oneself.

Once More into the Breach

The Stranger gave his reversed summary in order to assist Young Socrates in seeing that the diaeresis had not separated off competitors to the art of weaving for the title of curator of woolen clothing. It does not seem to have done the job, but instead it has strengthened the youth's conviction that they have successfully defined the weaver (280e5). In order to clarify the matter, and so presumably to reach our goal (280e6), the Stranger launches into a finer analysis of the art of clothesmaking rather than, as we might expect, of weaving. "He who begins the process of making clothes seems to do the opposite of weaving," which is a plaiting together or interlacing (*sumplokē*), a word elsewhere employed to refer to the community of Platonic Ideas. The initial act of clothesmaking is, in contrast, a *dialutikē* or "a separation of what is combined and pressed together, namely, the art of carding (*ksantikē*: 280e6–281a9). At 280a3–7, the Stranger said that since clothesmaking is the greatest part of weaving, we can take the two names as synonymous. Now he tacitly withdraws that identification and treats clothesmaking as broader than weaving. I should also note that we are concerned with the production of woolen clothes, but woolworking will emerge as a part of clothesmaking.

In the *Sophist,* carding, spinning, and weaving are classified together by diaeresis 5 as the discrimination of like from like (in other words, members of the same family); they are rejected in favor of purifying, or the separation of unlike from unlike (in other words, members of different families) or of worse from better. Here weaving is distinguished from carding because we are making a finer analysis in the hope of arriving at last at the elusive art of the statesman. We are, however, thus far still located apart from purification and, in particular, from the separation of the better from the worse. Why this should be so is not obvious. It could be argued with great plausibility that the statesman must purify the city of traitors and criminals by the appropriate penal code. Politics is both interlacing and separating, as it would seem.

The art of weaving is not carding, or separating the threads from their initial entanglement and straightening them out in preparation for the process of interlacing. But neither can it be identified with making the warp (*stēmōn*) and the woof (*krokē*), which involves a twisting of the carded threads. Furthermore, the arts of fulling (*knapheutikē*) and mending (*akestikē*) do not comprise the entire art of weaving, although they must be acknowledged as types of the care and servicing of clothing (281b3–6). Fulling is the art of cleansing and thickening cloth by beating and washing. The Greek word seems to have the same meaning. Previously the question arose whether the weaver is the only one to claim the title of maker of clothing. The point arises again here because the mender and fuller both participate in the process of repair, which has something to do with making because it is a remaking of the original. But especially after numerous repairs and alterations, one has, if not quite a new garment, certainly a different one from the original.

It would not be impossible to suggest political analogies to the mender and fuller from the contemporary state, for example, the justices of the supreme court, local and national legislators, political commentators, and lobbyists. In the Greek city, the analogy extends to all free citizens who gather together in the assembly to interpret and revise the laws. Stated in general terms, the city, and hence its citizens, must be repaired by menders and fullers, just as the normal epoch of the cosmos must be rejuvenated by the counternormal epoch, because of a loss of vitality and memory. But the repaired garment, like its political counterpart, cannot be entirely the same as the original, although it is certainly not entirely different. Since all living cities undergo repair, it is easy to see that political existence is both normal and counternormal, or more accurately, that it is both preservation or acquisition and also production.

And sure enough, the Stranger explicitly links the servicing and generating of clothing in his next statement about the basis of the dispute, with the crucial concession that the other arts will grant that weaving is the most important part of those activities (281b7–10). In this portion of the discussion, caring and servicing are once more united with nurturing, with the important difference that cleaning replaces feeding; mending and fulling are not quite rivals but adjutants to the weavers in the act of generating clothing—they stand somewhat closer than the weavers to the shepherds and herdsmen, as well as closer to the nurturers of individual animals, who assist in the process of breeding. The act of genesis is developed further by the introduction of those who make the tools for weaving and who thereby have some claim to a share in the art of clothesmaking (281c2–5).

In sum, producing, cleaning, and repairing (mending and fulling) are three distinct types of the "nurturing" of clothing, whereas the various aspects of weaving are subclasses of production. It looks as though the art of the statesman will then be some sort of internal as well as external rule; just as the actual weaver must rule over carding, preparing the warp and woof, and so on, so too the king must rule over the subcurators of the city. But reflection suggests that the example of weaving breaks down at this point because the political analogues to cleaning and repairing are also subordinate to the statesman's comprehensive care, whereas the weaver is no longer in charge of finished garments that require cleaning or mending.

This is in effect allowed for by the Stranger's next words. There is some truth in the contention that the definition of weaving reached by diaeresis contains the noblest and best part, but it will be neither clear nor complete until we separate off all the rivals to the weaver (281c7–d4). Once again the separation of like from like and unlike from unlike must be supplemented by the perception of nobility. The Stranger invokes the distinction between the noble and the base or humble, but he does not justify or explain it. If we did not understand that the art of the weaver is the decisive act in the entire network of arts associated with the production, cleaning, and repair of clothing, then we could not see the point of the analogy between weaving and politics on the one hand, and clothing and the city on the other. And in this case, diaeresis would be pointless or of interest exclusively as a formal exercise. Analysis depends on the intuition of analogies. But both the perception of analogies and the employment of diaeresis depend on the perception of like and unlike, or of what we called previously same and other.

A second major conclusion that follows from our cumulative analysis of the Stranger's heterogeneous exercise is that theory is tangled together with practice (which, the reader will recall, is practico-production). The more we separate theory from practice, the farther we are removed from human existence; the limit case is the contemplation of Platonic Ideas by pure noetic intuition. But the farther we are removed from human existence, the less accurately we understand it as it is actually lived. The perspective of the mathematician or the astronomer is not suited to the study of politics. And there is a deeper or more theoretical inference to be drawn. We cannot finally separate theory from practice because theory is itself in part practice. The pure viewing of Platonic forms is impossible for an incarnated soul, which must "recollect" these forms or view them in images, which are artifacts of the cognitive and perceptual process. And the expression of contemplation in discursive thinking, whether silent or spoken, employs a language, which is a conventional artifact in itself as well as a tool for producing more artifacts, which we call "concepts."

A third conclusion also follows from the attempt to untangle theory from practice. In the original diaeresis, the Stranger first separated off practice from gnostics and then divided gnostics into judging (*kritikē*) and commanding. This entails that the ability to command does not depend upon the ability to produce or to calculate (*logistikē* is a part of *kritikē*). But this distinction, which is crucial for politics, was soon lost in the subsequent stages of the division of biological herds and *technai* for tending to them, whether by nurturing or caring. It is, however, false to say that the statesman must know how to nurture the human herd, that is, how to breed citizens, feed and clothe them, teach them the various arts that are required for individual and collective existence, and so on. This was also concealed by the Stranger's paradigms. The shepherd is the physician, educator, and general tender of his flock. The captain must know the art of navigation, which is quite different from knowing how to command his crew and passengers; one may be a marvelous navigator and a terrible captain. Weaving is a productive or concatenative art, but the weaver does not issue commands about how those who wear her clothes should act or speak. Commanding is different from the *technai* exercised by the citizens, including those who are the commander's direct adjutants.

Different but not, of course, separate. Commands cannot be rationally issued in complete ignorance or to no purpose, and the purposes for which we command are deeds or speeches. The statesman must be acquainted with the capacities of human beings, in general, and his or her subjects or fellow citizens, in particular; statesmanship requires an understanding of the powers of the arts, but even more important is knowledge of the ends to which the arts may be addressed. These ends are not purely theoretical or gnostic; even universities and monasteries require practice in order to exist and function. In short, the distinction between commanding and obeying occurs within the interwovenness of theory and practice, not in a branch of one as separated from the other.

To return to the text, we must distinguish the art of the clothesmaker or weaver from its rivals, just as we have to distinguish the art of the statesman or king from its rivals. The Stranger will proceed with the assistance of another diaeresis, of which the basis step is *ta drōmena*, in general, "things that we do," but here used to refer in particular to acts of production (281d5ff). To be more precise, the Stranger begins with a very general diaeresis that identifies the criterion for the subsequent diaeresis of clothesmaking in particular. The general diaeresis proceeds as follows.

Step 1. We start with everything that we do of a productive nature. This refers to technical production, as is immediately clear from the context (281d5–9).

Step 2. Whatever we produce is by way of two *technai*, one of which is the cause of the genesis and the other the co-cause. By the latter, the Stranger refers to the arts that manufacture the tools required for the act of genesis; the cause is the art that actually produces the thing (*pragma:* 281d10–e5).

Instead of proceeding farther with this general diaeresis of what we do, the Stranger shifts to clothesmaking. To repeat, we are no longer dividing weaving, but what is called first "the production of outer garments" (*ergasia tōn himatiōn:* 280e7) and then "the genesis [via tools] of clothing" (*genesis peri ta amphiesmata:* 281e8–9).

Step 1. (Basis step) Clothesmaking is done by way of causes and co-causes (281e7–282a5):

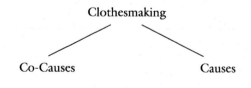

Clothesmaking

Co-Causes   Causes

(arts producing spindles,   (washing, mending, fulling =
shuttles, and so on)   adornment, and so on)

The arts listed in parentheses are examples of the subclasses. The causes are introduced as the arts that "tend and produce by hand" (*therapeuousas kai dēmiourgousas aitias*). But the examples listed are all of tending in the sense of nurturing rather than of generating clothing. In addition, *kosmetikē*, or adornment, is mentioned for the first time as the totality of which washing, mending, and fulling are parts. This coincides with 281b3–6, where fulling and mending were cited as parts of clothes therapy to be distinguished from the part that produces the clothing—namely, weaving. But it differs from that passage in listing adornment under the causes of clothing rather than under the co-causes. Production is now to be understood in a broader sense than in the slightly earlier passage. But this, together with the fact that weaving is now apparently a subclass of clothesmaking, in turn raises the question whether weaving is the single paradigm of the single art of statesmanship, or whether weaving is the noblest part of the paradigm of which statesmanship is the noblest part.

Step 2. At this point the diaeresis becomes complicated and hard to untangle. We are in the process of dividing the causes of clothesmaking, of which we have hitherto identified fulling or adornment. From this may now be distinguished "wool-spinning" (*talasiourgikē*), which includes "carding and spinning and everything concerned with the actual making [*tēn poiēsin autēn*] of the clothing" (282a6–9). So step 2 looks like this:

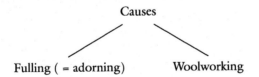

Note that woolworking falls under, and so is not identical with, making clothes from already prepared woolen cloth. But the important complication lies elsewhere. Within the subclass of causes, the further division distinguishes between the making and the adorning of clothing. There are in other words what look like two different senses of "co-causes" in this passage; one is coordinate with "causes" and the other is internal to it. This raises the question just noted about the inner structure of the art of statesmanship.

Step 3. Weaving is no longer visible as coordinate with fulling or adornment. It has been replaced by woolworking, which is about to be analyzed into its constituent arts. As examples of woolworking, the Stranger cites carding and spinning. But woolworking is made up of two parts or sections, each of which "is simultaneously a natural part of two *technai*." This odd situation is explained as follows. Carding and one-half of the use of the weaver's rod is engaged in division (*diakritikē*) of the threads, along with

whatever separates that which "lies together" or is compounded. This is one
of the two segments of woolworking. However, every art contains combination (*sunkritikē*) as well as division; we must therefore distinguish within
woolworking the combining arts (282b4–c8), in addition to the dividing arts
like carding.

This suggests the following diaeresis:

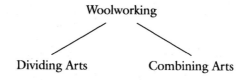

Woolworking

Dividing Arts   Combining Arts

Since carding (*ksantikē*) is an example of division, spinning (*nēstikē*) must be
an example of composition. Note that it makes no initial sense to say that
carding and spinning are the two halves of woolworking and that each belongs to two arts simultaneously, namely, division and composition. In what
sense, then, are we to take the Stranger's statement at 282b1–2 that each part
of woolworking belongs simultaneously and by nature to two different arts?
It sounds very much as though the Stranger is hinting at the presence of
diaeresis, which is both collecting and dividing, as the ground of woolworking (or, we may add, of anything else), which is itself or in its own identity
composed of both carding and spinning. The woolworker qua carder sorts
out the elements or results of diaeresis and selects those which are suitable for
the making of clothing; qua spinner, the woolworker weaves these elements
into the desired web or garment. In this interpretation, carding and spinning
each belong to two different arts, namely, woolworking and diaeresis.

Step 4. This seems to be confirmed by 282c5–8. We have two possibilities
here. Either diaeresis, consisting of dividing and collecting in some sense
other than carding or weaving, must be found in its entirety in each of these
segments of woolworking. Or else diaeresis is contained entirely within woolworking, but its dividing part falls together with carding whereas its collecting part falls together with spinning. On either alternative, diaeresis remains
the ground of woolworking. I believe that the Stranger has the second alternative in mind. This is why, having located carding within both woolworking
and division, we now put it to one side and turn to those parts of woolworking that are also parts of combination. The Stranger divides combination, and
a fortiori the second of the two segments of woolworking, into *streptikē*—or
making the warp and the woof by the twisting of threads—and *sumplektikē*—
or the interlacing of the warp and woof. This second subdivision is weaving
(282c10–d5).

Step 5. Thus far we have:

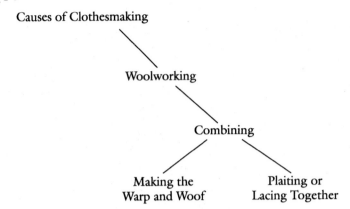

Causes of Clothesmaking

Woolworking

Combining

Making the
Warp and Woof

Plaiting or
Lacing Together

Young Socrates is hesitant but correctly identifies the making of the warp as a twisting of threads, and he quickly agrees that the making of the woof is also an example of the twisting art. The Stranger, however, suggests the need for a definition of twisting and plaiting together. A lengthened and broadened woolen thread (*katagma*) can be (1) twisted with a spindle to make a hard thread—this is the art of spinning the warp—or (2) dressed by a softer force to make loose threads that are then woven together into the warp (282d6–283a1).

Let us pause here to reconsider the diaeresis as a whole before we look at the concluding statement about weaving. The Stranger intends to prepare a paradigm of the distinction between the royal art of the statesman and his rival therapists of the human city. This distinction is performed by diaeresis, which is the fundamental human operation of articulating the cosmos into a determinate whole in accord with the phenomena or particular looks. Such an articulation requires dividing off one phenomenon from another and then collecting all those of a common look into a single separate family. From this standpoint, diaeresis is the method of perceptual and noetic vision and not simply a mechanical method for constructing concepts out of previously known elements.

But the Stranger is not explicitly concerned with diaeresis here. What interests him are the two models of weaving and clothesmaking or woolworking. These models are presented as though they were equivalent; no explanation is given for shifting from one to another. But in fact they are not equivalent. Weaving will turn out to be one part of the constellation of causes in the production of clothing. We have to decide whether it is the production of clothes or the art of weaving that is intended as the political paradigm. Both clothesmaking and woolworking are broader than weaving. Weaving depends on other arts, as the last diaeresis has made clear. Weaving is the last step, represented at the end of the dialogue as the combination of spirited and gentle souls into the web of the city. Souls, whether spirited or gentle, need to be nurtured by their parents, educated by their teachers, supervised by judges, priests, and other officials of the city, and civilized by their fellow citizens. As the broader art, clothesmaking gives us a richer articulation of the art of politics without isolating the royal art of the statesman. But weaving, the narrower art, which ostensibly identifies the statesman with complete accuracy, in fact fails to do this. It is radically incomplete, as can easily be shown.

The production of the warp or hard threads corresponds to the nurturing and educating of the spirited or hard-souled citizens, whereas the production of the woof or soft threads corresponds to the nurturing and education of the gentle citizens. But the model has no representation of commanding. The weaver and her affiliated artisans all produce clothing for the sake of merchants and clients on the one hand, and for members of the family on the other. It is here that we would have to begin looking for the art of commanding the production of clothing. And underlying the wholesale and retail production of clothing, as we might refer to the two, is the need of the body for protection against nature. The production of clothing is a technical matter, but the need for clothing is not; this is determined by a combination of natural necessity and *nomos,* whether written or unwritten. The natural factor is indicated by the metaphor of the herd, but that metaphor is in itself insufficient because human *nomos* is quite different from the behavior of nonhuman herd animals.

Once again we may conclude that there is and can be no single satisfactory paradigm of statesmanship. Such paradigms are either too general or too particular. This is not at all to say that the Stranger's various examples have been useless. One valuable lesson they teach is the inadequacy of analytical methods like diaeresis; another is the difference between the commanding and the productive parts of political caring. Nothing explicit is said about the quite different sense of diaeresis as the ground of intelligibility. I have teased out a reference to this sense from an unusually obscure passage that is certainly open to dispute. For my part, I regard the obscurity as characteristic of the Stranger's (and of Plato's) pedagogy.

Whether I am right or wrong in this element of my interpretation, there is no doubt that politics must understand human nature as well as man's technical capacity, which is to say that the statesman bridges the separation of gnostics from practice. But not even this dual understanding will suffice; it is also necessary to know how to command. This knowledge is in turn dual, since it includes possession of the tools for commanding but also knowledge of the ends or *phronēsis*. The commander must be a good speaker and charismatic leader, but he or she also requires sound judgment. And judgment can be divided into care of particular welfare and care for the common good.

The Stranger at last summarizes his treatment of weaving at 283a3–9. It is, he says, now clear to everyone what part of weaving we established at the outset as the topic for diaeresis. "When that part of combination [*sunkritikē*] within woolworking forms a web by straight, even-textured weaving, of the woof and the warp, we call the entire web woolen clothing, and the art that is concerned with this we call weaving." Again the Stranger assumes that clothesmaking and weaving are the same art. Apart from what has already been said, the summary draws our attention to the absence of division (*diakritikē*). Otherwise stated, the Stranger has silently resolved the earlier fluctuation between clothesmaking and weaving in favor of the latter. Assume for a moment that weaving is a satisfactory paradigm of statesmanship. What art corresponds to clothesmaking? Is statesmanship the final result of the diaeresis of some more general art or family of arts? It is not impossible that clothesmaking refers to the various ways in which human beings are protected by *technē* against the enmity of nature. In this case we might conceivably find the philosopher among those who are lurking in the tangled web of the diaeresis we have just studied.

The general significance of the paradigm of weaving is twofold. Politics is shown to be the art of commanding for the sake of a genesis. But the same is true of diaeresis, or what we call today conceptual analysis. Kant points out that every analysis is preceded by a synthesis. In Platonic language, every analysis is itself a synthesis or production of those articulations within the continuous web of human experience that are pertinent to the particular intention of the analyst. Since politics and diaeresis are both productive arts, the fundamental distinction between gnostics and practico-production, or as we say today, between theory and practice, exists in name only, and as such it is an artifact of human judgment or intention.

This is not to say that human beings produce themselves ex nihilo or that experience is pure construction. Just as human beings are produced by nature, so too the structure of intelligibility, or what the Stranger calls in the *Sophist* the elements of the whole, is given or discovered; it is acquired rather than produced. What we produce is the particular articulation of the structure. The difference between acquiring and producing corresponds very generally to the difference between the noetic apprehension of Ideas or pure forms on the one hand, and diaeresis on the other.

The picture of Plato that begins to emerge from the detailed study of the *Statesman* is rather different from the conventional accounts of Platonism. But it is not different from an equally careful study of any other major Platonic dialogue. Conventions arise from agreements that are a mixture of ideology and carelessness. They have their political uses, but philosophy is not politics. To make this point in a different way, the conventional picture of Platonism is largely a consequence of two factors. First, Plato's peculiar style and manner of communicating his doctrines have gradually been obscured by a major and continuous shift in literary taste, a shift that is rooted in a changing conception of subtlety or elegance. Second, Plato has been gradually assimilated into Aristotelianism; in other words, the poetical presentation of philosophy has gradually been replaced by the scholastic or professorial.

It may appear anachronistic to some readers when I say that the one thinker in the entire tradition of Western philosophy who is closest to what is today regarded as the rejection of Platonism is Plato himself. There is, however, no anachronism here but only the recognition of one of the main themes of the myth of cosmic reversal. It is precisely at the end of a cosmic cycle that we fail most drastically to understand the proximity of the end to the beginning. We could do worse than to think of Penelope, the wife of Odysseus, himself the prototype of the philosopher, as the human representation of destiny, who unweaves by night what she weaves by day.

CHAPTER SEVEN

Measurement

Introductory Remarks

IMMEDIATELY following the summary of the diaeresis of clothes-making, to which Young Socrates says "entirely correct" (*orthotata*), the Stranger asks: "Why ever did we not say straight out that weaving is the plaiting of woof and warp? Why did we go around in a circle making so many idle distinctions?" Young Socrates replies that he found nothing to have been said in vain. "No wonder," the Stranger responds, referring primarily to the conceptual richness of the intricacies of his presentation, but also, I suspect, to the young mathematician's delight in technical detail. It is, however, likely that the boy will later become subject to the sickness of doubting the pertinence of the elaborate discussion; "—and no wonder—" the Stranger says again, this time in the opposite sense. In order to protect him against this illness, he must hear a *logos* that is suitable to such occasions (283b1–c1).

The Stranger is thus well aware of the oddness of his long and confusingly repetitive as well as tangled exhibition. He therefore proposes to discuss the nature of excess (*huperbolē*) and deficiency (*elleipsis*) so that we can praise or blame what has been said at a greater than necessary length or with too much brevity. This *logos* is neither a diaeresis nor a myth. For the first time in the dialogue, we are about to be introduced to the exercise of *phronēsis*, good sense or judgment. This exercise is the art of measurement (*hē metrētikē*: 283c2–d2). It is related to dialectic, understood here as diaeresis, as the art of commanding is related to the *technai* of caring and nurturing. Just as the statesman needs good judgment in order to know how to arrange the occupations of human beings into a political whole, so too the philosopher must understand which methods of argumentation and analysis to employ for investigations of different kinds. Furthermore, both philosopher and statesman require myth in order to speak about totality and, in particular, about the three great wholes of the cosmos, the city, and the soul.

Let us take a preliminary view of the topic of measurement. As the Stranger will shortly indicate, there are two kinds of measurement—arithmetical and nonarithmetical. Arithmetical measurement proceeds by means of a standard that may be arbitrary or relative in itself, but which is absolute with respect to its application. We may measure lengths in feet or in meters, depending upon a conventional agreement. The convenience of measurements of this sort depends upon the relative size of the objects, just as the degree of precision of our measurements is relative to the nature of our sense organs. Measurements of motion are relative to the motion of the system of which we who measure are a part. And no doubt many other qualifications of this sort could be determined concerning the standard of measurement.

Once we agree to employ such a standard, however, and with every allowance for the fallibility of our senses, in each case of application there is just one correct answer to the question "How much is it?" There are many wrong answers, and in the case of extremely difficult standards there are approximations to the correct answer. But even when we give two values and say that the correct answer is somewhere between them, we do not mean to imply that there are two correct answers. In arithmetical measurement there is one and only one correct answer to the question of magnitude, whether or not we are in a position to obtain it.

We come closer to nonarithmetical measurement in the case of approximations because here sound judgment is required in order to determine the accuracy of our instruments, the weaknesses of our senses, the training we have received in the manipulation of complex instruments of measurement, and so on. But here too the use of judgment is directed toward coming as close as possible to what is in itself not an approximation. It is we and our instruments, so to speak, that are approximately suited to the task of determining the precise magnitude. And in the case of magnitudes that vary, it may be impossible for us to determine their precise length at a given instant, but whatever is extended must be a certain length at each moment of time, and we can determine the extreme points of the series of variations even if we cannot measure each point within the series at any given time.

In general, the differences between arithmetical and nonarithmetical measurement are two. The first is that in arithmetical measurement we have two terms: correct and incorrect; in nonarithmetical, we have three: excess, deficiency, and suitability. By "correct," I refer to the assignment of a number of the units of the standard that is being used for the measurement, only one of which corresponds to the length being measured. All other such assignments are incorrect. In nonarithmetical measurement, none of the three kinds of answers—excessive, deficient, or suitable—is correct in the sense that there is no one answer intrinsic to what is being measured, however difficult or even impossible it may be for us to find it.

The second difference is that the relativity of the standard of measure in arithmetical measurement does not alter the fact that such magnitudes, at least in everyday life, exist independently of the standard we use. A man possesses a definite height at any moment, regardless of the standard by which we measure it, and regardless of whether he looks tall to us but would look short to creatures of a different and taller race. Otherwise put, the magnitude in these cases is what it is, regardless of whether it is suitable for some human purpose or not. And in cases in which there is no possibility of obtaining a measurement of a magnitude as independent of a frame of reference, we can say at the least that there is still one correct answer relative to that frame of reference, whether or not it makes sense to speak of an absolutely correct measurement from any or all frames of reference. In nonarithmetical measurement, everything measured is excessive, deficient, or suitable with respect to a human purpose. Nothing is excessive, deficient, or suitable in itself. Every measurement of this sort is relative to a frame of reference, not because of relative motion but because the sense of the entity being measured exists only with respect to the intentional frame of reference.

It is crucial to emphasize that whereas measurement in the sense just indicated is relative, it does not follow that the standards are relative in the same way. What counts as a just act will vary from one circumstance to another, whereas the difference between justice and injustice could be fixed, and in fact it must be fixed in some intelligible or perceptible manner, or else we would be unable to distinguish between acts that are suitable or fitting and those that are unsuitable or unfitting in attempts to be just. In terms that are closer to dialectical exercise, some students require long discussions and others require short explanations; one kind of example will work with a student of one type and another with a student of a different type. But there is a difference between understanding and not understanding a topic, or between possessing technical competence in a method and not possessing such a competence. We cannot measure these conditions or skills with numbers, but we can perceive and judge them. In short, whereas the suitable varies from occasion to occasion, that for which it is suitable need not and in the last analysis does not so vary. Even in so difficult a case as beauty, you and I may disagree about beautiful speech, but it is beautiful speech about which we disagree, not about something that is itself varying from one identity to another.

What interests the Stranger in the *Statesman* is not how to obtain precise measurements of magnitude, but what we mean by "more" and "less" with respect to "just right" in the sense of "fitting" or "appropriate." Something is "just right" if it is an instance of *to metrion,* not "the mean" in an arithmetical sense, but rather "the moderate" in the sense of not too much and not too little. A magnitude of a certain definite extension might be just right in one context, say a blueprint, and too little or too much in another, say a house suited for human habitation or a miniature model suited to be a child's toy. The magnitude in this example would not change, but rather the purpose or intention of the user. A speech is excessive if its length interferes with the speaker's intention, for example, to communicate a given doctrine. But the same speech may be just right if the speaker's intention is to pretend to teach while in fact concealing the doctrine. There is, however, a crucial difference between these two examples. The magnitude of a line in a blueprint, or in its physical embodiment, is the same regardless of the purpose to which it is put. But a speech can be just right for a given purpose and vary enormously in length. We cannot fix the number of lines that Plato needed to write, or the number of words that the Stranger had to utter, in order to carry out his dialectical exercise as he intended it.

If a line is too long for some purpose, we can measure it and decide more or less precisely by how much it needs to be shortened. But the same does not apply to a speech of excessive length. The determination of how to make a speech that is just right in length depends on different factors from those determining the suitable length of a line. And none of these factors can be fixed with precision by measuring them with a standard ruler. In all cases involving suitable lengths for speeches, we must rely upon our *phronēsis.* We do not first measure the various capacities or faculties of our audience with standard rulers and then construct a speech that is just right for the occasion. We proceed with the speech, whether written or spoken, on the basis of our judgments of the natures of human beings of various kinds. And there is a fundamental difference between speaking and writing. In the case of speaking, we can redesign the length or structure of the speech as we talk, in response to our perception of the reactions of the audience. This is not possible in a writing which, however cunningly constructed, can only take into account the varying natures and circumstances of its potential readers up to a point and in an approximate manner.

It should be emphasized that in the case of nonarithmetical measurement, the assessment of the mean between excess and deficiency cannot be determined with precision. This is why there are no moral absolutes in Plato or Aristotle. The point is easier to see in the case of Aristotle, who spells out the general framework of excess-mean-defect and defines virtue as a mean between two extremes without formulating the mean in each case as a categorical rule or absolutely valid act. But the same point holds good for Plato; more cautiously, it holds good for the Stranger in the *Statesman,* as will become entirely evident in the last part of the dialogue, when he criticizes the rigidity of law and praises the extreme flexibility of *phronēsis.* The mean may be just right, or precisely what is called for, without being exact or measurable arithmetically. To summarize, when judging that one line is excessive or defective, that is, more or less than some other line, we have to perceive, measure, and compare two lines. When judging that an action is excessive or defective, we see only one act, namely, the act judged to be excessive or defective. And we measure this act, not by a fixed ruler or standard metric, but by an unquantifiable act of judgment.

Measurement and Diaeresis

After reiterating that the art of measurement is concerned with length, shortness, excess, and deficiency, the Stranger suggests a division of that art into two parts (283c11–d5). He thus gives the initial impression that we are about to be launched on yet another diaeresis. Let us be guided by this impression for the moment.

Step 1. Metrētikē is divided into (*a*) the part concerned with relative measurement, literally, with measurement "in accord with the community of greatness and smallness with respect to one another," and (*b*) the part "concerned with the necessary being [*ousian*] of genesis" (283d7–9). This language is far from pellucid, and Young Socrates does not understand it (283d10). Part a evidently refers to all cases of measurement in which there are two items, one of which is greater in magnitude than the other. Taken in itself, this description is not identical with arithmetical measurement; after all, an excess is more than a defect, which is conversely less than what exceeds it. If part b is supposed to refer to the establishment of the fitting in the sense of the moderate or the mean, the latter is more than the deficient and less than the excessive. But in this passage the Stranger does not refer to the fitting or the mean; instead, he invokes that which is necessary to genesis. What is it that is generated in this type of measurement? Is it the mean between the two extremes, either of which must be modified in order for the middle term to come into existence?

The Stranger asks whether it is the case that by nature, the greater is greater than nothing other than the less, and the less is less than nothing other than the greater; Young Socrates replies in the affirmative (283d11–e2). The Stranger then asks whether we must also assert as genuinely existing (*hōs ontōs gignomenon*) what exceeds and falls short of the nature of the mean (*tēn tou metriou phusin*) in both speeches and deeds, and furthermore, whether bad and good persons differ most from us in this respect. Young Socrates is not so sure: "it seems to be so" (*phainetai*: 283e3–7). The compound question is more difficult than its predecessor, first because it requires a commitment concerning the "genuine existence" of excess and defect, a phrase that sounds as if it is attributing the same status to these terms as to mathematical entities like numbers, geometrical figures, and proportions, or perhaps even like the "greatest genera" of the *Sophist*. Second, the Stranger now asks about the application of the tripartite distinction to human beings. Young Socrates may wonder whether, by equating the good with the excess and the bad with the mean, the Stranger has not stripped "us" or the mean of both attributes.

There are then two kinds of judgments corresponding to the two different *ousias* or natures of "great and small." In the first kind, we judge two entities with respect to one another; in the second kind, we judge each of them with respect to the mean (283e8–13). This second structure of measurement is applicable not only to human virtue but to the entire domain of *technē*: to the technical activities and to their works (284a5–6). As is so often the case with Plato, we think of Pascal's famous distinction between the *esprit géométrique* and the *esprit de finesse*. The Stranger's point is that both are required in technical activity, and not at all that the *esprit géométrique* or arithmetical measurement alone applies to *technē* whereas the *esprit de finesse* is reserved for the measurement of virtue and vice. In fact, the Stranger is not directly concerned with good and evil, which he mentions in order to illustrate the domain of the tripartite structure of excess, deficiency, and mean.

Statesmanship and weaving are thus on a par, not simply from an analogical or paradigmatic standpoint, but directly, as what we may call "intentional activities," not in the Husserlian but in the everyday sense that human beings intend to accomplish some purposes by engaging in them. A six-foot line is greater than a four-foot line, regardless of the intentions of the human being who measures and compares these two magnitudes. But a garment must not only have certain dimensions, which are greater or smaller than the dimensions of some other garment; it must possess dimensions that are suitable to its function of serving as human clothing. This particular garment must fit this particular man or woman; it cannot be too large or too small and still be just right in the sense of fitting comfortably. Greater (too large) and smaller are here measured in two different ways. First, they are measurable with respect to some other garment, entirely apart from the question of who will wear these garments. Second, they are measurable relative to the person who intends to wear them. The person is thus the mean.

The example of clothing is interesting because arithmetical measurement must be employed when fitting someone with a garment. This shows us that the two kinds of measurement are not opposed but coordinate in intentional activity. Both are subordinate to the intention. Measurement implies intentionality, but also sound judgment or *phronēsis*. It would be an egregious instance of bad judgment to select a garment without determining its fit but simply by establishing its dimensions. The purely theoretical knowledge that a suit is size 42 must be supplemented by the knowledge that this is my size. But this latter knowledge is also purely theoretical unless I intend to buy a suit. One could pursue this analysis by saying that my intention to buy a suit is the expression of the deeper intention to conform to *nomos*. I do not intend to go naked in the streets or to wear women's clothing, or perhaps to wrap myself in a sheet.

It is worth emphasizing that whereas intentional activity is relative to an intending person, it is not subjective or relative in the sense of lacking cognitive determinateness. This is why the Stranger uses terms like *ousia, ontōs,* and *phusis* in conjunction with excess, deficiency, and mean, and not simply with respect to arithmetical magnitude. Even when the former set of terms is applied to actions that do not issue in arithmetically measurable artifacts, these actions are measurable with respect to the intentions that motivate them. We can also measure the intentions in the sense that we judge whether they are appropriate or inappropriate.

The question is not here whether there is some set of eternally true intentions that bind, or ought to bind, all human beings. The doctrine of the mean is rooted in the structure of intentionality that defines rational behavior. There is no doubt that the Stranger, like Plato, has a certain general conception of how human beings ought to live, or that this general conception would be repudiated by others as historically relative or culture-bound or in some other equivalent expression. But one cannot repudiate the Stranger's general conception without replacing it by another interpretation of intentional behavior. To repudiate is to judge, even in the extreme cases of the nihilist or the madman.

The Stranger makes something like the point I have just developed when he goes on to say that the difficulties associated with applying the mean are "not nonexistent but existent" (*ouch hōs ouk on all' hōs on*) for the practices of the weaver, statesman, or any other technician. "When they save the mean, everything that they have produced is good and noble" (284a6–b2). This applies to the cloak or blanket of the weaver as well as to the commands of the statesman; the mean is good and noble because it conforms to the structure of intentionality. There is, however, an ambiguity in the Stranger's terminology. "Good and noble" seem to refer here to the successful achievement of the mean by any *technē* whatsoever. But some means can be used to fulfill evil intentions. This ambiguity is connected to an earlier remark in which the Stranger apparently associated the good with the excessive and the evil with the deficient, in relation to "us," or the mean. No doubt he is referring to the unusually good or evil in comparison with ordinary persons. But the mean can be good and noble in accord with two different standards of measurement. Let us call these the standards of technical efficacy and moral virtue.

The Stranger does not develop these standards separately, nor is he centrally concerned with moral virtue, as I noted above. But it is at least implied here that the effective statesman is also one who issues morally virtuous commands, and in the concluding part of the dialogue, there can be no doubt that this is the Stranger's meaning. Stated differently, the achievement of the mean by the weaver who produces a good and noble garment is not the same as the achievement of the statesman who issues a morally virtuous command. The same distinction can be made with respect to the weaver's activity. A properly produced cloak is an expression of technical proficiency but also of political responsibility. A cloak is good and noble if it is well made and fits properly; but it is noble and good in another sense entirely because it allows the maker and the user to express their appropriate roles as citizens. This distinction is blurred by the Stranger's unexplained use of "good and noble," but it is implicit in the use of the expression "political *technē*."

We can now see that the Stranger should have provided us with a diaeresis of *technē* and in this way with a justification for applying the term to the statesman. The word *technē* has a very general meaning in Greek because it refers to a way of doing something that carries out the actor's intention and not merely to deeds that issue in separate artifacts. But as Socrates regularly insists, there are good or noble and evil or base ways in which to carry out one's intentions. In the *Protagoras,* Socrates applies the expression *technē politikē* to the great sophist, not to himself. He claims that virtue is knowledge but denies that it can be taught. In this case, however, moral virtue in general, and so political virtue in particular, or the knowledge of how to govern virtuously, is not a *technē* that can be taught, as Protagoras claims to do. If weaving is an appropriate paradigm of politics, as the Stranger claims (and so if he has captured the mean in model theory), then politics is a productive *technē* that can be taught. We thus seem to arrive at a fundamental difference between Socrates and the Stranger.

This difference, however, is not entirely unambiguous. Since the Stranger does not distinguish between the two senses of goodness and nobility, we would be justified in claiming that he is concerned primarily with efficacy rather than with moral virtue, which latter he refers to only by the way to indicate the range of the standard of the mean. Surely Socrates would be compelled to admit that the statesman must employ the metric of excess, deficiency, and the mean from the two distinct if related standpoints of efficacy and moral virtue. After all, virtue is hardly well served by inefficient statesmen. Socrates would no doubt insist that politics is inseparable from considerations of virtue and vice, but he is not in a strong position to maintain that there is no political *technē*, especially since he associates political knowledge with philosophy and himself employs the model of *technē* when investigating the nature of philosophical *epistēmē*.

In sum, we must ask whether there are not two senses of *to metrion*, corresponding to the difference between technical efficacy and moral virtue. Instead of raising this question, the Stranger makes a puzzling comparison between the topic of measurement and the treatment of nonbeing with respect to the sophist. This comparison casts doubt on the natural status of the metric of the mean, despite what the Stranger now refers to as its indispensability for the art of the statesman. We recall that the theme of measurement was introduced not as part of that *technē*, but in order to prevent Young Socrates from falling ill at some future time by doubting the necessity of all parts of the investigation thus far. The theme of measurement seemed to pertain to the *technē* of dialectic or training in philosophical investigation, not to the *technē* of politics. Is there some connection between the Stranger's exercising of Young Socrates and the political art itself?

"Is it not the case that, just as with respect to the sophist we constrained nonbeing to be [*prosēnankasamen einai to mē on*], since the *logos* had escaped us at that point, so now one must constrain the measurement of more and less to exist [*prosanankasteon gignesthai*], not only with respect to one another, but also with respect to the genesis of the mean?" (284b7–c1). For a detailed discussion of the Stranger's treatment of nonbeing, I refer the reader to my book, *Plato's Sophist: The Drama of Original and Image*. Suffice it to say here that the Stranger forced nonbeing into existence by deriving it from the already existing *genos* or *eidos* of otherness (*to heteron*). The essential point of his analysis is that everything exists and is intelligible by virtue of its formal structure; examples of the most important elements or "greatest kinds" are being, sameness, otherness, rest, and change. As these elements are independent in a way similar to the independence of the letters of the alphabet, each exists by virtue of sharing in the element of being (having this element in its formal structure); so too each is the same as itself by virtue of sharing in sameness and is other than the others by virtue of sharing in the element of otherness. But to be other than the others is not to be them, even while being itself.

Let us restrict ourselves here to the elements or kinds just mentioned. The otherness or nonbeing of each element is not the opposite of its sameness or being; the opposite of being is nihilation or "the altogether not," according to the Stranger. And we have refused to speak of this, in obedience to father Parmenides (*Sophist* 258e6ff). To be other than something is not to be opposite to it. So otherness is other than—but not opposite to—being. Nihilation cannot be an element, *eidos,* or *genos* because as such it would be something; it would exhibit formal properties or at least one formal property, namely, nothingness. But it is self-contradictory to speak of a form of nothingness, since a form is a look or presence, whereas nothingness is complete absence. I put to one side the question of whether this is a persuasive argument. One might contend, for example, that nothingness is indeed visible precisely by its absence, if only in contrast with the visibility of the present structural elements. But granting the Stranger's analysis, in what sense has he forced nonbeing to be?

This question is not even visible to those who insist upon treating the Stranger's doctrine of nonbeing as a prototype of the Aristotelian doctrine of predication. As it happens, the doctrine of predication is itself deficient or circular because it assumes that we know what "not" means before defining it syntactically, just as is done to this day in formal logic. "Not" means "not true," but what does the "not" in "not true" mean? But the Stranger's doctrine is not one of syntax; on the contrary, he intends it as the necessary precondition for a rational explanation of syntax in general and of negation in particular.

A predicate can be negated with respect to a subject because the formal structure of that predicate, or the formal property of which it is a name, is not present in the formal structure of the entity named by the subject-term. When we say something like "the cow is not brown," we do not mean to say that the cow is other than the property "brown," because cows and colors are incommensurable. We mean that the color "brown" is visible as not being present in the cow's skin; some other color is taking its place. Suppose that the cow is black. Black is different from or other than brown, but as so different, it excludes brown from the cow's skin, which it colors. We do not see brown as absent from the cow by looking at or by naming the color black. The absence of brown is noticed by looking at that absence, whether because we were looking *for* brown and failed to find it, or because the very vision of the cow's black skin is accompanied by a vision of the absence of all other colors, including brown.

It is an equivocation to say that when we identify something as not something else, we mean that the first is "other than" the second and nothing more. "Not to be" is much more fundamental than "other" because two things cannot be other than one another unless they already contain negation in their formal structure, and by "negation" I mean the ontological element, not the syntactic operation. If this were not so, there would be no ontological gaps in the intelligible world; absences would all be filled up with presences, namely, presences of otherness. Persons could not be absent from a room without some other person being present. "False" would not be the absence of truth but the presence of an equally positive or existent quality; more generally, not-p would not be the absence of p but the presence of something else, even when no "other" place-holder for p is visible. And so on.

In one last formulation, nonbeing is not a matter of syntax. The reverse is the case; syntax is possible because being and nonbeing exclude one another in a way that is more than otherness but less than opposition. And exactly the same analysis can be presented at the level of the greatest kinds themselves. We need the altogether not or nihilation, regardless of any injunctions issued by Parmenides not to mention it, in order to provide otherness with its negativing power. Two things can be other only because both are positively what they are; the negation cannot be produced simply by saying "this is not that." The "not" refers only secondarily or indirectly to their otherness; it refers primarily to the nihilation that separates this from that. We cannot talk nothingness out of existence.

Stated with excessive brevity, this is why the Stranger's solution to the problem of nonbeing is a technical trick. He has forced otherness to do the work of negation or of nihilation. By forcing nihilation to assume the identity of otherness, which is capable of combining with the element of being, the Stranger has forced nonbeing to be. But there was a much more straightforward procedure available to him. He could simply have ignored Parmenides and stated the obvious: words like *not* are intelligible because they are the name of a form that is present or visible as much as forms like being, sameness, otherness, rest, and change. That form is absence, which is itself the manifestation within the cosmos of the *nihil absolutum* or pure nihilation that is so abominated by rationalist philosophers because it is apparently not amenable to *logos*.

To say that the *nihil* exists seems to be a contradiction. But on this analysis, it is also a contradiction to say that the *nihil* does not exist. We avoid the contradiction by the simple and straightforward recognition that being and nihilation are both elements in the constitution of the whole, cosmos, or world. In order to admit what is staring us in the face, and also to avoid contradiction, however, we must pay a price. And that price is to give up a rational ontology or coherent, consistent, and complete doctrine of being and nothing.

This line of analysis will remind many readers of Heidegger's criticism of Platonism, but there is a crucial difference between the two. I agree with Platonism that being is presence. I further disagree with Heidegger's restriction, in keeping with the Eleatic tradition as introduced by father Parmenides, of thought to finite negation. When Heidegger talks of *das Nichts,* he is referring to Platonist otherness, namely, the otherness of a *Seiendes* or *on* (a determinate existent entity) from *Sein* or Being. Being is present in its absence only in the sense that it is concealed by another presence: the existent being. I am referring here to the presence of absence, not to the absence of Being. I am therefore not, like Heidegger, in principle reiterating the Hegelian thesis that Being and Nothing are the same. On the contrary, I regard them as separate.

I am sorry to have been required to introduce so abstruse a question into our pursuit of the statesman, but the requirement was enforced by the Stranger himself. The Stranger admits that he and Theaetetus "forced nonbeing to be" as a desperate expedient required by the imminent loss of the *logos.* But why does he now say that he and Young Socrates must force into existence the doctrine of the mean? The forcing of nonbeing was based on a technical trick, namely, the interpretation of otherness as negation. Is the requirement to assert the genuine existence of the mean also the construction of a technical trick designed to preserve the rationality of *technē* altogether? This does not seem plausible; no tricks are required in order to learn how to farm the soil, to manufacture tools, clothing, or works of fine art, or for that matter to command human beings. We learn from experience, motivated by need and desire; *technē* must already exist in order for tricks to be devised that facilitate its progress.

In contrast, it does make sense to say that the mean does not exist antecedently to our efforts to achieve it. The metric of excess, deficiency, and mean is natural to human activity; it is ingredient in the structure of an intentional act. But if one does not act, the structure remains in potency. In this case, the mean is a possibility, but it will not come into existence on its own, or even in the way that plants grow and animals reproduce. Whether we are making shoes, painting a picture, or ruling a city, success depends upon artificial genesis. And what we must produce in order to succeed is different in each instance of intentional activity. No doubt the difference is less in the production of shoes than in painting or ruling, but even there one must take into account the condition of the materials and the tools, the design of the shoe, aesthetic refinements, and so on.

A complete analysis of this point would require us to go beyond the confines of the *Statesman* and to investigate the difference between the Greek conception of *techne* as intentional activity and modern technology or mass production. I restrict myself here to a general observation. The intentional forcing into existence of the mean is represented by the machines of modern production, although obviously enough the intentions of modern women and men are not identical with those of the ancient Greeks. Mass production is the expression of a non-Greek conception of human existence, but it is nevertheless a conception that renders actual the structure of excess, deficiency, and mean that the Stranger attributes to *techne*, which I have in turn interpreted as intentional activity. The problem we are now studying is therefore not historically relative or bound to a particular epoch, although it takes on different forms at different stages of human history. When Heidegger, for example, refers to the machine as the exemplification of the will to power that is intrinsic to Western European metaphysics, alias Platonism, he is committing himself to the view that the problem manifested in the modern machine is already visible in the ancient plough or the potter's wheel, whether or not it is understood by the ancient philosopher.

I will mention two passages from ancient texts that support the claim that the ancient thinkers did understand the problem. In Thucydides' *History of the Peloponnesian War*, Bk. I, Ch. 71, Sec. 3, the Corinthian representative at the conference in Corinth just before the start of the war is made to say that the necessities of political change require technical innovation. It is necessary in politics "just as in *techne* always to master what comes next." The second text is in Aristotle's *Politics*, Bk. I, 1257b25ff: "The art of medicine pursues health without limit, and each of the arts pursues its end in an unlimited way (for they wish to accomplish this to the greatest possible extent); although with respect to the end they do not proceed in an unlimited way (for the end is a limit to all the arts)." If *techne* is emancipated from the metric of the mean in praxis, as distinct from production, it will not cease to be governed by that metric in its individual productions, but production itself will no longer be regulated by politics. Instead, politics will be regulated by production. The Corinthian is thus the unwitting spokesman for modernity, whereas Aristotle is the conscious representative of antiquity.

Heidegger is in my view certainly wrong to equate the ancients and the moderns as proto-Nietzscheans. The modification of nature by *techne* is not an expression of the will to power so long as it is regulated by the natural ends of human activity. Aristotle was wrong to link these ends with a cosmological teleology; in contrast, his distinction between practice and production makes it easier for us to perceive the natural limits of *techne* than does Plato's doctrine, in which practice and production are not separated. Whatever Plato may have intended, the Socratic distinction between demotic and philosophical virtue, that is, the identification of virtue with wisdom (*Republic* VI. 500d4–9), when joined with the Stranger's view of politics as a *technē* gives rise to the previously noted ambiguity concerning the two senses of goodness and nobility. The mean of efficacy is distinct from the mean of moral virtue; but if moral virtue is wisdom and wisdom is *epistēmē*, of which the paradigm is productive *technē*, then it is not easy to detect a principle by which to restrict the continuous exercise of effective action. *Technē* cannot be regulated by wisdom if wisdom is *technē*, or in other words if *technē* is univocal. This is why I wrote earlier that the Stranger owes us a diaeresis of the senses of *technē* that distinguishes wisdom from productive efficacy.

Plato assumes, whether in the *Statesman* or elsewhere, that moderation—and not just the technical mean—is intrinsic to rational (and so to intentional) activity. In other words, despite the difference between theoretical and moral excellence and regardless of the attribution of divine madness to the philosophical nature, it is assumed in the dialogues that philosophical sobriety will preserve the subordination of *technē* to political justice, the principle of moral virtue, or that the madness of philosophy, if entrusted with political rule, will ensure the subordination of madness to sobriety. But this is a gratuitous assumption, as is suggested by the history of the participation of philosophers in politics.

What one could call Platonism gives rise to two opposing pressures in the domain of politics. On the one hand, there is the pressure of explicit constraint, namely, constraint by sound judgment and doctrine of the desires of the unphilosophical part of the soul or human race. On the other hand, since political activity is itself productive, or in other words since citizens must be produced, and since according to Plato all actual cities are not merely corrupt but sick, the door is opened to an infinite progression of philosophical attempts to produce a just city, attempts that fall sick as soon as they are actualized. This problem does not arise for Aristotle because he distinguishes first between theoretical and practical wisdom, thereby doing away with the need for philosophers to rule, and second between practice and production, thereby excluding the notion of the production of citizens. The political *technē* is for him concerned with the mean of efficacy and is subordinate to the mean of moral virtue. Otherwise put, the corruptness of actual cities must be countered by habituation in virtue, not by philosophical doctrine.

No doubt Aristotle's doctrine has its own defects, one of which is circularity (since only already virtuous cities can institute and preserve the habituation in virtue). But that is a topic for another investigation. We are attempting to understand the Stranger's remark in the *Statesman* that one must force into existence the metric of the mean. That this is not simply a figure of speech or literary ornamentation is quite evident from the Stranger's reference to the previous discussion of nonbeing. It is not enough, in other words, to force nonbeing as such to be. One must also force each instance of the ontological form of nonbeing (in the Stranger's account, otherness) into existence. This is especially obvious in the case of *technē*. Whereas we cannot act successfully except by bringing the mean into existence, if we do not act, the mean will not exist. And action is the exertion of force onto nature. It is not, however, an expression of what Nietzsche calls will to power, since it is perfectly reasonable for human beings to modify nature in order to exist, to flourish, and so to live well and even to be happy or blessed. The personal experience of unhappiness, or the perception of the unhappiness of others, is not a secure basis for the inference that the pursuit of happiness is an illusory mask by which we conceal from ourselves the underlying chaos.

All this being so, as the Stranger puts it, "without our agreement on this point, it is not possible either for the statesman or for anyone else who has knowledge about actions [*tas prakseis*] to exist indisputably" (284c1–3). Because the metric of the mean is intrinsic to the structure of intentional activity, if there is no such metric, then there is no such activity. And in this case, there is obviously no knowledge about *tas prakseis* or practico-production, of which politics is one type. Young Socrates accordingly agrees that they must proceed here as in the discussion of nonbeing. The Stranger then replies that this deed will be much greater than the forcing of nonbeing (284c4–6). Why is this? He does not explain, but the implication is evident that practico-production—and not just politics—is harder to understand than the structure of formal intelligibility. The ontological problem of nonbeing is resolved in one step by its equation with otherness. But the definition of intentional activity as inseparable from the metric of the mean must be confirmed for each type of practice. Furthermore, there is the problem of the difference between the mean of efficacy and the mean of moral virtue.

The Stranger says that eventually we shall require what has just been said about the mean in order to demonstrate or to exhibit it precisely (*pros tēn peri auto takribes apodeiksin*: 284d1–2). But for our present purposes, we can assume that we have spoken "nobly and sufficiently" (*kalōs kai hikanōs*), or in other words in accord with the technical mean of efficacy, inasmuch as the arts actually exist—which they could not do if the metric of the mean did not exist (284d2–8). This is obviously circular reasoning, since it assumes what remains to be proven about the nature of *technē*. Nonetheless, proofs must proceed in accord with the evidence when it is a question of empirical fact and not just logical deduction. We know enough about the arts on the basis of everyday experience to assume the reasonableness of the *logos* about the mean.

The Stranger now in effect repeats step 1 of the diaeresis (stated at 284d4–5), but with a different version of the right-hand element. Previously it was identified as concerned with the *ousia* that is necessary for genesis. By "genesis," the Stranger refers to production or to intentional (= technical) activity, not to nature. The right-hand element in the second version includes all *technai* that measure "with respect to the mean, the fitting, the timely, what is required [by a given situation], and whatever dwells in the middle between two extremes" (284e1–8). His point emerges if we put together the two statements: every technical genesis brings into existence a mean in the various senses of the term just indicated, which would not actually exist without an intentional productive act but which is not merely contingent upon this or that action because it belongs to the essence of activity altogether or as such.

Young Socrates observes, and the Stranger agrees, that the two kinds of measurement—arithmetical and nonarithmetical—are extensive and diverse. The Stranger adds that there is a coincidence between the observation of clever persons (*kompsoi* is normally pejorative in Plato) to the effect that measurement is concerned with everything (*pero pant' esti ta gignomena*) and what he and Young Socrates have just established. And yet, there is a difference between our results and the remark by the clever ones. They are not accustomed to divide in accordance with forms, and so they put both kinds of metrics straightway into the same class, believing them to be the same (284e11–285a6). Apparently the Stranger regards the doctrine of the mean to be his own discovery; one should note that Aristotle's innovation amounts to a narrowing of the domain of this doctrine to ethical virtue.

Oddly enough, the Stranger breaks off what seemed to be another diaeresis and shifts instead to a general praise of division in accordance with looks or formal differences. There follows a brief statement that is strikingly similar to Socrates' accounts of eidetic analysis in dialogues like the *Phaedrus* and *Philebus*. We cannot rest content with the isolated perception of community or difference but must articulate the community of forms into its differences and conversely bind together dissimilarities into likenesses of form (285a7–c2). I want to emphasize that, just as in the case of the diaereses themselves, there are no methodological procedures for seeing or perceiving communities and differences; instead, the method consists in seeing or perceiving how to collect and separate.

This must mean that the looks or forms are not themselves brought into existence as is the mean between two extremes, which is determined in each case by the individual practitioner of a particular *technē*. Furthermore, the same complex form might be divided into various arrangements of its eidetic elements, depending on the intention of the diaeretician. What this passage does not explain is whether there is a natural look corresponding to the *technē* of the statesman or the sophist, or in other words whether the Stranger's general remark about the division and collection of forms is itself accurately illustrated by the diaereses generated by him in the two dialogues of which he is the protagonist.

Praise and Blame

At this point it could seem that the Stranger is bringing to a close the discussion of measurement and beginning a new section of his demonstration: "After this *logos,* let us take up another one concerning the very topics we have been investigating as well as every exercise in discussions of this kind" (285c4–6). In fact, the Stranger is about to review the question of appropriate length for pedagogical speech, and so whether we ought to praise or blame the very long and complex exercise as it has thus far unfolded. He is in other words continuing with his therapeutical administration to Young Socrates of an inoculation or spell against future doubt (cf. 279c9). There is no occurrence here of the formulaic *palin eks archēs* (although it should be noted that not every appearance of *palin* is formulaic in this sense). So we remain within the part of the dialogue devoted to measurement.

Just as students are interrogated about the letters making up a word for the sake of spelling as a whole rather than for the spelling of that single word, so too our investigation into the art of the statesman has been conducted in order that we might become better dialecticians (*dialektikōterois*) with respect to all things (285c8–d7). As we have now learned from our study of the dialogue, this training is not in *methodology* in the modern sense of the term. To divide and collect is to see natural differences and to organize them on the basis of human intentions. Intentions are the gateway from theory to practico-production or *technē.* In order to pass through the gateway from theory to practice, we must produce artifacts of various kinds, including laws—written and unwritten—or commands uttered for the sake of the generation of citizens.

Weaving is of no interest to any intelligent person for its own sake; we studied it because it illuminates something about the nature of politics (285d8–9). But we cannot conclude that weaving is a paradigm, whether in the sense of a model or an example, of politics. On the contrary, weaving and politics are both examples of some other model. As a first approach to this model, both arts provide defensive screens against nature for the ensouled human body. Looked at from another standpoint, however, both are examples of the concatenative arts, of which spelling is also an example. The concatenative arts could be said to provide defensive screens either for the soul, like spelling, or for the body, like weaving. The Stranger associates politics with weaving and spelling without discriminating between the two subclasses or identifying the genus as explicitly as I have just done. He therefore blurs the central ambiguity of politics; it seems to straddle the division between the arts that defend the soul and those that defend the body. Thus far in the dialogue, the Stranger has emphasized the connection between politics and the body, as is obvious from the examples of the captain and the weaver. In the last part of the dialogue, he will emphasize the soul.

It goes without saying that if human beings were disembodied souls, the art of politics would be radically different from its actual form, if indeed it existed at all. But it might exist as the art of psychic community. From the most general standpoint, there is something defective about the paradigms of the captain and the weaver; both are primarily concerned with the defense of the body rather than with the improvement or care of the soul. From the standpoint of how things actually are, however, the paradigms are useful because they illuminate something about the centrality of the body to politics. One could say that philosophy, poetry and the fine arts, the pure or mathematical sciences, and even religion are primarily directed toward the care of the soul. There is no doubt that these activities intersect with the care of the statesman, but there is also no doubt that they transcend this care. To give only one example, the philosopher is primarily concerned with the pure Ideas which are the same for all, not with the laws which are common only to him and his fellow citizens. As is illustrated both positively and negatively by the *Republic,* the city is concerned with one's own, and the principle of one's own is the body.

To say that the body is central to politics is not, however, to deny the relevance of politics to the soul. It is merely to insist upon the obvious; the soul is political through the instrumentality of the body. Even from this standpoint, the paradigms of the captain and the weaver are defective; in short, the closer we come to the soul, or the farther we move from the centrality of the body, the more inadequate are our paradigms. I believe that this is the deeper meaning of the Stranger's assertion that there are easily exhibited sensible likenesses of some things, but that "there is no image of the greatest and most honorable beings that is made clearly for the sake of humans" (285d9–286a2). There are images of the body that can be easily exhibited without recourse to *logos*, as, for example, in mirrors and on the surface of still water or in painting and sculpture. There are also images of the body politic, this time drawn in words, like the myth of the divine shepherd or captain of the cosmos. But images are tied to the body; there are no likenesses of incorporeal forms because any presumed reflection or representation of such a form is just the presentation of that very form.

I therefore wish to suggest that what underlies the strange fluctuations in the argument of the *Statesman*—as well as the many errors, detours, repetitions, and apparently excessive detail—is that the political art is directed to the soul through the instrumentality of the body, and so that there are as many paradigms or exhibitions of sameness within otherness of the political art as there are bodily activities. The statesman is a defective image of the philosopher in the following sense: the philosopher is concerned with the whole and so with the body, but from the standpoint of the soul. The statesman is concerned with the soul, but from the standpoint of the body.

We are right to approach the art of politics via the body, but in the last analysis we cannot understand this art, or the body, except on the basis of an understanding of the soul. The statesman must understand the soul from the standpoint of the city, and this is an inadequate understanding of the soul. This means that in order to understand the city, and so the statesman, we must be outside or beyond both. The understanding of politics does not fall within the provenance of the statesman, odd though that may sound. It falls within the provenance, and I mean the extra-political provenance, of the philosopher. The multiplicity and so the dissimilarities of the images of the statesman can be reduced to community if not to unity by philosophy and by philosophy alone; that is to say, by *logos*. So long as the philosopher tells myths about politics, he or she is engaging in political rather than philosophical discourse. This is not to deny that philosophers may need to speak in myths to one another and to themselves when *logos* is defective or impossible. In sum, nothing that I have said here is intended as an assertion that a philosophical understanding of politics is possible, if by such an understanding one means a complete and coherent *logos*. In my view, there is no such *logos* of any totality, whether it be the cosmos, the city, or the individual soul.

According to the Stranger, the bodiless things, which are the most beautiful and the greatest, cannot be exhibited by perceptible images but only by *logos* (286a5–7). We may modify this statement as follows: if they can be exhibited at all, it must be by *logos*. But there is no dialogue dedicated to the philosopher; as to the hunt for the statesman, it is conducted by myths and images, including some that masquerade as *logoi*. The Stranger is like Socrates in that both engage in advertisements for the excellence of *logos*, dialectic, and the diaeresis of pure forms, but neither of them actually gives us a detailed example of these desiderata. The unexamined problem that underlies all of the Platonic dialogues is precisely the possibility of philosophy as it is described explicitly by the main interlocutors within the dialogues and as it is represented through the eikastic form of the dialogues themselves, which are embodied *logoi*.

The Stranger now includes himself among those who were, as he says, annoyed by the long speeches about weaving, cosmic reversal, and nonbeing, and this is why we have taken up the issue of measurement (286b4–c3). Note the emphasis in this context on the need to remember (285c2–3, 286b5, c5, d1). What we must remember above all is the reason that led the Stranger to speak at such length; this will enable us to praise or blame his speeches on the basis of the criterion of the fitting (*to prepon:* 286c5–d2). Presumably the reason to which the Stranger refers is that he has been training Young Socrates in dialectics (285d4–7). As we have now seen, "dialectic" is employed here in an extended sense to fit the investigation of body-connected topics.

The Stranger seems to overlook this aspect of his speech and to focus instead on diaeresis. In so doing, he also modifies his account of the mean or the fitting. It is our intention and not the neutral or technical calculation of the mean between two extrema that determines the fitting. The Stranger mentions three intentions and three corresponding senses of the fitting in increasing order of importance: (1) the intention to please, (2) the intention to resolve a problem quickly, and (3) "by far the most important and first is to honor [*timan*] the method itself that is capable of division according to forms" (286d4–9). Once again the Stranger refers to honor, thereby indicating that the method cannot testify to its own excellence or appropriateness. Honor belongs to the domain of intentions and purposes or ends; it is this domain that grounds *technē* and consequently method as well. It is the unity of gnostics and practico-production.

Those who object to the length of our speeches must therefore show how shorter speeches could have made those who hear them "better dialecticians" (*dialektikōterous:* 287a3). Provided that this term is understood in the light of the Stranger's own procedures, and not as a synonym for diaeresis, we may concur with his judgment.

CHAPTER EIGHT

Nomos

Possessions, Servants, and Regimes

WE come now to the last part of the dialogue: "Enough of this [namely, measurement], if your opinion is the same as mine. Let us go back again [*iōmen palin*] to the statesman and apply to him the previously discussed paradigm of weaving" (287a6–b2). This paradigm is applicable on the basis of the antecedent separation, thanks to diaeresis and its various modifications (including that of the myth), of the royal art from most of its kindred arts. The word translated as "kindred" is *sunnomoi,* which means literally "members of the same herd" or "co-feeders." The Stranger says that we have in fact separated the king from those *sunnomoi* that deal with herds (*tas agelas*). We are left with the arts that have a claim to be causes or co-causes with respect to the city, and these must now be treated by diaeresis (287b4–8). As usual, he will proceed in what seems to be an indirect manner.

The Stranger's metaphor suggests that there is a single "herd" of causes, namely, of commanding arts that issue in the genesis of living beings. This metaphorical herd can be divided into two main segments: (1) arts that deal with herds in the literal sense, and (2) arts that deal with cities. This distinction corresponds approximately to the division of tending into nurturing and caring. Nurturing can itself be divided into breeding and feeding. One might therefore expect caring to be divisible into two analogous segments. But if this were the case, we could immediately distinguish the king from those who challenge his title. These challengers include two distinct groups, referred to at 287b7 as "co-causes and causes." This expression in turn refers back to 281e7–282a5, as supplemented with 281b3–5. In the diaeresis of weaving, we found that cleaners and repairers challenged the weaver's claim to be the exclusive cause of clothing (281b3ff). Subsequently weaving was demoted to the status of subdivision of clothesmaking; the main division of clothesmaking was into co-causes, those who produce the tools used in clothesmaking, and causes, adorning (including cleaning and mending) and woolworking.

The arts listed as co-causes may be designated as external rivals to the king, whereas those falling under the rubric of causes must be designated as his internal rivals. This latter class is obviously ambiguous; if "adorners" are actually among the causes of the city, then they are not simply rivals but equal partners of the king. In this case there is no single art of the statesman. If then diaeresis is a fitting method at this juncture, it must separate off the internal and external rivals to the statesman. Assuming that "care" (*epimeleia*) is a univocal term as applied to politics, then we must isolate one single commanding art directed to the genesis of living beings that cares for these beings as citizens. And to the extent that the other arts, internal as well as external, are, so to speak, "citizens," they too must all fall under the care of the statesman.

If then we have been carefully following the details of the argument, it will come as no surprise when the Stranger says that it is hard to cut into two parts the "co-causes and causes"; otherwise, this expression is unintelligible. The Stranger assures Young Socrates that the reason for this difficulty will be evident as we proceed, but that we cannot at the moment employ the normal method of diaeresis. Instead of dividing into twos, we will proceed as do those who sacrifice an animal by cutting "limb by limb" (*kata melē*); this is as close as we can come to the desideratum of bisection (287b10–c5). The reference to cutting limb by limb reminds us of *Phaedrus* (265e1ff), where Socrates is describing the cutting of things "according to their forms, at the natural joints [*kat' arthra, hēi pephuken*], and trying to break no part in the manner of a bad butcher." Not even a good butcher practices the bisection of diaeresis; as to cutting at the joints, both butcher and priest must deviate from this procedure when they carve open the carcass. As is obvious, furthermore, both the butcher and the priest deal with corpses. Both diaeresis and the method of collecting and dividing by forms are inappropriate for exhibiting the animal as a living whole.

In the division we are about to perform, we shall be concerned with the classification of possessions, not of living beings. Our intention is to eliminate rivals to the king, and the first step in doing this is to attach the toolmakers or co-causes of the city to a classification of nonpolitical arts. The Stranger thus alludes initially to the earlier diaeresis of clothesmaking, in which we separated toolmakers from adorning and woolworking. So here toolmakers must be separated off into one class; "without these neither the city nor the art of politics could come into existence" (287c7–d4). This reconfirms the treatment of the city as an artifact. But the toolmakers make the tools, not the city. In other words, they are, together with their tools, possessions of the king. The king uses these tools indirectly by commanding them to be used in the construction of the city.

It might plausibly be said that everything is a tool for producing something or other (287d7–e1). If this is so, then of course it would be impossible to distinguish between toolmakers and some other class. The suggestion is quite interesting in its own right, especially as it seems to confirm the thesis that everything in the city is a possession of the king. But the Stranger does not comment directly on the suggestion. Instead he shifts to the list of possessions (*ktēmata*), in which those used for a genesis are distinguished from six other kinds, of which the first is explicitly said not to be used for the sake of a genesis, like tools, but rather for the protection (*sōterias*) of things that have been produced by the demiurgic arts (287e1–6).

The reference to the demiurgic crafts is a reference back to 279c7, where we began the diaeresis of "everything that we make by the demiurgic crafts and that we possess." That class was divided initially into "things for the sake of doing something" and "defenses [*amuntēria*] to avoid undergoing something." All possessions in this diaeresis are manufactured; their use is active or passive. We were concerned with passive artifacts; as a result, we arrived at weaving, a passive model of the political art that excludes the art of making war but not that of making instruments for self-defense. In the present list, all items are either manufactured or modified by human labor. Passive artifacts are presumably not tools, if tools are for the sake of a production. Tools are the first item, and the list includes all things that furnish the bodies of things (Plato has no single word for "matter"); these "raw materials" as I will call them could be said to be prepared, for example, by mining, forestry, and so on, for the sake of a genesis.

The list must therefore be constructed independently of the previous distinction between action and passion. It is a list of the possessions of citizens, and hence of the city that is commanded by the king. If commanding is possessing, then all possessions of the city are possessions of the king. Rather than to try to separate the art of the king from all the rest as the last step in a diaeresis, we would be better advised to begin with the royal art as the *summum genus* and to articulate the descending hierarchy of the arts in terms of the various political functions. Although it is plausible to infer from the Stranger's presentation that commanding is possessing, this is not how he describes his procedures. According to him, the purpose of the list must be to help us arrive at the king by a series of separations, not all of which are diaereses in the technical sense of the term. A crucial consequence of the new list is that the king now includes among his possessions tools used for making war, although the Stranger never makes this explicit. For him to do so, obviously, would be to expose his paradigm of weaving as entirely inadequate. There is then an oversight, intended or otherwise, in the statement at 287a6ff that we are about to apply our paradigm of weaving to the task of identifying the art of the statesman.

Tools count as the first kind of possession; in particular, they are possessions that we make in order to bring into existence something other than the tools. For example, the producer of spindles makes these in order that weavers may make woolen clothing; but the spindlemaker does not (at least in that identity) make woolen clothing. Our list is thus seen to possess one item consisting of tools and six items of what I will call nontools, inasmuch as they do not produce anything. This is the first of three lists of seven items each that the Stranger will propound in what is the seventh part of the dialogue that deals with the training of Young Socrates by the Stranger (and in this enumeration I exclude the prologue, which is not part of that training). The lists are of possessions, servants, and political regimes, respectively. It should be stated that there is an ambiguity in the list of regimes because there is no name to describe one of the two forms of democracy arising from the distinction between law-abiding and lawless regimes. The Stranger will thus speak of five names of actual regimes, but the lawless democracy makes a sixth and returns to the discussion in due course. I repeat that servants and regimes could also be regarded as possessions of the king.

Now we are ready to inspect the list of possessions, which goes like this (287d6–289a5):

1. tools (what is an *organon* of something: 287e5)
2. receptacles
3. vehicles
4. defensive bulwarks (*problēmata*)
5. toys
6. raw materials
7. nourishment

Item 4 appeared in the third step of the diaeresis of productions and possessions. Item 5 consists of the artifacts of painting and music; these are manufactured "solely for our pleasure" (288c3). Items 2 through 6 should contain all possessions that are not tools and so are not manufactured or possessed in order to make something else. The Stranger presumably considers raw materials as passive rather than active; we use them to make "synthetic forms" out of what has not been combined (288e3–4). Something of this sort can also be said of nourishment, which we use for our self-construction. Item 7 refers to nurturing, and so to farming, hunting, gymnastic, medicine, and cooking (288e3–5). These are now considered in such a way as to exclude them, along with the other items in the list, from the political, commanding, or possessing art.

In general, there is some overlap, either explicit or implied, between this list of possessions and the previous division. But we cannot superimpose one list onto the other, nor is it easy to see how the items we are inspecting would be sorted out under the classes in the diaeresis. The diaeresis of artifacts was constructed with the intention of isolating the art of weaving. In the list, weaving is included under the class of the production of defensive bulwarks in item 4. Manufactured possessions can be classified by more than one schema. Furthermore, the thesis that tools are always employed for the sake of a genesis is never explained or adequately established. In the original diaeresis of manufactured possessions, the artifacts employed for defense or for preventing an action are as much tools as the artifacts employed for the sake of doing some deed. In sum, the diaeresis was intended to produce a paradigm of the statesman; the list does not have that role, except in the negative sense that it eliminates possible rivals of the statesman. Not all divisions (see 287b8: *diaireteon*) are diaereses.

As usual, the Stranger has no sooner presented us with the appearance of precision than he is forced to modify it. Nearly all possessions were mentioned or allowed for except tame animals. This class obviously corresponds to the collection of classes of herd animals who are commanded by human beings (see 261d3ff). We recall the Stranger's original objection to the division of this collection into the two segments of human and brute herds. In the course of our analysis, we found that his objection was unwarranted. The Stranger virtually admits this by dividing tame animals into herds and slaves (289b8). Herds refer to brutes; if all citizens are the possession of their commander, then they are all slaves. But even if they are not, the distinction between brute and human is employed in the division of possessions. It is also immediately pertinent to the task of separating commanders who are not statesmen from those who are. In order to arrive at this diaeresis, we would have to rectify the earlier error of referring to the nurture of all herds, including tame humans.

Before arriving at this distinction, the Stranger summarizes the items on the list. In so doing, he presents us with a new puzzle. Initially the Stranger proceeded directly from tools to the second item on his list, receptacles. Now, however, he distinguishes between "the firstborn form [*to prōtogenes eidos*], which ought in all justice to have been placed first," and "after this, tool *[organon]*, receptacle, vehicle, defensive bulwark, toy, nurture" (289a9–b2). This seems quite clearly to be a correction of the list; tools are now the second item. But what is the "firstborn form" that the Stranger unjustly omitted in constructing the list a moment ago? Let us return to 287c10ff with this problem in mind.

The Stranger begins by referring to toolmakers, who are distinguished from woolworkers in the diaeresis of clothesmaking at 281e7ff. These are here referred to as co-causes; I have designated them as external rivals to the king. The Stranger says now that their work is not to be attributed to the political *technē* (287d4), although the city could not exist without it. He then adds that it will be hard to separate this family (*genos*) from "the others" because whoever says that each existing thing is a tool for something or another seems to speak persuasively. This must mean that it is hard to separate toolmakers from nontoolmakers, for example from woolworkers or statesmen. But even granting that everything is a tool or instrument for generation, why should this cause a difficulty for the separation of political from nonpolitical generation? It is true that we have to separate off the adorners or fullers (cleaners, menders, and so on) from those who make tools. But this should not be difficult because they work on the cloth itself rather than make tools for such work.

Tools are employed either to do something or to prevent something from being done. They are, so to speak, either active or passive. If every being is a tool (see *Sophist* 247d8–e4), there are no nontools, but one may still separate the active from the passive families. If commands are tools used for making others act, then all those who obey these commands are passive, regardless of whether they or their tools do something or prevent something from being done. The Stranger does not express himself in this manner, but the suggestion is entirely compatible with his argument. It also allows us to identify the firstborn form as the class of commands or active tools that are the possessions of the statesman, produced by him to carry out his intentions, whether themselves active or passive, offensive or defensive.

The tending of herds, whether as nurturing or caring, and so of brutes or humans, was a division of the commanding branch of the gnostic arts. We can bring together the paradigm of the captain and that of the weaver by identifying commanding as a type of toolmaking. We would then require an entirely different diaeresis from the ones supplied by the Stranger. The new diaeresis would present the human animal as a toolmaker, in other words, as *homo faber*. We could then divide tools into two kinds, commands and instruments for carrying out commands. I will not insist that Plato intends us to reproduce this line of reasoning. The suggestion I am making is a plausible inference from the evidence of the Stranger's argument, which requires us to think through the underlying connection of a series of terms that includes, among others, the following pairs: shepherd and captain, captain and weaver, toolmaker and woolworker, active and passive tools, commanding and producing.

Granted the difference between commanding and producing, yet bearing in mind that commands are for the sake of generating something, it is natural to arrive at the insight that commands are not the genus of which tools are a species, but that they are themselves a species of the genus of tools. The division of the epitactic arts is thus a diaeresis of toolmaking. If the statesman falls under commanding rather than pure knowing or gnostics, he too must be a toolmaker. And this remains true even if we regard the statesman as straddling the division between gnostics and practico-production. Another advantage of this way of looking at commands is that it illuminates the distinction between them and the intentions that produce them. Intentions are the activity of *phronēsis*, which is not subject to diaeresis because it has no inner structure. *Phronēsis* is the toolmaking activity; once it acts, we can divide or analyze the structure of the action. But the actor is distinct from each of its actions, which are not bound by the laws, whether of *technē* or of the political regime.

Two final observations: in order to keep the number of items on the list at seven, the Stranger omits raw materials from his summary. And in referring to "the idea of coinage," which includes seals and stamps, as an example of items not yet included in his list, the Stranger says that its members can be dragged into one line or another "by force" (289b7). Just as in the case of nonbeing and the measurement of the mean, we are free to impose our will onto the articulation of experience; how we articulate this experience is dependent on our intentions. Since seals and stamps are a metaphor for Platonic forms, the implications of the passage just cited are both evident and should raise unorthodox thoughts in the mind of the reader.

Since the possession of tame animals is subsumed under the tending of herds, which is listed under nurture, we are left with slaves, or the tending of human beings who are neither herd animals nor citizens (289a7–8, b8–c2). The Stranger then links slaves with servants and prophesies (*manteuomai*) that those who dispute with the king for his very fabric (in other words, the city) will come to light here, just as the spinners and carders disputed with the weavers. All other disputants can now be rejected as co-causes, and so it follows that spinners and carders are the internal rivals to the weaver and serve as the paradigm for servants and slaves. This is interesting on two counts. First, the Stranger refers us back to the very tangled diaereses of weaving and clothesmaking (281a2ff). Carders, makers of the warp and woof, menders and fullers (including cleaners), as well as toolmakers, were all identified as co-causes of the art of weaving (*sunaitias:* 281c4). In the diaeresis of clothesmaking that followed from an anticipatory step at 281d5, the toolmakers (the makers of spindles, shuttles, and so on) were identified as co-causes, and the washers, menders, and fullers were included among the causes (281e1–282a5). In this diaeresis, carding and spinning were subclasses of woolworking, which is itself a branch of the causes. Carding was discarded as the separation of threads; spinning or combining was divided into the making of the warp and the woof on the left-hand side and plaiting or weaving on the right.

In sum, spinners and carders are listed among the co-causes at 281a8ff but among the causes at 281d5ff. In the later and more detailed passage, they are included together with cleaners, menders, and so on under the rubric of fullers. So there is some confusion in the Stranger's analysis of weaving as to exactly how he wishes to separate co-causes from causes. On the whole, however, his line of analysis culminates in the separation of toolmakers from producers, which latter class includes all forms of preparing the cloth, including all versions of fulling or adorning such as cleaning and mending. But now the fullers have been dropped without explanation. It is true that in the diaeresis they were also rejected, but only after having been separated off from the class of causes. Those who prepare the cloth participate directly in the production of clothing as fullers do not. But whether we count them as co-causes or causes (and the Stranger does both), they are certainly an example of the class of servants and slaves, and hence they should be lurking somewhere in the interstices of the passage we are now studying.

The second interesting point in this passage is that the rivals to the king should finally be located in the class of servants and slaves rather than among free people. This raises the following possibilities. (1) The king is one-half, or belongs to one-half, of a division of the class of servants and slaves. From this standpoint, kings, shepherds, captains, and so on are the servants or slaves of those whom they command because they must spend all of their time in caring for them. (2) The class of human beings must be divided into servants and slaves on the left and free people on the right. We would then have to divide the subclass of free people in order to find the king. (3) All human beings except for the king are servants and slaves. In this case, however, why are human beings not contained as a separate item in the list of possessions? Question: In which segment of any of these diaereses is the philosopher to be found?

However this is to be resolved, the Stranger is about to provide us with another list of seven items, this time of servants and slaves. Perhaps the reader will indulge me in another amusing calculation. There are seven cases of divisions, whether diaereses or lists, in the *Statesman*. These are: (1) the diaeresis of the *technai* (ten or eleven steps, depending on whether we follow the longer or the shorter way); (2) the diaeresis of everything done and acquired (eleven steps); (3) the diaeresis of clothesmaking (five steps); (4) measurement (two kinds); (5) possessions (seven kinds); (6) servants or slaves (seven kinds); (7) regimes (seven kinds). If we allow ourselves the liberty of following the shorter diaeresis of ten steps, we have seven diaereses or divisions with a total of forty-nine distinct stages, or seven times seven. The choice between eleven and ten in the diaeresis is a typical Platonic maneuver, in which precision, even the precision of a joke, is blurred just sufficiently to leave a shadow of ambiguity over the appearance of clarity.

We now approach more closely those who have survived our long process of elimination. The Stranger sharpens his terminology by using the term *huperētēs* (servant) to stand for the entire class. Here is the division:

(1) One type, called "greatest" to define the degree of servitude, consists in purchased slaves; these are opposite in function or condition to the royal art (or so I understand the reference to "the opposite of what we suspected" in 289d6–e2). It is a striking feature of the list of servants that it contains no reference to enslaved prisoners of war. I noted earlier that the paradigm of weaving fails to express the martial activities of the statesman's art, which we ourselves must infer from the tangled threads of the exposition.

(2) Free men who undergo voluntary servitude; these are all types of merchants who exchange goods for profits and who travel on land and sea (a rebuke to the original diaeresis, which classified human beings as exclusively land animals: nature is again subordinated to *technē*: 289e4–290a3).

(3) Wage earners, who are prepared to serve anyone who will pay them (290a4–6).

(4) The family (*ethnos*) of heralds, clerks, and other such officials (290a8–b6). Immediately after identifying this family, the Stranger interjects the query: Surely his prophecy that the king would be found "somewhere here" was not a dream; and yet it would be odd to try to find him among the servants (290b7–c1). So it is not quite clear whether we are separating off servants from the king or heading toward the king as a unique type of servant.

(5) We must now draw closer to the remainder of the class of servants; presumably the smaller number includes types that are harder to identify than the previous kinds. First we see those who possess a sort of servile knowledge (*epistēmēs*) about prophecy (*mantikēn*). The Stranger himself has just delivered a prophecy; we must presume that he would not classify himself among

the servile hermeneuts of the gods. This suggests that there should be a diaeresis of the mantic art; something like it is supplied by Socrates in the *Phaedrus,* but the Stranger does not follow suit (290c4–7).

(6) The race (*genos*) of priests. They know how to give presents that are to the liking of the gods and how to satisfy our wishes by asking the gods for good possessions on our behalf. This account of priestly duties reminds us of Diotima's description in the *Symposium* of the intermediate hermeneutic function of Eros. But the Stranger is very far from Eros. He identifies these functions of sacrificing and requesting as servile (290c8–d3).

The Stranger goes on to say that we are now on the scent of the king. Both prophets and priests exhibit pride in their actions and acquire a solemn reputation because of their magnitude. So it is plausible to regard them as rivals of the king. And indeed, the Stranger adds, the king of Egypt must be a priest; one also finds a link between priestly and political duties in Greece (290d5–e8). Prophets and priest are thus related, but nevertheless they are distinguished by this comment. The Stranger then says that we must investigate these elected kings and priests and their servants, as well as another large crowd that is now visible (291a1–3). In this transition to the seventh type of servant, the Stranger suggests that we are not yet finished with type 6 and presumably also type 5. But nothing more is said about them in the dialogue.

(7) The large crowd is a *pamphulon genos,* a race of many families, as we might translate this expression. The Stranger claims to have initial difficulties in discerning their looks and power because they are changing back and forth into one another. Many resemble lions, centaurs, and other beasts of this sort; others resemble satyrs and the weak and wily beasts. The word translated as "wily" is *polutropoi,* applied by Homer to Odysseus. It is worth noting that Socrates was said to resemble a satyr and that he frequently identifies himself with Odysseus in the dialogues by means of quotations from the *Odyssey.* As if to elicit this recollection in us, Plato has the Stranger refer to his young interlocutor by name at precisely this point: "O Socrates, I have just now identified the men" (291a8–b4). This is the first time he has mentioned Young Socrates' name since 284e11.

Young Socrates asks for the identification of this odd vision, and the Stranger, after observing that it is ignorance that makes things look odd, says that the troop he sees are those sophists who are most experienced in the affairs of the city and who are the greatest sorcerers. It will be difficult but necessary to separate them from the genuine (*ontōs on*) statesmen and kings (291b5–c5). As will be made clear later, the Stranger is referring here to the rulers of actual cities, not to sophists like Protagoras or other professors of wisdom. Because this is not explained at the outset, the Stranger's turn to the question of types of regime seems abrupt. Before making this turn, he does not further clarify whether the seven kinds of servants qualify as possessions. The transition from possessions to servants by way of the example of tame animals suggests that this may be the case. Even if it is, however, servants, as tame human beings, constitute a class of possessions of sufficient importance to merit their own list. Another open question is whether servants as a whole are a family of images of some set of originals, of which the statesman is just one type.

Why does the Stranger take up the seven kinds of regime at this point? To answer this question, we have to look ahead. The Stranger will identify six kinds of actual regime, all of which are imitations of the seventh, which is alone genuine but which exists only in speech, not in deed. The ruler of the seventh regime must then be the only genuine statesman. Otherwise put, only the genuine regime is ruled by a genuine statesman; the other rulers must be sophists, who were identified yesterday in the conversation with Theaetetus as magicians and masters of disguise, but who nevertheless deny the existence of images or themselves claim to be originals. How can the seventh ruler and the seventh city be the only genuine ones when they do not exist? The answer must be that they exist as the paradigm, in the sense of the model, of the actual but defective or eikastic cities.

The Stranger will distinguish between legitimate and illegitimate regimes but, paradoxical as it may sound, his analysis leads to the conclusion that even existing legitimate cities are not genuine in the sense that they are not ruled by the genuine statesman. The genuine statesman is not a person or a human being at all, but rather *phronēsis*. The genuine regime is therefore not a regime at all because it lacks a constitution or both written and unwritten laws. The Stranger will defend the paradoxical conclusion that *nomos* is the image of *phronēsis*, or that the rule of law, although tautologously legitimate, is what he calls in the *Sophist* a fantasm, namely, an inaccurate image that is so proportioned as to appear to be accurate to the human eye.

The list of regimes begins at 291c8. The Stranger starts with the arithmetical principle of the number of rulers. He asks Young Socrates: "Is it not the case that monarchy is for us one of the kinds of political rule?" Young Socrates affirms that this is so, and the two further agree with no delay that two more such kinds are "the domination of the few" (*tēn hupo tōn oligōn dunasteian*) and "the rule by the multitude [*plēthous*], the name of which is democracy" (291c8–d8). What I have called the arithmetical principle could also be designated as the commonsense criterion; it leaps directly to the eye and was a commonplace in ancient Greek political discussion. So too with the next extension of the list: "Investigators today refer to forced and voluntary obedience as well as to poverty and wealth together with law and lawlessness as these come to exist in the aforementioned regimes, thereby dividing two of them into two kinds for each; they call monarchy by two names as though it had received two forms: tyranny and kingdom." The second division is of the city that is ruled by the few; its parts are called aristocracy or oligarchy. Democracy is the only regime not to undergo a change in name, whether the poor rule the rich by force or with their consent, and legally or illegally. There is, nevertheless, a difference between a law-abiding and a lawless democracy. We thus arrive at six types of actual regimes but only five distinct names (291e1–292a3).

It is very striking that in this discussion, the Stranger's analysis is entirely orthodox, unlike the peculiar categories and neologisms that he produced in his previous diaereses and classifications. This is especially obvious in the case of democracies, all of which are traditionally called by the same name. The investigation of types of regime is not amenable to the innovation required by the investigation of the art of the statesman. It is not hard to understand why this should be so. The classification of regimes proceeds according to very natural principles, which have just been mentioned by the Stranger. But this classification tells us nothing about the art of the statesman. For example, the distinction between one, few, or many rulers does not explain to us what these rulers are to do or what commands they are to issue in order to make the city endure and flourish.

In response to the Stranger's questioning, Young Socrates sees nothing to make us deny that any of the regimes just noticed is correct (*orthēn*) or right. This answer is unsatisfactory to the Stranger, who refers back to the original diaeresis of *epistēmē* and asks whether we are to abide by it. He reminds Young Socrates of their agreement that the royal principle was a kind of knowledge, namely, knowledge of judging and commanding (*kritikēn . . . kai epistatikēn*: 292a5–b11). This is incorrect. In the diaeresis, judging and commanding resulted from the division of gnostics, but the political art was placed under commanding, and judging was discarded (258e4–5). The Stranger silently reunites judging and commanding in preparation for his introduction of the theme of *phronēsis*, by which he makes explicit what I have previously been calling "intentionality." He also omits the distinction between autepitactics or the uttering of one's own commands and the anonymous art that includes the function of the herald (292b12–c4).

I said a moment ago that the classification of regimes does not illuminate the art of statesmanship. This point is now made by the Stranger. It is not the number of rulers, the willing or forced adherence of their subjects, or their wealth or poverty that determines the scientific character of their rule

(292c5–d1). The Stranger here omits the distinction between law-abiding and lawless regimes. This apparently trivial point will assume considerable importance, because the Stranger is about to claim that the only genuine regime is one in which there are no laws because every decision is made by *phronēsis*, in other words, by sound judgment of each particular situation (and here we should think of the previous discussion of the measurement of the mean).

We must now determine whether knowledge concerning the rule of human beings comes into existence in any of these actual regimes, a knowledge that is very close to being the hardest and greatest to possess (*ktēsasthai*: 292d2–4). This is a crucial passage. Hitherto we have argued that political knowledge is a *technē*, and as such it brings into existence something that would not otherwise exist. The paradigm of weaving makes it clear that the city is an artifact. One might still resist the inference that man is not by nature the political animal, on the Aristotelian grounds that art completes nature, at least in this case. But this counterargument depends on an affirmative answer to the question whether the knowledge of statesmanship comes into being in actual cities. If all actual cities are "crooked" or sick, and so only imitations of the genuine city, and if that city exists not in fact but only in the speeches of the philosopher, then it can hardly be the case that man is by nature the political animal. This Aristotelian definition depends on the rejection of the Platonic thesis that the only genuine city is one ruled by philosophy, a thesis of which the Stranger is about to promulgate his own version. It should also be noted that *epistēmē* is here called a possession, but it did not appear on the list of seven kinds of possession.

What I have called actual kings are those to whom the Stranger refers as men who pretend to be, or who persuade many that they are, statesmen but who must be distinguished from the wise king (*tou phronimou basileōs*: 292d5–7). No science, least of all statesmanship, could be possessed by a large number of persons; a city of a thousand men could not even produce fifty skilled draughts players, let alone kings, Young Socrates observes. And only he who possesses the royal *epistēmē*, whether he rules or not, may be called a king (292d1–293a1). The Stranger praises his pupil for reminding him of this point and adds that they will have to look for the correct rule whenever it occurs in one, two, or, in any case, a very few persons (293a2–4). He then uses the physician in order to illustrate the principle that "any kind of ruler whatsoever" is correctly defined by the possession of knowledge and not by the willingness of their subjects, the use of written laws, or their own wealth or poverty (293a6–c4). In this connection, one should compare the otherwise surprising remarks of the Athenian Stranger in *Laws*, IV. 709e6–

710e2, where he holds that a good tyrant is the quickest instrument for making the city blessed.

Just as the physician cuts the body and causes us pain for our own welfare, so too with the statesman. As Socrates says in the *Gorgias* (504c5–d4), the order and harmony of the body is health; the order of the soul is justice and moderation. Human beings are subject to disease by nature; one species of natural disease is manifested in political life. There is a fundamental difference, however, between the diseases of the body and those of political life. The diseased person wishes to be cured and will normally if not always submit willingly to the cuts and pains of medicine. Even if the patient is unable to endure these cuts and pains, he or she wishes to be healthy, and in the same sense of that term as is understood and intended by the physician. This is not true in the case of political disease.

The Stranger perhaps assumes that every normal person wishes to live in a just, well-governed city, and that since this can be achieved only through knowledge, all citizens acquiesce in principle, even if not knowingly, to the cuts and pains of philosophy or political *epistēmē*. But this is again dubious. There is no agreement between the nonphilosopher and the philosopher as to what constitutes political health, as there is in the case of the patient and the physician. The fundamental question must be raised whether a rule can be called healthy or correct if it is contrary to, or even if it is obtained without, the will of the citizen. Is politics truly an *epistēmē*, or is it defined instead as *praxis* in the Aristotelian sense? How can there be political "correctness" without political virtue, and is not virtue dependent upon willing or intending? It may be true that everyone wills or intends only what is good, but that does not mean that the good is the scientific, regardless of whether he or she who wills intended the scientifically correct result. For this reason the art of politics, understood as commanding, would have to be supplemented by the art of rhetoric and not by the art of pure philosophical rhetoric alone.

Interlude

Before we turn to the study of lawless *phronēsis*, it may be useful to pause for a general reflection on the results of our analysis thus far. We recall that weaving, the paradigm of the political art, was a subclass of the making of defensive screens. This suggested that politics is an artifice for protecting human beings and, in particular, the human body, against nature. At 288b1ff, however, defensive screens, including clothing, are counted as the fifth of seven classes of possessions having nothing to do with politics. This tells us that there is a defect in the paradigm of weaving. Weaving or clothesmaking produces protections for the body; I note that these protections are not only against nature (for example, the weather) but also in accord with custom (for example, the prohibition against public nudity). Protection against the violation of custom is as it were the middle term between protection of the body and that of the soul. But weaving is also defective as a paradigm of the protection of the body because it is a peaceful, feminine art of the household, whereas the statesman must fight offensive as well as defensive wars.

If politics is the care of the entire human being, that is, of the soul as well as the body, then it can easily be shown that there is no political *technē*. This was apparent in the defects of our paradigms, which all turned out to be examples of an inaccessible model rather than the model itself. But it will be helpful to make the point by way of a reflection on the soul. There are, I suggest, three kinds of human difference—bodily, intellectual, and those stemming from the character. We normally call these last "ethical." In the *Republic*, Socrates divides the soul into three parts or functions: intelligence, spiritedness, and desire. In this matrix, the character or *ethos* would correspond most closely to spiritedness, which is assigned the task of regulating desire in accord with the dictates of intelligence. It is interesting that the Socratic tripartition has no obvious equivalent to what we in the post-classical or Judaeo-Christian tradition call "spirit" or "spirituality." This is partly associated with the fact that piety is not one of the four cardinal virtues (nor is it a virtue for Aristotle). But that is not the whole story.

We can see this by considering, for example, the German distinction between *Geist* and *Seele*, which is somewhat sharper than what we normally understand in English by the equivalent terms spirit and soul. The *Geist* is a kind of blending of Greek spiritedness (*thumos*) with a cultural formation or expression of ethical, political, artistic, and religious formation (*Bildung*). *Seele* has a variety of meanings but is distinguishable from *Geist* in the sense of the soul as understood by the Judaeo-Christian tradition. But this has to be qualified in two ways. *Seele* can also refer to character or spiritual inclination, and *Geist* certainly reflects the religious conception of "spirit" (for example, the Hebrew *ruach*, "breath" or "wind").

From the Socratic standpoint, *Geist* is in the domain of *nomos*, custom or law, rather than of nature (*phusis*). Spiritedness enforces the commands of intelligence. These commands in turn define the particular expression in the city of the artistic, religious, and moral, as well as the political behavior of the citizens. One could also say that *Geist* has something to do with the Platonic doctrine of Eros. Eros is a very ambiguous power that can be detected in all three parts of the soul, which loves honor and pleasure in addition to the Ideas. There are also indications that Eros transcends the human soul, for example because it is described by Diotima as intermediate between the divine and the mortal, and so as peculiar to neither but instead the bond of the cosmos or whole.

There is no mention of Eros in the *Statesman*. The word literally appears only once in the dialogue, at 307e6, where it refers to an excessive desire for peace, not to sexuality or the love of the beautiful. There are also no occurrences of the word in the *Sophist;* obviously the Stranger differs importantly from Socrates in his lack of interest in this topic. Questions of sexual reproduction are assimilated into discussions of the nurturing of herds in the *Statesman,* which also contains no mention of the doctrine of Platonic Ideas. The closest we come to such a reference is to the "bodiless beings" with which diaeresis is said to be concerned. But diaeresis is a neutral method of classification, not a love for what it classifies.

When the Stranger will come to speak of hard and soft natures, which the statesman must weave together in order to construct a city, the reference is to something like the degree of spiritedness in the Socratic sense. Hardness and softness constitute jointly a natural difference; hard and soft souls are like threads or the warp and the woof used by the weaver to make clothing. But just as warp and woof do not plait themselves together without the intervention of the weaver, so too the hard and soft souls do not blend by nature. If there is any possibility of the overcoming of the separation between theory or gnostics on the one hand and practico-production on the other, its root will not be spiritedness.

But neither can it be desire, since this part of the soul is endlessly diverse. If we were to adopt as our political principle the freedom of desire, the result would not be unity but chaos. Even democracies depend on the restriction of desire, as commanded by the intellect and enforced by spiritedness, for their existence. It therefore looks as though the unity of human existence, or the overcoming of the division between theory and practice, if it is possible at all, must come from the activity of the intellect. But this in turn is possible if and only if the citizens are all in agreement with the laws—written and unwritten—of the city; differently stated, the unification of the individual soul depends on the unity of the city, or on conformity to the regime on the basis of intelligence.

How is this conformity to be obtained? The Stranger has excluded the rule of the gods by situating political existence in the normal epoch when human beings, despite the presence of the Olympians, must govern themselves. Conformity must therefore "grow up" out of human nature as an innate tendency of the embodied soul to arrive at common *nomoi* that are also just and rational. Unfortunately, human beings grow up within already corrupt or sick cities that are marked by widely divergent laws, customs, and desires. If there is any sense in which one could speak of natural agreement or unity, other than the biological sense, it could only be as the result of historical progress or through the imposition of force based upon *epistēmē*. There is no historical progress of this sort in the Platonic dialogues; both Socrates and the Stranger arrive at the the alternative of enforced *epistēmē* as the only conceivable solution.

To be conceivable, however, is not the same as to be possible. In the *Republic,* among the many difficulties that stand in the path of the coming into existence of the so-called beautiful city, perhaps the outstanding is the need to expel everyone over the age of ten in order to start afresh with the children. It should be obvious that parents would not surrender their children voluntarily to philosophers; they would have to be murdered. But who would do the deed? Certainly not the one or two would-be founding fathers. A police force would be required, and this could be obtained only by lies and compromises with human brutality or incredulity. If this is the basis of justice, then certainly injustice is preferable. As to the Stranger, he excludes the possibility of the rule of intelligence, not because it is unjust, but because it is impractical. Even if it were possible, the rule of *phronēsis* or intelligence would be like that of a tyrant, not a king.

In sum, the royal art is much broader than weaving. As to the other arts, they all, whether offensive or defensive, have political uses, but none is the political art. So too with the distinction between free citizens and servants or slaves; there is something servile about the practice of statesmanship because the king must devote himself entirely to the welfare of his subjects, yet it would be an exaggeration to call the king a slave. We must conclude that the art of the statesman comprehends all other arts and aspects of the human condition. The genuine statesman is more like the sophist or sorcerer who is continuously changing his shape than like a shepherd, captain, or weaver. There is no single or definite, and so definable, paradigm of the statesman. In fact, there is no such person as the genuine statesman.

This may sound paradoxical, but it is actually quite obvious. We can define the weaver, the shepherd, the manufacturer of defensive screens, and so on. This is because each has a definite task that is expressed as a *technē*. But the statesman, if he or she existed, would have every task. In order to organize all tasks into a harmonious regime, one in which there is a unity of theory and practice, the statesman must know enough about every task, and so every *technē*, to grasp its function and uses and how it fits into the hierarchy of ends constituting the political expression of human existence. This is necessary because the statesman is technically or professionally responsible for humanity as a whole. But there is no *technē* that is responsible for, or that corresponds to, the whole.

Each *technē* is defined by a definite intention, task, method for achieving the intention, set of relevant materials, tools, and so on. If we consider the whole, in the sense of the totality of human activity, there are too many ends and methods for achieving them to be mastered by any one person. And if the totality of human activity corresponds to the whole or cosmos, then the "end" of that whole must be the same as its comprehensive order or structure and so must resemble Hegel's absolute, which, if it falls within the domain of a single *technitēs*, is the concern of the speculative logician or wise man, not the statesman. Even in Hegel the ostensible overcoming of the split between theory and practice is intelligible only at the level of the whole, and not at the level of human existence where the wise man remains a professor or civil servant who subordinates himself to the Prussian monarchy and the Lutheran church.

These reflections lead inevitably to the conclusion that if there is a genuine king, his or her activity cannot be technical at all, but must instead be the activity of *phronēsis* or commanding judgment. This is why the Stranger suppressed the division between commanding and judging a short while ago. Let us now see how he develops the consequences.

Phronēsis and *Nomos*

Because the only correct regime is the rule of those who truly know, all others are incorrect, spurious, or false images of the one true original. This regime is the seventh on our list. Its relation to the regime in the *Republic* is immediately indicated by the Stranger. The "physicians" who rule the city may purify it by killing or banishing some of the citizens, or by sending out colonists as bees swarming from the hive, so long as they are acting with knowledge and justice. Young Socrates accepts all this as reasonable; his only objection is to the Stranger's earlier statement that laws are irrelevant to the question of the genuineness of the regime. The Stranger responds by implying that he was about to question the superfluousness of laws and proceeds to a consideration of this topic (293d4–294a4).

The Stranger begins by acknowledging that *nomothetikē*, the art of lawmaking, is in a way a part of the royal art. "But it would be best if the kingly man were to rule by *phronēsis* rather than that the laws should rule." Young Socrates does not see why this is so. Perhaps his mathematical training makes him a partisan of rules (294a6–9). The reason, according to the Stranger, is that the law is incapable of arranging things in the best possible way by applying what is best and most just in a precise way to all occurrences in the city. Human beings and their deeds are dissimilar to one another; human affairs are never at rest and so do not admit of a single rule to cover them all (294a10–b6). Stated more fully, no particular rule that covers a type of occurrence is capable of accommodating itself to the differences from occurrence to occurrence within that type. The Stranger brings this out in an unusually strong denunciation of the defects of law: "The law strives toward something that approaches this, just like a stubborn and ignorant man who will allow nothing to be done contrary to his own arrangements [*taksin*]; he allows no questions to be asked, not even if something new should come to pass that is superior but contrary to the *logos* that he has himself established" (294b8–c4).

I want to comment first on the word *dissimilarities* (*anomoiotētes*) at 294b2. This word first appeared in the myth when the Stranger referred at 273d5ff to "the unending sea of dissimilarity" into which the cosmos will dissolve unless it is rescued and rejuvenated by the co-rotator of the counternormal epoch. At 285b3 it occurred again, with reference to the dissimilarities of every kind that the master of diaeresis must separate in accordance with bonds of similarity or, in other words, in accordance with forms. Human experience, in short, is threatened with dissolution into the unending sea of dissimilarity, not only because of the intrinsic debility of the aging cosmos, but because of the heterogeneity of human speeches and deeds. Human life is continuous change within a continuously changing cosmos. But these changes are discontinuous. We can separate out the dissimilarities within our own lives by dividing and collecting in accordance with looks or forms. This diaeresis will be of some assistance in regulating the dissimilarities within the cosmos that threaten us with destruction, but we do not have sufficient control over nature to effect more than a holding operation. Death and destruction are the inevitable result, although they will be followed by birth and construction; these two stages of the cycle of human existence have always recurred and they will always recur.

It is not in keeping with Platonic terminology to apply the term *nomos* to nature. The only such application occurs in the *Gorgias* (483e2–3), where Callicles uses the expression to designate natural justice as the right of the stronger to have more than the weaker and the better more than the worse. Let us use the language of the myth instead and say that the cosmos and human beings are each regulated, even within their dissimilarities, by *phronēsis*, which somehow escapes destruction in both phases of cosmic reversal. When the divine demiurge makes the cosmos or when the co-rotator seizes control of the tiller, neither god employs a *technē*. Human *phronēsis* is thus analogous to, if not identical with, divine *phronēsis;* the genuine statesman, who is an example of the god in its two identities as demiurge and co-rotator, rules neither by *technē* nor by *nomos,* but by *phronēsis.* Or rather, he or she would so rule if a genuine statesman were possible (and no doubt the same must be said of gods). The wisest human beings employ the nomothetic *technē* to construct laws that will be surrogates for the direct inspection by *phronēsis* of each individual event in the city. This is also the view of the Athenian Stranger in the *Laws; phronēsis* is the highest of the divine goods (I. 631c5–6), but the human possessor of *phronēsis* must rule in accord with law (III. 690b7–c3). If it should happen that someone with a divine nature were to acquire the rule, he or she would not require to be ruled by laws. "For neither *nomos* nor order of any kind is stronger than knowledge" (IX. 875c3–7). In keeping with the *Sophist,* we could also say that the laws are fantasms of *phronēsis,* or false images artfully constructed in such a way as to look like the original to human vision.

The Eleatic Stranger's criticism of *nomos* amounts to a secularization of politics. The customs of the city cannot be the genuine expression of the will of the gods, but at most a simulacrum. One thinks here of Socrates' criticism of writing in the *Phaedrus.* Speech is superior to writing because it can accommodate its assertions to the nature of the immediate audience. The voice of *phronēsis* is capable of innovation; writing is always the same, and *nomos* is the least mobile of writings. It is "always simple" because it has one meaning and so cannot properly be applied to life, which is never simple (294c7–8). The Stranger is himself guilty of oversimplification in this passage because writing is open to interpretation, but he might reply that interpretation is the innovative voice of *phronēsis.* When the Stranger speaks of "the new" he is not thinking of innovation or progress in the modern sense, but rather of the variability of circumstances that call for different responses to situations that *nomos* would judge in the same way. The Stranger takes it for granted that *phronēsis* is not revolutionary but prudent as well as flexible. Nevertheless it is fair to say that the rule of *phronēsis* is open to radical change in a way that the rule of *nomos* is not.

Why then are laws necessary, even though they are not perfectly correct? In addressing this problem, the Stranger turns once more to *technē.* It should be noted parenthetically that by associating *technē* and *nomos,* the Stranger does not necessarily forget the element of judgment in the arts. He does however wish to emphasize the dependence of *technē* on rules and codified procedures. The rules and procedures for making shoes are not the same as those for sailing a ship; furthermore, in each case these rules and procedures are defined by the nature of the product to be manufactured or the deed to be accomplished. The freedom to improvise or interpret in the arts is restricted by the nature of the intention and the means to the end. In the imaginary kingdom of *phronēsis,* human nature is not fixed like the nature of leather or wood and canvas. Even the motions of the wind and the sea are subject to technical procedures of a more or less determinate sort. Experience shows that such and such a maneuver is called for under such and such circumstances. In the case of human beings, the standard maneuver may be inappropriate for reasons that go beyond the circumstances of the act or speech under judgment.

The example chosen by the Stranger to defend the rule of *nomos* is that of gymnastics: exercise of the body. Unlike the weaver, whose *technē* is defensive, the athletic coach prepares the body for competition and victory, and so for the acquisition of honor, a crucial political characteristic that has thus far been neglected. According to the Stranger, the coaches cannot accommodate the rules of conditioning to each individual body but must impose on all the order that they deem suitable to the majority (294d7–e2). This is of course why those who are contending for the highest honors in their sport must have individual trainers. The Stranger applies his analogy to politics and significantly refers to "the watchman of the herds," thereby tacitly assimilating human beings to tame brutes and so continuing the emphasis on the body (294e8–9). The lawgiver is unable to give to each individual person "precisely what is fitting" (*akribōs heni hekastōi to prosēkon:* 295a2). At 284a5ff, the Stranger maintained that abolition of the measurement of the mean would destroy the arts, including the art of politics. How are we to reconcile these two passages? Is not the art of lawgiving an expression of the measurement of the mean or fitting?

We could of course make a distinction between what is fitting for large numbers and what is fitting for the individual person. In our associations with individuals, we are able to adapt our speeches and deeds to the particular nature and circumstances of the person and the occasion. The lawgiver adapts his or her laws to the particular circumstances of a given people or tradition but is unable to fine-tune these laws to the needs of each citizen. This is why the written law must be supplemented by equity, a point not mentioned by the Stranger. But the deeper problem follows from the difference between politics and arts like shoemaking or sailing. What is fitting for the making of shoes, and even for the art of the captain, must be selected from a much narrower range of possibilities than is the case with politics. The legislator of shoemaking must accommodate to the exigencies of leather, nails, thread, and the shape of the human foot. But the statesman must take into account all parts of the body, not to mention the soul and its multitudinous needs, desires, and intentions.

In short, the laws of the city are already a statement of the fitting. But it is impossible to legislate for each individual citizen; law is necessarily addressed to kinds of persons, speeches, or deeds. The law is guided by the *eidē* or forms of individual instances, not by the instances themselves. But just as the philosopher does not apprehend the particular instance by viewing the Idea, so the law fails to discern the circumstances that require its own modification. *Noēsis* or the pure apprehension of forms must be supplemented by *phronēsis* or sound judgment of particular cases. This explains why Socrates spends relatively little time on the laws of his just city in the *Republic*, whereas in the *Laws*, the Athenian Stranger legislates to a degree that the modern reader finds tedious, as a result of which the dialogue is seldom studied carefully. In a city ruled by philosophers, laws are a radical compromise, even more, a fundamental defect; no matter how wise the legislator, his or her wisdom cannot govern directly but is represented by custom and written law. The impossibility of the rule of *phronēsis* can lead to a different but related failure if the legislator tries to overcome it by making laws that are as detailed and as close to particular cases as possible. The result is counterproductive: particulars are transformed by the law into generalities, and the burden of legislation is so great as to destroy the freedom and dignity of political life.

The Stranger exaggerates the opposition between law and *phronēsis*, as is clear from his association of the determination of the fitting with the latter but not with the former. In so doing, he indicates the fundamental shortcoming of technical models or approaches to politics. We can express this shortcoming in a still more radical way. The noetic apprehension of pure forms is not based on rules or methods; on the contrary, all methods for dividing and collecting in accordance with kinds are based on the direct apprehension of the looks of the kinds. But the judgment of the particular is also not based on rules or methods; there is no rule of prudence and no method for seeing what is required in the individual case. This is an odd, even perplexing situation. If rules and methods apply neither to the general nor to the particular, when do they apply? Perhaps the answer is that rules and methods are applicable exclusively to the constructive *technai*. There is no right or wrong way in which to see something, but once we have seen it, there are determinate procedures for moving from what we have seen to the genesis of something else, whether a speech, a deed, or a physical artifact. If this is so, then diaeresis is constructive; it is not the definition of Ideas but the invention of concepts.

The measurement of the fitting is thus a feature of human construction or production; the mean pertains to artifacts that we generate in order to fulfill an intention. The term *artifact* must be extended to refer to speeches and deeds, as well as to separate entities like shoes and defensive screens. And this already follows from the Platonic separation of the arts into gnostic and practico-productive. Practice is itself productive because in carrying out political, ethical, or (to employ a modern term) social acts, we are engaged in the process of self-construction. It was in a sense obvious from the outset, but we have shown in conclusive detail that the usual understanding of Plato as a kind of proto-Aristotelian is false. It results from the habit of reading Plato through the eyes of Aristotle, but also from a failure to read the texts carefully, as well as from a mistaken notion of the difference between the ancients and the moderns.

This difference, at least so far as Plato may be taken to represent the ancients, is not between the theoretical viewing of eternal forms and the radical mastery of nature by construction and the will to power. But this is not to say that Heidegger is correct in his interpretation of the Ideas as themselves constructions imposed onto Being by the classical prototype of the will to power. For Plato it is not the Ideas that we construct but ourselves. This process of self-construction is of course not as radical as the modern version because it does not take itself to originate ex nihilo. Plato agrees with Nietzsche that man is the not-yet-completely-constructed animal, but he denies Nietzsche's principle that chaos is at the heart of beings. I discuss this more fully in my book *The Question of Being*.

To return now to politics, the Stranger says that the lawmaker cannot sit beside each person and tell him or her what to do at each moment in life (295a9–b2). In fact, he is referring to *phronēsis,* which is here personified as the genuine statesman. Actually, there is a sense in which *phronēsis* does guide us throughout our lives, not by sitting at our side but by residing within our souls. By the same token, the laws also guide us in this way, not by sitting at our side but by surrounding us from within and without, in other words, by the daily work of habituation and education. In a free city, or one which, although corrupt by Platonic standards, can nevertheless be counted as a political association, there is a constant quarrel between *phronēsis* and the laws that increases in intensity with the maturity of the citizen; it is a function of his or her ability to think independently and so to read books like Plato's *Statesman*.

The Stranger, of course, means by *phronēsis* not the judgment of every citizen but the faculty in its highest or purest form. This faculty does not exist, or if it does, it can be found incarnated only in the one, two, or few persons who are entitled to be called the genuine statesman. Throughout the dialogue, the Stranger refers to statesmanship as a *technē,* but he is now in the process of showing the inadequacy of that appellation. *Phronēsis* and *technē* are entirely distinct from one another; hence too *phronēsis* is distinct from *nomos,* which is a product of *technē. Phronēsis* is the genuine king; *technē,* including the art of the lawgiver, is the tool employed by the king to compensate for the fact that he cannot rule in his own person. If we follow the explicit terms of the Stranger's investigation, we find that there is no genuine city because the rule of the genuine king is impossible. It is impossible, not simply because the king cannot sit beside each person and tell him or her what to do, but because the citizens would not obey the king. Instead, they would regard him as a madman or at best a potential tyrant. Lacking an army of sufficient loyalty to enforce his authority, the genuine king does the next best thing. He assumes the mantle of the prophet, founding father, or lawgiver and rules through the instrument of the written and unwritten laws of the regime or constitution.

In other words, the king does sit by the side of each citizen and issue a stream of instructions; he does this in the form of *nomos*. But this king, the genuine statesman, need not be and usually is not the person who holds the title of king in the actual government. The king who himself obeys the laws of the founding father is rather a herald. As to the tyrant or revolutionary who changes the original laws, he substitutes himself for the original lawgiver. But this is to say that he becomes an original lawgiver himself. His technical productions, like those of the original founding father, may then be subjected to critical analysis by students of politics like the Stranger. The comparative evaluation of two sets of laws is conducted on the basis of a philosophical doctrine of human nature; interestingly enough, no such doctrine is contained in the *Statesman,* beyond practical indications like the need to weave together hard and soft natures into the fabric of the city. It is true but only a first step to say that the wise man is the genuine king. The second step is to describe the wisdom that such a king possesses. Presumably that step would be taken in the investigation of the philosopher. It is typical of Plato's wisdom, as well as of his sense of humor, that this investigation, if it ever took place, was not recorded.

Politics is oriented toward the body; but philosophy, or the genuine art of statesmanship, is oriented toward the soul. It sounds odd, but it is nevertheless correct to say that the genuine art of statesmanship is neither an art nor is it directed toward the city. Not only is it the case that all actual or historical cities are corrupt, but so too are all philosophical utopias or cities that claim to be just or wise because they exist in the speech of philosophers. Even these cities in speech must be constructed on the basis of human nature, which is not complete but which nevertheless exists, and in a peculiarly self-contradictory manner that is manifested in the difference between the soul and the body. *Phronēsis* cannot rule because it is parceled out to the individual citizens and prevented from uniting by the boundaries of corporeal existence.

That is why Socrates must expel, in other words kill, everyone over the age of ten before he can institute his rule of philosophers.

The Stranger indicates the political priority of the body to the soul by discussing the impossibility of the rule of *phronēsis* by means of the examples of the gymnast and the physician. If they are about to leave town on a trip, they will write out their instructions to those under their care. These writings serve as "memoranda" (*hupomnēmata*), the word employed by Socrates in the *Phaedrus* (276d3) when he speaks of writing as memoranda to assist the failing memories of old men. If the physician or gymnastic trainer returns to town sooner than anticipated, he will examine his patients or students and change the instructions if circumstances have changed (295b10–d7). This is not entirely compatible with the Stranger's earlier remarks on the inability of the gymnast to accommodate his general rules to the bodies of his individual students. A change of instructions is not the same as the overthrow of the laws; furthermore, most such changes, especially in the case of medicine, will be on an individual basis, not with respect to a large group.

It would be absurd for the practitioner of genuine science and art not to change the rules when circumstances change (295d7–e3). The Stranger seems to suggest that the same absurdity applies in the case of political legislation, but he shifts his position as he goes along, and for good reason. In this passage, the Stranger grants the malleability of *technē* and *epistēmē* and leaves himself open for the inference that their rules and methods are subject to endless progress. In addition, he continues to employ the terminology of herds and their tending. Most important for our present purposes, he begins by assuming that the laws should be changed whenever circumstances make it reasonable to do so (295e4–296a2). This is quite contrary to the doctrine of the Athenian Stranger in the *Laws*, which warns against the disastrous consequences of any changes, however small, in the legal code (VII. 797a1–c9). It seems that he does not regard the art of legislation as a *technē* in the usual sense.

So it looks as though the consequence of the Eleatic Stranger's distinction between *phronēsis* and *nomos* is that political laws are to be altered whenever circumstances warrant, for reasons that are analogous to the shifting of the winds that lead the physician to alter his prescriptions. This is the course of reason or good judgment in all arts and sciences, including the art that is the surrogate or simulacrum of the genuine political knowledge. Let us watch carefully how the Stranger develops his argument. He has just asked Young Socrates what the many say about the right of the lawmaker to change legislation on the basis of knowledge furnished by the one who legislates with *technē*. The young man replies that he does not remember (295d7–296a6).

The Stranger reminds him that the many give a reply that looks good on the surface (*euprepēs*). Whoever believes himself to possess laws that are superior to those already established may legislate for them if and only if he persuades the city, but otherwise not. "Is this not correct?" asks Young Socrates, apparently missing the point of the Stranger's reference to "the many." "Perhaps," the Stranger replies (296a7–b1) and then proceeds to reverse direction.

The Stranger poses a general question and then applies it to the statesman by way of the example of the physician. What do we call the imposition of the superior by force without persuasion? This question is not so difficult to answer; it refers to the rule of the technician over the nontechnician. If I am in need of expertise, I must rely on the specialist who possesses the knowledge that I lack, and with which he forces my acquiescence because I am too ignorant to be persuaded by a technical explanation. But the Stranger refines his question to apply to politics. He starts once more with the physician. We are to suppose that a physician knows what is best for his patient and that this knowledge is contrary to the accepted technical wisdom of the discipline. What are we to say if the physician forces the patient to follow the superior treatment instead of persuading him or her, adult or child? Should we or the patient who has been benefited refer to this as a harmful error that is contrary to *technē*, what is known today as "unprofessional conduct," or is this the last name to apply to such conduct? Young Socrates affirms the latter response (296b1–c3).

This is a peculiar example that requires analysis. The question is not that of a physician who has "state of the art" knowledge or who has made a major discovery not yet known to other practitioners and who then persuades the patient to accept this apparently unorthodox treatment with the assurance that it will ameliorate his condition, perhaps even save his life. In this relatively straightforward case, the patient relies on the known or perceived expertise of the physician; furthermore, the patient wishes to be cured by the physician, not to be given traditional remedies. In the example posed by the Stranger, the physician does not persuade the patient, whether by technical exposition or the force of his own reputation, to accept the novel remedy. Nor does he presumably trick the patient by telling him a noble lie. Perhaps he ties the patient down on the examination table and forces the medicine down his throat. It is even possible that the patient does not wish to be saved or would prefer for religious reasons to undergo the traditional treatment rather than violate some sacred belief, as would be required by submitting to the new treatment.

Let this suffice as a specification of the example. What name would we give to the physician's behavior? In order to answer this question, we would, I believe, have to make a distinction between the medical or technical and the moral or political aspects of the action. If we allow the assumption that the physician acts from correct knowledge, then there is no error from a technical standpoint. It could be argued that the use of a new and unorthodox drug or experimental surgery carries grave risks for the patient and should not be applied against his or her will. But this is a moral or political consideration and not one of the physician's technical knowledge of medicine. And even if there is no risk, the same distinction applies. We would all agree, philosophers as well as "the many," that under normal circumstances a patient has the right to accept or to reject treatment. This agreement is obviously moral or political; it certainly does not follow from the *technē* of medicine. There may be exceptional circumstances under which we would sanction the physician's behavior—for example, if the patient were carrying the virus of a terrible plague that would threaten the lives of many or all citizens but nevertheless refused treatment. But again, these circumstances are moral or political, not medical.

What does this example teach us? Not, I believe, that physicians have the right to force novel but efficacious remedies on unwilling patients, but rather that *technē*, like diaeresis, is morally neutral. There is no moral right that accrues merely from superior technical knowledge. But neither is there a *technē* that will allow us to resolve the question of whether the physician's behavior was justified. His behavior was not a harmful scientific error, but that is not to the point. Or is it? Does the Stranger wish to argue that superior knowledge gives the physician the right to cure the patient in the technically best way, even against his or her will? What, in other words, is the political point that the Stranger intends to convey by his example?

According to the Stranger, "the many" would not accuse the physician of acting in an unscientific or technically incompetent way. But if someone were to act contrary to the rules of the political *technē*, this action would be called shameful, evil, and unjust, as Young Socrates entirely agrees (296c4–7). The Stranger must be referring to action contrary to the popularly accepted version of the political *technē*, since the genuine art is unknown to the many. However, if he is referring here to himself and Young Socrates and the genuine political art, then condemnation in this case would contradict the point of the example of the physician. In the immediate continuation, the Stranger asks us to consider someone who forces persons to act contrary to the written laws and ways of the ancestors, but thereby to behave more justly, nobly, and better than previously. Would it not be entirely absurd to accuse such a person of subjecting the others to shameful, unjust, and evil treatment? Young Socrates once more wholeheartedly agrees (296c8–d5).

For reasons that have already been given, there is no analogy between the correct technical behavior of the physician in the previous example and that of the statesman or lawgiver (who cannot quite be identified with the statesman but stands to him as does the art of lawgiving to the *phronēsis* of the genuine king). The analogy is rather between the moral and political behavior of the physician and that of the lawgiver. The people in the second example already have their laws and desire to retain them. The essence of politics is not that the technician shall impose superior laws onto already existing cities, but that citizens are defined as such by the act of choosing their own laws. The Stranger could maintain that the citizens acted more or less in ignorance, or that they have been habituated to accept laws the defects of which they do not understand. But this does not alter the situation. Once they accept these laws, whoever imposes different ones onto the city is a tyrant, and political life in its fundamental character of freedom to rule and be ruled has been replaced by slavery.

The one thing that counts is that "the wise and good man manages the affairs of the ruled." Whether he uses persuasion or force is as irrelevant to the justice of his acts as whether he is rich or poor, whether he acts in accord with written laws or without them (296d6–e4). This shows that the immediately preceding passage at c4–7 was directed against the ignorant many. The Stranger falsely argues from the technical justification of the physician who heals by force to the political justification, and so to the justice, of the rule by force of the wise and good man. But there is a missing premise in this argument. It has to be shown that rule by force can indeed be wise and good, or in other words, that it is just. The assumption that force can produce virtuous actions is not only gratuitous; it is also absurd because virtuous acts must be performed freely. The comparison with the captain of a ship is thus faulty (296e4–297b3). A city is in fact not really like a ship because the functions of the citizen are not the same as those of the crew or passengers. It is not the job of either to perform virtuous actions but instead to complete the voyage safely. Perhaps one could say that the captain's art is defensive and for that reason is related to the art of the weaver.

It is impossible, the Stranger continues, for a multitude (*plēthos*) to possess the knowledge required to rule the city in accord with intelligence. We must search for "our one correct regime" in a small number, either in a few or in one person (297b7–c2). We should note that there are many ships, and so many captains, although the nature of sailing is such that it would be disadvantageous and probably impossible to have more than one captain on each ship. Because there are many cities, there must be more than one person who possesses the knowledge of statesmanship; otherwise there could only be a small number of well-governed cities, and perhaps only one. I think this supports the distinction between the statesman and the philosopher in the strict Platonic sense. The Stranger does not argue that only he possesses the royal art, but that it cannot be possessed by more than a very few in each city. If this is right, and it seems to be supported by the text, then this opens the way to Aristotle's distinction between philosophy and the political art.

More immediately, it does seem to be possible to train a reasonable number of captains; this being so, it would certainly be possible to have more than one captain on some if not all ships. One might wish to have a co-captain in reserve for long voyages in case the captain should fall ill; this is the principle that is followed on commercial airlines. The reason why there can be only one captain in authority at any given time is not the difficulty of the art but rather the dangers of sailing, which leave no margin for debate, and the fixed nature of the destination of the voyage, which is not a matter of chance or philosophical speculation. It is all very well to speak of nobility, goodness, and justice, but the Stranger has said nothing about the destination of the ship of state. Debate and speculation seem to be part of the voyage, not obstacles to its accomplishment. This is another important reason for the disanalogy between the captain and the statesman.

In any case, the Stranger establishes as his seventh type what I will call the epistemic city, of which all other regimes are better or worse imitations (297c1–4). Young Socrates does not understand, and the Stranger goes on to explain. Cities of the six traditional regimes must make use of the written laws (*tois tautēs sungrammasi*) of the epistemic city if they are to survive destruction by conforming with the traditional notions of praiseworthy conduct, however far such conduct may be from what is entirely correct (297c5–d7). This is an important statement. It is now assumed that the epistemic city has written laws. One cannot even imagine a city without laws, that is, a city ruled entirely by the voice of *phronēsis*. As I said previously, even the city in speech is a defective version of the genuine art of statesmanship.

Once having admitted that the rule of *phronēsis* is impossible, the Stranger draws the inference that the "second best" procedure is not to disobey the laws of one's city, on pain of death or extreme punishment (297e1–6). Has he forgotten his previous sharp criticism of *nomos*? Not at all; the criticism remains in force. It follows from the impossibility of constructing a city of *phronēsis;* the epistemic city, with its regime of technically correct laws, is already a "second" choice, although not one that is available to residents of actual cities. Those actual cities that survive by imitating the laws of the epistemic city are accordingly not imitating the lawless city of *phronēsis*. Or rather, it is a dictate of *phronēsis* that laws be obeyed as a simulacrum of the living intelligence. Human existence is a life of simulacra or inaccurate images proportioned to our defective and perspectival vision. But the Stranger is not a follower of Nietzsche or his contemporary French interpreters. The statesman who is wise in the human sense of the term can see and enter into the perspectives of the nonphilosopher; it is this transperspectival vision that enables him or her to construct the appropriate simulacra.

CHAPTER NINE

The City as Simulacrum

Back to the Icons

I use the term *simulacrum* to refer to an expanded interpretation of what the Stranger calls in the *Sophist* a *fantasm* (*fantasma*). A fantasm is an image that alters the original proportions in such a way as to exhibit an inaccurate copy of the original, yet one that looks accurate to human vision. This image is employed primarily in architecture, sculpture, and painting. But the notion can be extended to refer to any construction that is intended to mediate between inaccessible originals and human existence. The rule of *phronēsis* is an original in the following sense: it is the archetype of communal human activity. Because *phronēsis* rules without laws but by making a judgment that is unique in each case, or at least determined in each case by the particular circumstances that cannot be known in advance, it is impossible for the Stranger or anyone else to give a *logos*, in other words, a detailed description or account, of *phronēsis* or its decisions. One can say that all human beings ought to act prudently, judiciously, or wisely at all times; one might even be able to arrive at a widely accepted general description of prudence, judiciousness, or wisdom, although even this is dubious. But one could certainly not describe the political structure of the application of wisdom because there is by definition no such structure to describe.

We have now shown that all talk about the science or *technē* of politics is distinct from the rule of *phronēsis* or is already an accommodation of that rule to the necessities of incarnated existence. Not only is it an accommodation; it is also a reversal of the original. The rule of *phronēsis* is literally lawless, whereas lawlessness is a technical defect; the science of politics rules by laws that are to be obeyed on penalty of death or severe punishment. The original does not lose its ideal function or intrinsic nature; but it is either inaccessible, or accessible only via its technical reversal, in a way reminiscent of the counternormal epoch, which is accessible to us only by prophetic myths recounted in the normal epoch. A myth is a story; it is a fiction, something that is not true. And yet this untruth, which we hesitate to call a falsehood, is able to communicate deep truths.

Even this, however, is only an approximation to the actual situation. The myth of the *technē* of politics is designed to exhibit how we may render possible the impossible rule of *phronēsis*. Unfortunately, the *technē* of politics is itself a further myth, or an element in the original myth. This is obvious from the intrinsic moral or political neutrality of *technē*, as well as from its radical incompleteness. Human existence cannot in its foundations or horizons be technical; it must be prudential or, as I put it previously, intentional. The odd truth is that we are governed by *phronēsis* even when we lack it or violate it. There is no such thing as a technical rule of human life; even technocracy is ruled by the prudential judgment that the technically regulated life is better than its alternatives.

At best, then, the expression "political *technē*" is ambiguous and rests on an equivocation of the term *technē*. At worst, it is a self-contradiction. Whereas there are *technai* that apply to the various activities pursued within the city, politics is intrinsically nontechnical. This fact is concealed within Plato's assimilation of practice to production or, rather, by his failure to distinguish between the two. I say Plato, not the Stranger, because the point is to be found throughout the dialogues, regardless of the identity of the main speaker. In contrast, Plato is certainly not entirely mistaken to think of laws, and so of citizens, as productions or constructions of human intentionality. This is a point that seems to have been missed or knowingly suppressed by Aristotle. The difference between practice and production holds in principle, but not in practice. More precisely stated, practical excellence is definable only as relative to the existence of a city of a certain type, and this city has been brought into existence in accord with the intentions of the lawgivers and founding fathers.

It is not by chance that Aristotle's definition of the virtues leaves it undecided in any particular case what a virtuous act should be. The individual case is to be decided by *phronēsis*, exactly as the Stranger holds. But the Stranger adds a step in the analysis that is missing in Aristotle. He shows us that the rule of *phronēsis* is impossible in the sense of compelling us always to do the prudent or appropriate thing. Therefore we require a "second best" paradigm, the rule of *technē* as exemplified in obedience to the laws of the city. Unfortunately, it is also impossible to apply this paradigm because there are no laws of political activity; *technē* is indifferent to virtue and vice. The upshot thus far of the Stranger's analysis is that we imitate the political *technē*, which is itself a reversal or simulacrum of the rule of *phronēsis*, not by enacting wise laws, but by obeying the laws we possess. *Nomos* is then indeed the imitation of *technē*, but it is once more a simulacrum rather than an accurate copy. It hardly requires emphasis that one may obey bad laws as well as good ones, or more to the point, technically deficient as well as sound laws.

That we have not strayed away from the orbit of the Stranger's argument is shown, among other considerations, by the close connection between commanding and obeying. If politics is an autepitactic art, it cannot function unless there is someone to obey the commands that the statesman has produced in the form of laws. But the various paradigms introduced by the Stranger have the net result of presenting the statesman as a tyrant, of whom the archetype or paradigm in the sense of the model is *phronēsis* and of whom examples are the divine co-rotator or shepherd, the captain of a ship, the weaver, the physician, and the gymnastic coach. In this series of examples, *phronēsis* is continuously inverted into *technē*, with the net result that politics is conceived with increasing intensity as an art of defending the body against the ravages of nature. The one exception to this generalization is the gymnast, who trains the body to win honor; but the exception proves the rule because the source of the honor is again the body.

Let me repeat the major conclusion of this study. The paradigm of the art of politics is not an art, and it is inaccessible to the polis or state. What gets applied from the paradigm of *phronēsis* is the abstract structure of commanding and obeying. Every attempt to fill in this abstract structure with politically applicable content must have recourse to *technē*, the stepwise and so teachable procedure for carrying out human intentions by producing an artifact, whether in speech or in deed (including such deeds as the products of the handicrafts). The *technai* in question are tools of human intentionality. It would be tempting to identify intentionality with *phronēsis*, but the problem is that some intentions are prudent or wise and others are not. All this being so, it is vain to speak of "a solution to the political problem" or "the unification of theory and practice." Given the impossibility of codifying *phronēsis* or furnishing content to the general invocation to act wisely, we can scarcely state the problem. As to the unification of theory and practice, if this could be achieved, it would transform human beings into speeches, very much in the manner of contemporary philosophies of language, whether analytical or postmodern.

Let us now follow the Stranger's request and "go back once more to the images [*Eis de tas eikonas epaniōmen palin*] with which it is always necessary to represent [*apeikazein*] the royal rulers" (297e8–9). Exactly as I noted above, it is impossible to present or exhibit the royal ruler in his own persona because this persona is a myth. The Stranger has to remind Young Socrates that the images are those of "the noble captain" and the physician. The adjective *noble* is added here for the first time; the reference to the physician is by way of a quotation from Homer, the first time in the dialogue that a citation from poetry occurs. I refer to these images as simulacra simply to have a distinct term for copies of copies. From what one could call the standpoint of orthodox or traditional Platonism, it is the Ideas or archetypes that possess genuine existence (*ontōs on*). A copy of an original is ontologically defective; a copy of a copy is a mere phantom of existence. Human existence in this sense is neatly captured by Shakespeare's couplet in the *Tempest:* "We are such stuff as dreams are made on, / And our little lives are rounded with a sleep."

The Stranger attributes nobility to the captain and the authority of Homer to the physician. He also ignores the shepherd and the weaver. The image of the shepherd is defective because it refers to nonhuman animals. The fundamental difference between the weaver on the one hand and the physician and gymnast on the other is that the former prepares defensive screens or clothing for the body, whereas the latter two both modify the body directly. In addition to these two distinct types of *technē*, which are both directed primarily to the body, there is a third type that neither produces separate artifacts nor modifies the body; its product is virtuous activity, and the paradigm of the master of this type was *phronēsis*. Because the paradigm is inaccessible in the sense just described, the Stranger is left with the physician and the gymnast.

There follows a long passage reminiscent of *Republic* VI. 488a1–489a2. The Stranger asks us to imagine an assembly of citizens called to protest the harsh treatment meted out by captains and physicians to those who are subject to their respective arts. The assembly agrees that we will no longer submit to this abusive conduct but will ourselves legislate about medicine and navigation, whether or not we know anything about these matters. Furthermore, new rulers of the city are to be chosen each year by lot, and it is these rulers, whether selected from the rich or the entire people, who will command the ships and treat the sick, both in accord with written rules. At the end of the year, judges are chosen, again by lot, in order to decide whether the captains and physicians of the preceding year have acted in accord with the written laws or ancient ways (298a1–299a6).

The most obvious purpose of this passage is to introduce a long diatribe against the political behavior of the Athenian democracy. The criticism depends on the assumption that there exist political technicians analogous to captains and physicians, who are being absurdly ignored as the genuine captains and physicians are not. Certainly it would be relatively simple to distinguish a fraudulent from a genuine captain; let us also grant that despite the state of ancient medicine, the same holds true of the physician. A captain is someone who demonstrates knowledge of the art of navigation by exercising it successfully; this is done by navigating ships safely on more than one occasion in order to show that the first time was not by good luck. Similarly, a physician is someone who demonstrates technical knowledge by improving health, whether through the cure of diseases or by their prevention (and here he is associated with the gymnastic coach).

But what do genuine statesmen do? If we apply the Stranger's analogy, the statesman must prevent the city from being destroyed, whether by the natural elements, wild beasts, or the armies of other cities. And yet this could be accomplished by a tyrant. It was also accomplished by the Athenian democracy as long as Pericles lived. The criticism of the democracy has a point only if it can be shown that the popular assembly is incapable of producing virtuous activity or, in other words, of caring primarily for the soul. More precisely, the Stranger would have to strip his criticism of its excessive and question-begging rhetoric and to demonstrate both that there is a knowledge of virtue that is accessible to very few persons within a city—perhaps only to one—and that this knowledge cannot be taught to the multitude like a *technē*. But all this is made difficult, if not impossible, by the image of the captain and the physician. One could say that the arts of navigation and medicine are more difficult than those of weaving or the other handicrafts. Yet no one could claim that they are so difficult as to be accessible only to a very few within each city.

In fact, to the extent that the Stranger's diatribe against the democracy is plausible, it draws its strength from the passions of the multitude, not from the analogy between politics and *technē*. Is it technical ignorance or the voice of passion that prevents us from listening to the voice of *phronēsis*? Would a knowledge of navigation or medicine make the multitude better qualified to exercise prudential judgments about which voyages have virtuous outcomes or who will live a good life if he or she is cured by the physician? Not even expertise in the *technē* of the lawgiver, assuming such a *technē* to exist, could moderate the passions of an unruly soul. It is extremely odd that, precisely while showing the unruliness of the multitude, the Stranger talks as if it were due to a lack of technical knowledge. This is a thesis of the scientific Enlightenment. Once again Aristotle's doctrine of the need to habituate the citizenry in virtue is more plausible than the Stranger's analysis.

The Stranger continues his satire on Athenian democracy with a discernible allusion to Aristophanes' *Clouds*. In the city Aristophanes describes, whoever studies navigation or medicine in a way contrary to the written rules or teachings will be called neither a captain nor a physician but rather one who talks about the stars (*meteōrologon*), or, in other words, someone who ignores human affairs and speaks in a foolish and pretentious manner like a babbling sophist (299b2–8). Again the satire turns on the assumption that technical innovation is possible in politics, just as it is in the natural sciences. Here as earlier when the Stranger refers to "written laws" (*ta grammata*), he means those passed by the multitude with respect to subjects that they do not understand. The investigations that go contrary to these writings are those that are directed toward the discovery of the genuine rules and procedures of navigation and medicine; so too the genuine statesman would be condemned for treason if he were to investigate the genuine rules and procedures of politics.

After a further ironical allusion to Socrates' current status in Athens (he is, as we recall, under indictment on the charge of having corrupted the young; see 299b8 and c4–5), the Stranger concludes with a long list of sciences ranging in type from mathematics through horse breeding to the playing of draughts, all of which, he emphasizes with some bitterness, would be destroyed if they were conducted in accord with laws passed and written down by the untechnical multitude (299c6–e4). Young Socrates is properly outraged and notes that life, "which is already hard, would become unlivable in the future" (299e5–9). We hear in this response an anticipation of the argument by which human beings have come to rely on *technē* and research (*zētein*: 299e7) for the amelioration of the human condition.

More important to our assessment of the Stranger's account is the shift in his attitude toward writing. He began with the premise that the genuine statesman, namely, the voice of *phronēsis*, would write nothing down because writings cannot respond to the change that characterizes human existence. Since *phronēsis* is possessed only by one, two, or a very few, it is necessary to reverse course and write down all the laws of the regime, so they may have uniform application. But now, in the satire on democracy, writings are debased to the status of untechnical products of passionate ignorance. There is no explicit contradiction here because the writings recommended by the Stranger are those he would attribute to the genuine statesman or lawgiver. However, there is still a problem. Either these laws will be preserved continuously in unchanged form, in which case they cannot do justice to the changing circumstances of human life. Or else they will be changed; but once the genuine statesman is dead, the danger exists that he will have no successor, and even if he does, a change in the laws leads eventually to a change in the regime, with the great likelihood that sooner rather than later laws will be passed and written down by the ignorant, who, if not quite the multitude, are certainly many in comparison with those very few persons who presumably know what they are doing.

The Stranger's scorn for writings is then directed against the ignorance of tradition as well as of the contemporary popular government in Athens. How are these traditional laws to be abolished, if not by force? Now we see the pertinence of the previous denial that the distinction between force and voluntary obedience has any bearing on the right of the wise to govern. If the Stranger's training in dialectic is something more than mere talk, and even if it is not, since words have practical consequences, the Stranger is under suspicion of inciting to revolution. This point supervenes over the problematic of *phronēsis* versus *technē*. Even if the genuine knowledge of politics is a *technē* in a sense quite different from that of navigation, medicine, or weaving or, rather, if it is different from these, it must answer the question whether the imposition of *phronēsis* by force is itself just. More sharply stated, the question is whether the use of force to impose the judgments of *phronēsis* is itself an act of *phronēsis*.

In sum, the model of *technē* has the following implication for politics. Not only are there rules or laws of correct statesmanship, but these are subject to continuous change. The rules or laws may be written down, but this does not lend them permanence; or rather, to regard them as permanent, for example because they have been formulated by the founding fathers, is to deprive them of the power to adapt to changing circumstances and so to acquire new knowledge and more efficient procedures. If writing is the attribution of permanence and stability, then in the essential sense, the rules and laws of *technē* are unwritten, or in the process of being continuously rewritten with the advance of knowledge. On this model, politics is continuous change; it is therefore more like the Athenian democracy than the Stranger seems to admit.

Obedience to written rules is then an evil, if the writings are the work of ignorance and interfere with both *phronēsis* and *technē*, albeit in somewhat different ways. But the previously noted impossibility of a government by *phronēsis* makes written laws necessary, and laws gain their authority from the permanence of tradition. It is therefore politically more dangerous to violate the laws—especially for personal gain or out of ignorance—than it is to obey them (300a1–8). This leads the Stranger to yet another shift in his stated position. Earlier when discussing the need for technical knowledge in politics, he attributed the written laws to the multitude and, in general, to ignorance. Now he says that the laws have been written after long experience and careful consideration and that the many have been persuaded to vote for them; any violation of the laws is thus a much greater error than may be embodied in the laws themselves and the disruption of affairs consequent upon disobedience will be much more extensive than that due to obedience (300b1–6).

The best regime would be rule by *phronēsis*. Because this is impossible, we must have rule by law. The laws of *technē*, although written down for convenience, are changing, and in that sense unwritten or in the process of continuous revision. But the laws of the city cannot be continuously revised, for this is tantamount to the continuous destruction and rebirth of the regime or to permanent political stasis. The Stranger shifts away from his previous acknowledgement of the need for innovation in *technē*, and he now insists that the second best choice, after *phronēsis*, is to preserve inviolate whatever has been written or legislated on any point whatsoever, whether by one person or many (300c1–3). Taken literally, this is an absurd injunction; most likely the Stranger is thinking ahead to the political application of this principle. He also postulates that these *nomoi* have been written down as imitations of the truth in each case, by persons who possess as much knowledge as possible (300c5–8), thereby sanctifying tradition. By so doing, the Stranger preserves consistency with his earlier denunciation of democracy. He can now advocate a stable regime in which it is forbidden to anyone, one or many, to change the laws.

But this extreme formulation must be modified if the paradigm of *technē* is to be retained. Changes must be made as knowledge advances, regardless of what has been written down (300c9–d2). Whereas all who advocate change are of the opinion that they do so to make things better, only persons with knowledge (*entechnoi*) are able to imitate the paradigm of truth. And we have already established that this knowledge is available to a very few in each city. It follows that the true or seventh regime is the monarchy ruled by the epistemic king. I remind the reader that this "best" regime is already a reversal or image of the original paradigm of *phronēsis*. But it too is inaccessible or unachievable; the best we can accomplish in human affairs is to imitate the scientifically or technically governed monarchy. And in this case, nothing must be done contrary to the written laws and ancestral customs. "Most nobly spoken," Young Socrates says in concurrence (300d4–301a5).

We have moved from the abolition to the absolute authority of writing by a series of steps that require a shift from criticism to praise of tradition. The reversals and contradictions by which the argument is woven together result in the interpretation of political existence as an image of an image, or a simulacrum: a ghostly efflorescence of genuine truth and being.

The Stranger continues with his application of the model of the epistemic city to the actual or historical regimes. When one person rules in imitation of the genuine king, the result is a monarchy. When the rich imitate him or her, it is an aristocracy, but when they are scornful of the laws, it is an oligarchy. The Stranger then recurs to monarchies and repeats that whoever rules in imitation of the knower is called by the same name of king, provided that he or she rules by laws, despite the fact that these laws are opinion rather than knowledge. In other words, he excludes the name of tyrant as applying to the rule of one person in accordance with laws. The possibility that these laws are, in fact, not imitations of the truth or that they write down bad or false opinions is not mentioned. In the original discussion of the various regimes, the Stranger noted that there is a difference between law-abiding and lawless democracies, but that the same name is applied to both. Here he is distinguishing between law-abiding and lawless regimes, but he is guided by the conventional names and so overlooks the case of the lawless democracy. As a result, he treats explicitly six rather than seven regimes. He will reinstate the seventh below.

The tyrant rules in accord with neither laws nor customs and thus cannot be identified with the king who rules in accord with bad laws, as just noted. In fact, the tyrant is prepared to violate the written laws on behalf of what he or she claims it is best to do, thereby imitating the epistemic king, but badly (301b10–c5). We now have five regimes with traditional names and a possible sixth that is anonymous (the lawless democracy) and not mentioned here. All five (or six) arise because human beings do not believe that any one person could be worthy of the power that belongs to the epistemic king; apparently they believe that a person with this power would become a tyrant in the usual sense of an absolute ruler who commits injustice and kills his subjects at his pleasure. Nevertheless, the Stranger assures Young Socrates, the epistemic king would be received with affection and entrusted with rule, if he or she were ever to appear (301c6–d6).

"But now," that is, in actual cities, the genuine king does not grow up naturally (*emphuetai*) like the ruler of the beehive, with body and soul immediately distinguished from the others; we must therefore write laws that follow in the tracks of the true laws of the epistemic city (301d8–e4). This important passage shows that healthy political life is not natural. Existing cities are all sick, and nature does not grow a political physician from the stock of citizens as it grows a queen bee in the hive. It therefore comes as no surprise that cities that are built on the faulty foundation of unscientific laws and habits should be filled with evils. In other words, what was a moment ago praised as the product of experience and careful counsel—namely, the written laws produced by the founding fathers—is now condemned as the product of ignorance. It looks as though the deliberations of the careful counselors are not much better than those of the popular assembly (301e6–302a2).

It is therefore amazing how strong the city is "by nature" (*phusei*). This has to be read together with the previous assertion that cities do not grow suitable rulers by nature. What is natural here is the sick or disordered city. This is why Plato never refers to man as by nature the political animal. He is made by nature to live together with his fellow human beings, but this nature is divided against itself and produces a botched product, which must be corrected by human artifice. A sick city is better than none, and lawgivers can be ranked by the degree to which they ameliorate this illness. Taking them as a group, they are all imitators of the epistemic king who personifies the model of *technē*, and in that sense they produce cities and citizens by their legislation (302a2–b3). I regard it as likely that the expression "by nature" has no ontological significance in the present passage but is used to refer to the essence or power of the city. In this sense, an artifact also has a "nature." Hence the comparison here to ships. But even if we consider the city as the natural expression of the need of human beings for one another, the results are defective "by nature." Even those ships that survive the storm produce seasickness in their passengers and crews.

The Stranger asks next as a side issue (*parergon*) to the present discussion, yet one that perhaps guides us in whatever we do, which of the incorrect—in other words, actual—regimes is least bad to live in, although all are bad, and which is the easiest (302b5–9). The criterion of difficulty and ease is not the same as that of virtue and vice or justice and injustice. No doubt the Stranger has this in the back of his mind, but his actual wording seems to be influenced by the paradigm of the city as a defense of the body. He replies to his own question as follows. Of the three types of regime, the same is both the hardest and the easiest. The Stranger is referring to monarchy, and in so doing he returns to one of his original distinctions, that between rule by law and lawlessness. There are then indeed six imitative regimes, of which the monarchy, aristocracy, and democracy in the traditional sense are law-abiding; the tyranny, oligarchy, and hitherto anonymous democracy are lawless. It is interesting that the distinction between wealth and poverty is not mentioned here. Unlike the political thinkers of the Enlightenment, the Stranger does not require comfortable self-preservation (302c1–e2).

When we investigated the correct regime, it was unnecessary to distinguish between lawfulness and lawlessness because the ruler was *phronēsis* in the first instance and its reversed image, the epistemic king, in the second. The king writes down laws and presumably follows those that have been written down by other knowledgeable legislators, but he is also free to violate them when he discovers something better. In actual monarchies, when the king obeys good written laws, this is the best of regimes (and presumably "best" means "easiest"); a lawless monarchy (in other words, a tyranny) is the hardest and most oppressive (302e4–12). I note that the lawless tyrant is a caricature of the rule of *phronēsis*, whereas the law-abiding king imitates part of the epistemic king because he obeys the law but does not change it for something he deems better.

The Stranger carries out his evaluation of the remaining regimes in terms of their power to oppress their citizens or to make their existence easier. This power is in the first case inversely proportional to the number of rulers. Thus oligarchies are second to tyrannies with respect to this power because they lack the concentrated authority of the monarch but are less diffuse than democracies. In the second case the proportion is reversed. Aristocracies are less easy to live in than monarchies because the power to lighten the burden of existence is more focused in the latter than in the former, and hence it is more concentrated. Democracies are the hardest of the law-abiding regimes to tolerate because no single citizen has much power to alleviate the burden of existence; conversely, they are the best of the lawless regimes. To this the Stranger adds the following refinement: when all the regimes are marked by licentiousness (*akolastōn men pasōn ousōn*), presumably the last degree of lawlessness, then "life in a democracy triumphs" (303a2–b3). As to the seventh city, it is set apart from the others as god is set apart from human beings (303b3–5). In other words, it is impossible for human beings.

In applying the results of his long examination of *nomos* and types of regime to the unfinished diaeresis of the causes of the city, that is, of the class including the statesman and his internal rivals, the Stranger has very harsh words for the rulers of all actual cities. As the supervisors of the greatest images (*eidōlōn megistōn*), they are themselves such images, "and since they are the greatest imitators and magicians, they are the greatest of all sophists" (303b8–c5). This language supports my interpretation of the actual city as a simulacrum, the greatest of all images because it is not a representation of an original but of another image. To this I add that the epistemic statesman is himself an image of the original of the rule of *phronēsis*. Hence the persistent confusion about the relation between freedom from and obedience to laws in the case of the epistemic king, a confusion that radiates down into the Stranger's analysis of actual statesmen and their regimes.

Weaving a Conclusion

Our consideration of the rivals to the king has thus far "been for us very much like a drama" in which a troop of satyrs and centaurs appeared, but which we have disposed of with much difficulty (303c8–d2). At 291a8ff, centaurs were associated with fierce beasts and satyrs with weak and cunning ones; together, these groups constituted the sophists, who busy themselves with political affairs, or actual statesmen. But now there is yet another type of "relative" (*sungenes*) of the statesman, closely resembling him and harder to separate off than the mixture of wild and tame beasts with which we have just finished. The Stranger compares the process of diaeresis to the separation of gold from its encrustations, both common and precious in their own right. We have removed the common arts and are left with the "precious" or "honorable" (*ta timia*) rivals: the general, the judge, and the political orator (303d4–e5).

Why are the practitioners of these arts more honorable and closer to the genuine king than actual statesmen? The reason is this: the general, judge, and orator each practice a genuine function that is essential to the care of their fellow citizens, and none of these functions is a simulacrum or image of something else or more original. This is easier to see in the case of the general and the judge than in that of the orator, but the Stranger notes that the latter "co-navigates the affairs in the city by persuading [the citizens to be] just" (303e6–304a2). We would require generals, judges, and orators even in the epistemic city, which is governed by law for the most part and not by the fiat of the king. By and large, this is also true of the other *technai* that have figured in the discussion, such as navigation and medicine. These arts are genuine expressions of human need and would be practiced in the just city in exactly the same way that they are practiced in actual cities. They become ambiguous only when they are used as examples of the political art.

The Stranger turns next to the task of separating the honorable arts from the genuine king. In general his procedure is straightforward, but there is one odd point. The Stranger says that he will make manifest the king by means of music (304a6–7). What he in fact does is to single out the learning of music and the handicrafts and to distinguish this from the knowledge of when we ought to learn these arts and when not. This is the first time that music plays a role in the discussion. It is prominent in Socrates' analysis of pedagogy in the *Republic;* in particular, music makes the soul hard or soft, depending on which modes are employed in the education of children. *Mousikē* refers to the interconnected arts of music, dance, and poetry. These arts are not as apt for the role of political paradigm as navigation and medicine, but their actual political function is much greater. It is therefore appropriate that they appear as we come to the end of our search for the royal art. Even while linking them to the handicrafts, of which weaving is presumably one, the Stranger gives prominence to the musical arts and thereby points to what we would call the aesthetic dimension of *technē* or, in Platonic language, the connection between beauty, play, and nobility.

Important as they are, music and the handicrafts are subordinate to the knowledge of when they must be learned and when not. This judgment is then applied to all forms of knowledge; knowledge of whether we ought to learn or not must guard and rule all other knowledge, as Young Socrates agrees (304b1–c3). And the same is true of the art of persuasion, which addresses mythical tales to the multitude or mob instead of teaching them. The knowledge of when this is to be done or, more generally, of when the people are to be persuaded to act or not to act is more powerful than—and must rule—the art of persuasion and speaking (304c4–d7). The general principle is then applied to the arts of rhetoric, warfare or generalship, and judging. The Stranger says explicitly of the judge that he is the guardian of the laws and the servant of the king, but the same could be said of the rhetor and general. Music and the handicrafts seem to have been forgotten here; they guard the laws in the extended sense that beauty plays a decisive role in pedagogy (304d8–305c8).

It thus turns out that the internal rivals to the king, those who actually do participate as causes in the continuous production of the city, are a type of servant. Apparently there is only one free man in the city: the commander. Everyone else obeys his commands and so must be classified as servants. There is one possible exception to this conclusion: the philosopher, who seems to be neither ruler nor ruled in the usual senses of those terms. If, of course, the philosopher should succeed in becoming a lawgiver, or let us say an adviser to the lawgivers or genuine statesmen, then it would be plausible to call him a philosopher-king. With this possible exception, we are now in a position to say that none of the forms of knowledge advanced by the Stranger is the art of the statesman, which "ought not to act itself, but to rule the arts that are capable of action" (305c9–d2). The verb translated as "to act" is *prattein*. The art of the king is neither *praxis* nor *poiēsis*, according to the Stranger's conclusion, but a type of *epistēmē* or *gnōsis*, although not *kritikē* or pure theory.

Do we now actually understand the knowledge that constitutes the art of the genuine statesman? What kind of knowledge is it that is no particular *technē* and no type of practico-productive activity, but that issues commands for the sake of the genesis of the city and everything that participates in the regime? One is tempted to say that the art of the statesman is the art of politics. But what is politics? The closest the Stranger comes to answering this question is in his extreme criticism of *nomos*; genuine political life is obedience to *phronēsis*. And this in turn means carrying out human intentions in a fitting or appropriate manner. How do we decide which manner is fitting or appropriate? If the answer is merely "on the basis of the circumstances," then the metrics of the mean will sanction any action that carries out a human intention efficiently. No one could doubt that the Stranger intends the circumstances themselves to be measured by the standards of goodness and justice, and so too of truth in the sense of what is best for human beings. Perhaps the most important inference that one must draw from the *Statesman* is that the art of politics, to the extent that it is a *technē,* cannot carry out this highest and most noble form of measurement. Knowledge of the good may be embedded in *phronēsis,* but it will not be extracted by *technē,* not even by the *technē* of diaeresis.

The statesman "rules all of the arts and cares for (*epimeloumenon*) the laws and everything in the city and weaves them all together most correctly." This is the final definition of the art of politics (305e2–6). The Stranger will bring his exercise of Young Socrates to a close by discussing this definition in the light of the paradigm of weaving (305e7–306a3). In order to do so, he must bring to light a serious difficulty. The virtues seem to be at odds with one another, and this could be attacked by those who attempt to persuade us with the opinions of the many. Not surprisingly, Young Socrates does not understand (306a5–11). Nor do we, at least initially, since the Stranger seems to be taking sides with Protagoras against Socrates in denying the unity of the virtues. But how could it be said that those who maintain this unity do so by employing popular opinions?

In the dialogue bearing his name, Protagoras holds to the view, by no means unreasonable in itself, that the virtues oppose one another in some cases; for example, courage is not identical with wisdom (*Protagoras* 329d3–e6). Socrates claims, on the contrary, that all virtues are one, namely, wisdom or knowledge. Thus courage, for example, is knowing whom and what to fear. The two theses can be made compatible by employing the Socratic distinction, noted above, between philosophical and demotic virtue. In ordinary political terms, courage is not and ought not to be an expression of wisdom but rather of patriotism. The soldier must obey his orders without subjecting them to philosophical elenctic. The philosopher, in contrast, is not about to enter into battle to defend the city; he or she is engaged in leisurely inspection of claims that this or that deed or event is a reasonable object of fear. The quarrel between Socrates and Protagoras is thus a quarrel between critical and epitactic gnostics. Since Socrates claims both that virtue is knowledge and that it cannot be taught (*Protagoras* 361a5–d6), he is in principle in agreement with my own conclusion that the rule of *phronēsis* does not admit of discursive analysis or definition by diaeresis.

Although it may be true that we sometimes hold, in an everyday and thus popular sense, that the virtues are unified or at least harmonious with one another, I suspect that the Stranger is teasing Socrates when he suggests that those who defend the unity of the virtues do so with vulgar arguments. The serious component in his criticism is that if the virtues were genuinely unified, the art of the statesman would be either superfluous or quite different from what it is in actual practice. Intrinsic to the paradigm of the weaver is the counterthesis that persons of opposite virtues must be woven together by the art of the statesman, and so that the unity or harmony of virtue is a political artifact.

The Stranger illustrates his unpopular contention that one part (*meros*) of virtue may differ in a certain manner from the look (*eidei*) of virtue in general with the example of courage and temperance or moderation (*sōphrosunē*). The terms *meros* and *eidos* remind us of the Stranger's warning to divide only by parts that are looks or forms. Let us therefore restate his present point in the light of the previous warning. The *eidos* is *aretē*, which may be translated as "excellence" or "virtue." The parts (*merē*) are courage, temperance, wisdom, and so on. One *meros* not only may, but certainly does, differ from another; even if the virtues are intrinsically one, this unity manifests itself in differing ways. If however the difference between two parts is that of a part to the *eidos* or look, then we must have discovered two looks. The part that differs from the look of the *eidos* cannot then be a virtue.

If the Stranger has not forgotten his earlier distinction, which he said was of central importance to diaeresis, and if he is not simply speaking carelessly in the passage under scrutiny, then we have to find a sense in which a part of a given *eidos* can differ "in a certain manner" (*tina tropon*) from that *eidos*. The metrics of the mean is of some assistance here. So long as we do not quickly identify every virtue with wisdom or knowledge, it is fair to say that what is a virtue under some circumstances may be a vice under others. This is especially true in times of great danger, such as war or revolution. It is plain that courage may be a virtue in resisting the enemy where moderation is a vice. Under these circumstances, moderation, without being deprived of its status as a part of the *eidos* of virtue, "in a certain manner" looks different from that *eidos*. We are led to this conclusion by two premises. It is unreasonable to deny that moderation is a virtue, and it is unreasonable to deny that under certain circumstances moderation is a vice. Another and more profound inference to be drawn from this analysis is that virtue is relative to the determination of the fitting or appropriate, and therefore to *phronēsis*. Otherwise put, the demotic virtues are relative to wisdom or knowledge, which alone is virtue in the philosophical sense.

We can perhaps now better understand the Stranger when he tells the "marvelous *logos*" about courage and moderation, namely, that they are "in a certain manner" enemies and that a state of political discord (*stasin*) exists between them. This last term brings out the point that they are related but that under certain circumstances they may oppose one another (306a11–b11). Citizens of the same city become involved in political intrigues and form factions, nor is it infrequent that members of the same family will take opposite sides. This is the metaphor underlying the Stranger's discussion. We normally say that the parts of virtue are friendly to one another, but closer investigation reveals that in a way there can be a difference between one virtue and its relatives (*tois sungenesin*). The Stranger tries to resolve the difficulty by identifying another look that is to be found in the parts of virtues. He speaks of the parts of this look as *eidē;* in other words, the new look, "the noble" (*ta kala*), must itself be a higher and more complex *eidos* (306c4–8).

We begin with the noble and cut it into two opposing *eidē*. The first of these is sharpness or quickness, whether in body, soul, or speech and whether in actual persons or in artistic imitations. We praise this *eidos* and give it the name of *andreia*. This word should be translated here by "manliness," which is more extensive than courage but includes it. The second *eidos* consists of other praiseworthy actions, which we describe as gentle, slow, or more generally *kosmiotēs*, well-ordered or proper behavior. This term replaces *sōphrosunē*, which the Stranger employed initially to name the opposite of courage or manliness (306c10–307b3). The praise that we give to each *eidos* depends on the circumstances: the right moment or the appropriate degree of sharpness or gentleness. When either of these praiseworthy forms is manifested at the wrong time, we blame it (307b5–c2). This being so, the noble cannot belong to those things that are always and intrinsically praiseworthy. In fact, there seems to be only one candidate for that title: *phronēsis* is always appropriate or at the right time because it is always needed to pass judgment on the suitability of our deeds and speeches.

The souls that are marked by sharpness on the one hand and propriety on the other are thus like warring parties in their difference from each other (307c2–7). Each side praises its own defining attributes, and this leads to enmity between individual representatives of the two forms that is unpleasant enough but which is a game or joke in comparison to "the great disease" that affects the city when this enmity spreads to all aspects of private and public life. The gentle persons try to live in an orderly and quiet way, "tending to their own affairs" (*ta sphetera autōn prattontes:* 307c9–e4). This is almost literally the definition of justice arrived at by Socrates in the *Republic*. The workers must work, the guardians must guard, and the philosopher-kings must rule. But the point now being made by the Stranger arises in the

Republic when Socrates makes use of the noble hound to explain that the guardians must be fierce or sharp with their enemies and gentle or orderly with their friends. The Stranger is tacitly pointing out that Socrates admits the impossibility of finding sharpness and gentleness in the same human being by citing the hound as an example. Otherwise put, in order to breed human hounds, we require the nurturer of tame herds (see 289a7ff); but brutes cannot be woven together to make cities or citizens.

The gentle souls are excessively inclined to peace, for which they have an inappropriate Eros; as noted previously, this is the only appearance of the word *Eros* in the dialogue. As a result, these souls make the younger men excessively unwarlike, and the city often passes from freedom to slavery without noticing it (307e4–308a2). Conversely, those who lean toward courage are excessively warlike and cause either the destruction of the city or its enslavement by the enemy (308a3–9). The net result of an excessive or inappropriate influence of either defining virtue is the same: slavery. Gentleness and sharpness are distinct forms of the noble, but they come into conflict with one another only when dominating the city in their excessive states, as the Stranger indicates will occur if they are not properly balanced by an external factor. In other words, an excessively quick city is as sick as an excessively gentle one. The statesman can cure the disease by the art of weaving together the two types of citizen. Only at the end of the dialogue will he suggest that it is also possible to weave together quickness and gentleness within the soul of the same person. I will return to this point at the proper place.

The Stranger then leads Young Socrates to affirm the conclusion that the two families (*genē*) "are always marked by the greatest enmity and stasis with respect to each other" and so that "not the least parts of virtue differ from each other by nature, as do the deeds of those who possess them" (308b2–8). If this is so, then the statesman must act contrary to nature or by means of the art of political weaving in order to preserve the city from ruin. And this is the final step in the Stranger's argument. It is true that a few lines later he speaks of "the truly genuine political art in accord with nature" (308d1), but the meaning is clear from the context. It is not the city or product of weaving that is natural, but the materials from which it is woven. No synthetic knowledge ever constructs anything voluntarily, no matter how trifling, out of bad and good materials; instead, it rejects the bad wherever possible and works with the serviceable and good elements, thereby producing a one out of many, with a single power and form. So too with the "demiurgic" (supplied from 308c7) art of statesmanship. It will put individual persons to the test by play and assign them to appropriate teachers; the leaders of these games and modes of instruction are like the carders and those who prepare the threads to be woven by the weaver (308d1–e2).

I call the reader's attention to a flaw in the Stranger's use of the paradigm of weaving. The carders and their colleagues straighten out and separate the threads before they are woven into a fabric; but the testing of citizens must be conducted within the city. It is true that children can be tested by adults, but these must have been tested in turn, and eventually we arrive at the need to sort out potential citizens before the city is constructed. This brings us to the problem of the founding, a problem that Socrates could not resolve without violence when speaking of the just city of philosopher-kings. Since the statesman will necessarily be working with already grown human beings, he must begin to spin his web with defective material. Every attempt to purify the web by taking it apart and respinning it must lead to a perpetual Penelope's web, which is another way in which to see the perpetual political entanglement. The web of politics is spoilt before the weaver sets to work.

The Stranger puts a good face on things by emphasizing the need to regulate nurture and education by supervising the parents and teachers. So long as they produce good citizens, they will be permitted to continue their tending. As to those who have no courage and moderation nor any of the other attributes that tend toward virtue, but whose evil nature leads them toward atheism, hubris, and injustice, the statesman will cast them out into death, exile, and the greatest dishonor (308e4–309a3). It is not certain from this statement whether the parents and teachers must possess both courage and moderation or at least one of these. If they are each representative of one or the other forms of the noble, then they will each make very poor teachers. But the Stranger's analysis has made no mention thus far of the possibility of finding both virtues in the same soul; the whole point of political weaving is to bring together into one city individual persons who are each stamped by one defining attribute or the other.

Those whose natures allow it will be woven into the city as citizens. Those of an ignorant and base nature will be slaves. The royal weaver uses the natures that tend more toward courage as the warp of the city, and those who tend more toward orderliness or propriety (*to kosmion*) as the woof (309a8–b7). Again, the individual souls are natural; the city is not. There is another problem here; obviously the slaves cannot be woven into the web, yet they cannot be left altogether outside it. The Stranger no doubt thinks of slaves as possessions of the citizens, but entirely apart from all questions of justice or compassion, the existence of human beings in the city who are not and cannot be citizens leads to a blurring of the line between tame brutes and human beings. Slavery is a conceptual or philosophical, as well as a "political" in the sense of moral, problem.

The Stranger passes next to a description of the act of weaving. The statesman first binds the eternal part of the soul with a divine bond to which it is related, namely, a true belief (*alēthē doksa*) about the noble, just, and good things and their opposites; the human part of the soul is bound together with human bonds. These are not described immediately (309c1–8), but shortly thereafter, at 310a7ff, they are identified as the bonds of marriage and procreation. It is not stated whether the just and the good belong to the noble or separate forms. And most important, there is no *technē* or *epistēmē* of the noble, just, and good. Their perception belongs to the faculty of *phronēsis*, which is of course present in different degrees to persons of differing natures. It is presumably present in the fullest sense within the soul of the genuine king or lawgiver, to whom alone it is given to produce the aforementioned bonds within the citizens who receive the proper education (309d1–4). Whether these are one person or two, the king and lawgiver act "by the royal muse" or, in other words, by poetic prophecy rather than by diaeresis or discursive dialectic.

Now the Stranger introduces the power of weaving gentleness into the soul of the naturally courageous person, and courage into that of one who is by nature gentle. Again, this cannot occur by nature; we must therefore assume that the mixture cannot be bred, as in the case of hounds. The blending occurs by the influence of the divine bond of true belief concerning the noble, the just, and the good. In other words, it occurs through the education of the children, in accord with the muse who has inspired the king. Nothing lasts from the weaving together of the bad with the bad or the good with the bad. If we apply this general rule to the present case, we must not form our city by weaving together the excessively sharp or quick with the excessively gentle or decorous, or either of these with someone in the proper condition of the mean. Since human beings are born into one or another of the families of the quick and the gentle by nature—but not into both—it is likely if not certain that left on their own, or in what one could somewhat metaphorically call a state of nature, they will all deteriorate. And this is what happens in actual or badly woven cities, in which the divine bond is improperly constituted or nonexistent.

The successful construction of the city thus depends on the application of the royal *technē*, suitably supplemented with musical inspiration, to the souls of children. Parents and teachers will be employed as instruments of transmission if and only if they have themselves been properly nurtured. I have already noted the problem that this raises. The genuine king must begin with excellent and so unspoiled natural materials. But nature spoils its own materials in the case of human beings. I infer from this that it is impossible to blend gentleness and quickness in the appropriate manner within the soul of the actual citizen; at best, one could only approximate to this in a more or less defective image. But it is not impossible to weave together the quick and the gentle before they are spoiled by nature, or to produce a city that contains the quick as the warp and the gentle as the woof. It is not impossible, but it is unlikely because to do so requires a genuine king or some reasonable approximation thereto. This potential philosopher-king (since that is who we are describing) will require something more than the excellent natural qualities attributed to him by Socrates in the *Republic* or the Stranger in the *Statesman*. He or she will also require a completely obedient police force, extreme ruthlessness, and good luck, to mention nothing else.

To come back to the Stranger's exposition, we need not deny that "music hath charms to soothe the savage breast," if I may cite Plato's most intelligent student. With the assistance of the Muses, we may do something to mitigate the harshness of the naturally quick person. But not even the Stranger dares to suggest that the same music, or art of weaving, can make a naturally gentle person quick. Instead, he says that the gentle person when woven with the divine bond will become "temperate and prudent" (*sōphron kai phronimon:* 309e5–8). Now we can appreciate why the Stranger shifted from *sōphrosunē* at 306b3 to gentleness, decorum, and so on, whereas he retained *andreia* even while adding additional descriptive terms to the designation of this form. Thanks to the divine bond, the temperate person becomes temperate: this is the upshot of the Stranger's doctrine once we penetrate beneath the shift in the name of this form of virtue. But temperance is the opposite of courage or manliness, not the result of blending courage and temperance.

There follows a complicated passage: "In those who are wellborn and who have from the beginning been nurtured in such characters, in these alone it has been implanted [*emphuesthai*] in accordance with nature through the laws, and for these this is the medicine according to *technē,* and as we said before, this bonding together of parts of virtue that are by nature unlike and are maintained in opposition to one another is more divine" (310a1–5). The main point here is that *nomos* modifies nature; indeed, this modification is in accord with nature. Human nature is such that it must be modified by *technē* if it is to survive and prosper. But the aforementioned modifications will be possible only in the case of well-nurtured natures; a proper upbringing is required as a precondition for the implanting of the divine bond by the genuine king. The Stranger's analysis is as circular as Aristotle's explanation of the necessary precondition for virtuous citizens, namely, a virtuous upbringing.

The human bonds—marriage and procreation—are not very difficult to conceive or to install. The crucial point here has to do with the choice of proper mates for breeding. Most people fail to act in accord with a correct doctrine on this score; they tend to pick someone like themselves in search of immediate gratification; in other words, the orderly or gentle persons look for mates of the same disposition, and so too with the courageous. The results, as we have in effect already seen, are disastrous. If courage breeds true and is unmixed with the temperate nature, the offspring are eventually altogether mad; if, however, the souls that are filled with an excess of shame continue to breed from one another exclusively, the children are eventually too lethargic and so are utterly maimed by feebleness (310a7–e3).

The royal art of weaving, in sum, must unite the quick and courageous with the gentle and moderate in marriage in order that their children will become like the noble hounds referred to in the *Republic* and exhibit a blend of both virtues, so as to overcome their mutual opposition as well as the self-destructive consequences of unmixed breeding. I do not need to emphasize again that none of this can transpire unless the king has complete control over every aspect of political life. As the Stranger puts this, the citizens must be of one *doksa*, namely, the opinion about the noble, the good, and the unjust as implanted in their souls by the king. The sole task of the art of royal weaving is never to allow the temperate to be separated from the brave character. The web is fulfilled in the production of citizens who combine the hard and the soft elements in their souls, thanks to common opinions and, in particular, to common honors and disgraces (310e5–311a2). At the same time, Eros is entirely subordinated to politics, and in fact it is not even mentioned here.

The offices of the city must be distributed in the following manner. A person who possesses both the hard and the soft elements will be selected for offices held by individuals, whereas for joint commissions, persons of both classes will be selected (311a4–6). This shows that the breeding of unlike kinds will not always produce the desired blend; eventually the race will degenerate despite the vigilance of the breeders. The importance of breeding, incidentally, shows that shepherds or grooms will be required for the human beings in their identity as herd or pack animals; in this sense, the discussion of the nurturing of herds in the diaeresis was not entirely off the mark. We should note that the courageous souls are deficient in justice, a quality possessed by the gentle souls but at the expense of quickness or sharpness (311a6–b5).

"This then is the completion": we come at last to the end of the exercise with a restatement of the political art of weaving. The web of politics clothes both free citizens and slaves in a common life of concord and friendship (311b7–c6). Apart from Young Socrates' closing benediction, the last word is devoted to *technē*. I cannot prove it, but I suspect that the reference to the concord and friendship of free citizens and slaves is an indication of the defect in the web of politics. By this I refer not merely to slaves in the usual sense of the term, but to the actual status of the citizens themselves. The *technē* of weaving is finally revealed as a tool designed to carry out the intentions of the genuine statesman, who is personified as *phronēsis*. But this means that the genuine art of politics has no political application except through images and simulacra or, in other words, that there is no solution to the political problem, if the problem is that we exist in the modality of simulacra. The highest form of political existence, ironically enough, turns out to be the transpolitical existence of *phronēsis* or, in other words, philosophy.

Bibliographical Appendix

The bibliography is selective and contains only those books and essays on the *Statesman* that I have found of unusual interest. In the remarks that follow, reference to individual works will be by the author's last name and date of publication.

BIBLIOGRAPHY

Benardete, S. "*Eidos* and *Diaeresis* in Plato's *Statesman*" in *Philologus* 107 (1963): 193–226.
————. *The Being of the Beautiful* (Chicago, 1984).
Brague, R. "L'isolation du sage" in *Du temps chez Platon et Aristote* (Paris, 1982), 73–95.
Crosson, F. J. "Plato's *Statesman:* Unity and Pluralism" in *New Scholasticism* 37 (1963): 28–43.
Dorter, Kenneth. "Justice and Method in the *Statesman*" in *Justice, Law, and Method in Plato and Aristotle,* ed. S. Panagiotou (Edmonton, 1987), 105–22.
Griswold, C. "Politikē Epistēmē in Plato's *Statesman*" in *Essays in Ancient Greek Philosophy,* ed. J. Anton and A. Preus, vol. 3 (Albany, 1989), 141–67.
Klein, J. *Plato's Trilogy: Theaetetus, the Sophist and the Statesman* (Chicago, 1977).
Lachterman, D. R. "Review of Klein, Jacob, *Plato's Trilogy*" in *Nous* 13 (1979): 106–12.
Manasse, E. M. *Platons Sophistes und Politikos* (Berlin, 1937).
Miller, M. H. *The Philosopher in Plato's Statesman* (The Hague, 1980).
Mohr, R. "Disorderly Motion in Plato's *Statesman*" in *Phoenix* 35 (1981): 199–215.
Morrison, J. S. "The Origins of Plato's Philosopher-Statesman" in *Classical Quarterly,* n.s. 8 (1958): 198–218.
Plochmann, G. K. "Socrates, the Stranger from Elea, and Some Others" in *Classical Philology* 59 (1954): 223–31.

Scodel, H. D. *Diaeresis and Myth in Plato's Statesman* (Gottingen, 1987).
Tejera, V. "The Politics of a Sophistic Rhetorician" in *Philosophy and Social Criticism*, 5, no. 1 (1978): 1–26.
———. "Plato's *Politikos:* an Eleatic Sophist on Politics" in *Philosophy and Social Criticism*, 5, no. 2 (1978): 108–25.

REMARKS

No doubt because of its initially recalcitrant nature, the *Statesman* has been the object of surprisingly little detailed analytical attention. Of the five books cited above, only two are devoted exclusively to the *Statesman,* and one of these is a monograph on certain aspects of the dialogue. Although it is true of Plato in general that one cannot understand his dialogues by fragmenting them into analytically convenient segments, it is especially necessary in the case of the extraordinarily intricate later dialogues to see them as a whole. As I have tried to demonstrate, this requires grasping all of the details, and so it imposes on the commentator the famous hermeneutical circle. One must view the details in the light of the whole, and the whole in the light of the details. But there is no real circle here; the whole is not invisible or concealed by the details. It comes into initial sight after a number of readings and continues to sharpen in focus as we master the details.

The most careful and in many ways the most profound works in the select bibliography, Benardete (1963) and (1984), illustrate the danger of separating the interpreter's two obligations. It should be said at the outset that Benardete's writings are enormously valuable. His (1963) is the best single publication I know on the *Statesman.* Following the path-breaking work of Leo Strauss (itself anticipated by Heidegger, as we now know from the recent publication of his *Sophist* lectures of 1924/25), Benardete subjects the diaeresis section to an intensive analysis that picks out decisive general features, of which I mention the following: (1) gods and mortals are defined without reference to transgenerative eros; (2) the division is not by natural kinds but by arts, and so it is concerned with *technē* rather than with *phusis;* (3) the diaeresis of weaving omits to explain how the parts of the art fit together temporally to produce a wool cloth; in other words, there is no real presentation of the art of the statesman; (4) human beings are eidetically whole as wholly partial, that is, it is human nature to be able to produce all of the arts, and so to mirror the whole, precisely because human beings are the not yet fully constructed animals, as Nietzsche puts it (my comparison, not Benardete's).

This is extremely illuminating, and Benardete understands very well

Plato's odd style and his sense of humor, which is not only elitist (as would be said today) but in the service of a sense of beauty that eludes the usual geometrical representations attributed to him. Unfortunately, within the limitations of an article in a learned journal, Benardete was unable to consider in similar detail the entire dialogue; he thus has the tendency to leap to general assertions about the dialogue and Plato's comprehensive teaching that often look like non sequiturs. One therefore turns with keen anticipation to his mature study (1984) of the trilogy *Theaetetus, Sophist,* and *Statesman* (which also contains translations of the three dialogues). And here, I think, one will be disappointed. Again, as almost always with Benardete, the work is necessary for the serious student of Plato. But the style has deepened, and in my view it has descended, from an astringent attention to detail, salted by extreme and penetrating generalizations, into a willful obscurity and manner-ism that seems to be somehow modeled on Plato's own baroque prose while capturing only the eccentricity. More precisely, the general study is too gen-eral; ostensibly constructed from detailed observation, it is instead too often a string of assertions not grounded in an accurate representation of the text.

I restrict my observations to what I take to be the most valuable of Benardete's comments in this section of his commentary: (1) whereas the *Sophist* is dedicated to the punishment of Socrates, the *Statesman* seems to be devoted to his revenge against the Eleatic Stranger; (2) the separation in the diaeresis between gnostics and practice is almost immediately followed by the process of rejoining them; (3) unlike Aristotle, the Stranger never says that people are political animals; and correlatively, (4) there is nothing natural about the city's well-being, which depends on political science; (5) "no weaver has ever been an element of his own web" (142), by which I take Benardete to indicate that the dialogue never overcomes the initial separation between ruler and ruled as represented by the shepherd and the divine demi-urge. In addition to these five general points, there are of course numerous beautiful insights along the way, too many to be cited. But the general interpretation is too brief and too condensed to give us a rich and plausible interpretation of the dialogue, and it never rises to the level of intensity and precision exhibited by the earlier monograph. These two works have my highest recommendation.

Also important and well worth detailed study is Miller (1980). So far as I am aware, this is the first book-length study of the *Statesman* in English (excluding editions such as those of Campbell and Bury). Miller shares the conviction of the "Strauss school" (as it is inaccurately called) concerning the substantive importance of the dramatic structure of the dialogue. One would think that this conviction would constitute the minimum requirement for competency in a Plato scholar, but that was not the case in English-speaking countries when Miller published his book, nor is it really the case today, despite a spreading tendency to accept Strauss's thesis without giving him credit for it. In any event, to make the elementary if necessary observation that Plato wrote dialogues rather than treatises is one thing; to understand the dramatic form is something else again. Miller makes out a compelling case for his reading by taking seriously all parts of the dialogue and by embedding his detailed comments within a hypothesis about the dialogue as a whole, and hence as a unit within the Platonic corpus.

Here are some of the most important of Miller's results: (1) there is an analogy between the trilogy (*Theaetetus, Sophist,* and *Statesman*) and the stages of Socrates' trial (the point of the analogy being the difference between the philosophical and the nonphilosophical judgment of Socrates); (2) the Stranger is not only the judge who mediates between Socrates and Athens (as well as Theodorus), but he is also Socrates in disguise, come home like Odysseus to reclaim his throne; (3) the method of diaeresis is defective on a variety of accounts, of which I note Miller's assertion that there is no positive contrary to human beings' essential common character, as well as his recognition that (5) the diaereses are humorous and not seriously meant. However, Miller also holds that (6) the Stranger mediates between the geometry of Theodorus and the philosophy of Socrates, and this leaves it unclear to me whether the diaereses play a serious role in this portrait of mediation, as well as whether the Socrates on trial does not also practice geometrical thinking (among other types), and so in what sense he requires mediation with Theodorus. Miller wisely observes that (7) the myth, in addition to its metaphysical and political significance, shows the hidden crisis of communication in the dialogue. What will Young Socrates do when Socrates dies and the Stranger leaves town? The same point must be addressed to each reader of the dialogue, as I am sure Miller would agree. Miller holds that (8) the figure of Young Socrates is intended by Plato as a warning against Pythagoreanism. The universal point to the dialogue is rather to show (9) "the diaeretic method of dialectic" (69). Unfortunately, Miller does not explain how this squares with the unserious and indeed humorous nature of the diaeresis section. Why should the unserious be the essence of the philosophical method? Does this mean that philosophy is humorous play? Finally, (10) Miller notes the incomplete nature of the discussion and, in particular, the failure to characterize the wisdom of the perfect ruler. Such a completion, he says, requires that the interlocutor be philosophical; Young Socrates is not ready for it. I doubt that this is correct. As I have argued, there is no science of ruling and no perfect ruler. Nor, I think, will Young Socrates ever be ready for a non-Pythagorean discussion. Otherwise put, if philosophy is serious play (to put the best face on Miller's analysis) and the statesman (presumably the philosopher) transcends the polis, as Miller also holds, then is not ruling a kind of unserious play? Miller's book is necessary reading for every student of the *Statesman*.

The remaining items on my bibliography can be considered more briefly. Manasse (1937) is especially interesting and has been almost completely neglected, abroad as well as in America. He writes somewhat impressionistically, and one misses a more precisely defined structure to his comments, which are nevertheless extremely subtle and illuminating. I note especially his recognition of the connection between *poiēsis* and *epistēmē* in the later dialogues, as well as his observation that there is no separation between Being and acting in the *Statesman*. Manasse thus sees the artefactual status of the city, especially in the light of the paradigm of weaving. He also sees, but does not adequately explain, that the *Statesman* "relativizes" the *Sophist*. This book is highly recommended. The same should be said for the work by Scodel (1987), my former student, who criticizes some of the details of my interpretation of the gods in the myth of the reversed cosmos but is on the whole in agreement with the general spirit of the present work. I cannot be so enthusiastic about Klein (1977), which manages to transform reticence into vanity; but for a more positive assessment of the last work of an extremely intelligent and learned scholar, see Lachterman (1979).

I will discuss briefly the remaining authors in alphabetical order. Brague (1982) provides an elaborate philological analysis of readings and interpretation of a single short passage in the *Statesman* (271d3–6) dealing with the demiurge's retirement to the cosmic lookout tower. In a brief but rich paper, Crosson (1962) holds that the *Statesman* contains a "strikingly modern" theory of democracy; he also defends the unity of Plato's thought and notes that Socrates and the *Republic* are constantly in the background of the discussion in the *Statesman*. Dorter (1987) notes illuminatingly that the Stranger comes to resemble Socrates more closely after the diaeresis section; he is also very good on the failure of diaeresis with respect to due measure or value. Griswold (1989) presents a good discussion of diaeresis. He sees the shift, unmentioned by the Stranger, from *gnōsis* to *praksis*, and he develops Crosson's point by providing a plausible interpretation of what he calls the Stranger's defense of democracy. In a much-cited and stimulating article, Mohr (1981) develops the thesis that in the *Statesman*, the phenomena are in and of themselves a positive source of evil, moving erratically without psychic causes. I was less convinced by this than by his assertion that the alternating cycles of the myth are dramatic representations of constitutive factors obtaining simultaneously in this world. Mohr also holds that the figure of the demiurge and the associated creation of the cosmos should be taken literally, another point on which we disagree. Morrison (1958) contains a useful study of the Pythagorean background of Plato's conception of the philosopher-statesman. Plochmann (1954) is a valuable reminder of the fact that the five other main speakers in the Platonic corpus each complete an aspect of Socrates' method of philosophizing. Finally, Tejera's two papers (1978) are excellent on the various puns and literary allusions in the *Statesman*, as well as in developing the correct perception that there is for Plato no political science. I found more difficult his claim that the Stranger is intended to represent sophistry. This thesis would have been more persuasive if Tejera had faced up to the sophistical component within philosophy. Nevertheless, Tejera does us a service by forcing our attention toward facets of the Stranger's procedures that are normally either neglected or automatically assumed to be signs of Plato's new position.

Index